POMP, CIRCUMSTANCE, AND UNSOLICITED ADVICE

GEORGE WEIGEL

POMP, CIRCUMSTANCE, AND UNSOLICITED ADVICE

Commencement Addresses
and
University Lectures

IGNATIUS PRESS SAN FRANCISCO

Cover images:
Mortarboard
© iStock/ivmirin
Wise Owl
© iStock/bazilfoto

Cover design by Roxanne Mei Lum

ISBN 978-1-62164-791-1 (PB)
ISBN 978-1-64229-355-5 (eBook)
Library of Congress Catalogue number 2025931512
Printed in the United States of America ♾

For Fran and Mary Kane

CONTENTS

PREFACE

The Catholic Church invented what we know today as the "university."

Beginning in the eleventh century and accelerating at a rapid pace throughout the High Middle Ages, Catholic scholars and students gathered in Bologna, Paris, Oxford, Cambridge, Prague, Kraków, Salamanca, and other urban centers to engage in study, academic mentoring, and debate. The cast of characters involved included saintly men of genius like Albert the Great, Thomas Aquinas, and Bonaventure, and scholars of the caliber of Roger Bacon, Robert of Sorbonne, Duns Scotus, and Alexander of Hales. This new form of intellectual institution led to an explosion of knowledge in the arts and sciences, including theology.

That debate—rigorous and public—was a prominent, even defining, feature of the medieval Catholic university is worth pausing on briefly, because one of the many black legends about Catholicism is that it stifles intellectual exchange and academic rigor. Precisely the opposite was true in those early universities, where distinguished scholars were expected to defend their work through the method of the *Quaestio Disputata*: a public debate on a "disputed question" in which a professor would lay out his argument and then be required to deal with criticisms mounted by both fellow scholars and lowly students. Western civilization is unique in its capacity for self-criticism; that capacity has been crucial to the West's contributions to world civilization, not least in science; and the medieval university with its rounds of *quaestiones disputatae* solidified that distinctive cultural commitment to reflect critically on things that matter, no matter how uncomfortable that reflection may sometimes be.

In a word, Voltaire and other Enlightenment bomb-throwers did not create the West's ability to be self-critical. The medieval Catholic university did.

American colleges and universities date their origins to the founding of Harvard in 1636. As that foundation was followed by others—William & Mary, Yale, St. John's, Princeton, and so forth—residues of the medieval European Catholic university were still discernible in these New World institutions of higher learning. Thus, Harvard's original Great Seal, adopted in 1643, displayed the word *Veritas* (Truth) surrounded by the motto *Christo et Ecclesiae* (For Christ and the Church)—and not simply because Harvard and other early American colleges and universities were originally dedicated to training Protestant ministers. The university, it was broadly understood, was in the truth business: It existed to explore the truths given in divine revelation, the truths that could be discovered by reason, and their interaction.

That this is no longer the self-understanding of many Western institutions of higher learning is to state the obvious, and in the third decade of the twenty-first century the obvious has become the painfully obvious.

For the meltdown of civility and rationality displayed on many "elite" American campuses, long ignored by society in general, became unavoidable and unmistakably clear when, in January 2024, the presidents of three such institutions (Harvard, the University of Pennsylvania, and the Massachusetts Institute of Technology), bewitched by anorexic concepts of "free speech" and "academic freedom," found it impossible to condemn calls for genocide on their campuses, saying that it was all a matter of "context." Years ago, Father Richard John Neuhaus used to wonder aloud when Harvard, having long ago jettisoned *Christo et Ecclesiae* from its Great Seal, would go the full Pontius Pilate and put a question mark after *Veritas* on its heraldic self-identifier. But even so keen an analyst of American culture as Father Neuhaus, who died in 2009, might not have been able to imagine that "Truth" would be replaced by the "Context" beloved by "critical theory" and other forms of cultural Marxism.

The implosion of American universities in 2023–2024 was but the most recent expression of what French philosopher Julien Benda called *la trahison des clercs*, the "treason of the intellectuals," in a 1927 book by that title. Benda believed that European scholars and their universities were descending into various forms of racism and extreme nationalism: a fear both embodied and confirmed by the behavior of Europe's most famous twentieth-century philosopher, Martin Heidegger, who swore fealty to the Nazi Party and acquiesced in the banning of his mentor Edmund Husserl, a Jew, from the use of the library at the University of Freiburg. Benda charged that the treasonous *clercs* (an image reaching back to the medieval university, populated as it largely was by clerics) had given the world an age of political hatreds, intellectually organized. And if ideas have consequences, as they always do, then the recent self-immolation of "elite" universities—at which American parents can spend almost half a million dollars to have their children turned into raving anti-Semites who demand that student staples (one imagines yogurt and pizza) be delivered to the university offices they are illegally occupying—does not bode well for the future.[1]

Thankfully, there are institutional countersigns to this madness, and they include the colleges and universities that honored me by asking me to deliver their commencement addresses or that invited me to lecture on their campuses. The commencement addresses gathered here touch on the challenges facing college and university graduates in the first quarter of the twenty-first century. The lectures celebrate authentic Catholic higher learning, authentically Catholic genius, and the capacity of the Catholic mind to address some of the gravest issues of global public life today.

In each case, I hope that what I have written is a call to renewal in higher education, which is essential to the overall restoration of a culture of reason at a politically overheated, culturally decadent, and dangerous moment in Western civilizational history.

Part One

Commencement Addresses

THE VOCATION OF THEOLOGY

St. Mary's Seminary and University, School of Theology, Baltimore, Maryland, May 11, 2000

Dear Graduates:

Over the past several years you have become participants in a conversation, the living dialogue of theology, that has shaped the civilization of the West, and indeed the civilization of the entire world, for millennia. Too much of our contemporary high culture has forgotten its debt to theology—and truth to tell, some contemporary theologians have acquiesced in their own cultural marginalization. This forgetfulness and theology's occasional acquiescence in it reflect profound misreadings of theology's mission and the theologian's vocation. For salvation history, the story of God's action in history, does not run parallel to world history; salvation history *is* the history of the world, read in its proper depth and against its most ample horizon. The task of theology in the twenty-first century will be to help the world to remember its true story—the story whose chapter headings are Creation, Fall, Promise, Prophecy, Incarnation, Redemption, Sanctification, and Glorification.

In that story is found the path to genuine human flourishing.

In that story lies the fulfillment of the human aspiration to freedom.

In that story is the satisfaction of the human longing for the truth.

In the last quarter of the troubled twentieth century, which saw unprecedented slaughters and the greatest persecution of the Church in history, God raised up Christian witnesses whose names and example will inspire fellow believers—and indeed all people of good will—for many years to come. Some of them were theologians, for amidst its sorrows the twentieth century was a time of great theological creativity. One of those witnesses, who has also made significant contributions to the Church's theological understanding and to the Church's theological address to the world, was elected Bishop of

Rome in 1978, after which he conducted one of the great teaching pontificates in history—teaching that he also embodied in his personal witness to Christ and the Gospel. This naturally raises a question, at the commencement exercises of a school of theology: What does the pope from Poland—who was aptly described by a French journalist as also being a "pope from Galilee"—have to teach us about the vocation of theology in the twenty-first century?

Let me suggest that there are four lessons for theology to be gleaned from the pontificate of John Paul II.

The first lesson is that *doctrine is liberating*. In the biblical view of reality, truth binds and frees at the same time. This is a difficult notion for our contemporary culture to grasp. For the better part of two generations now, our culture has been dominated by the idea of freedom as personal autonomy—"I did it *my* way," as Frank Sinatra sang, in the theme song of this ultimately degrading concept of freedom. If theology is to help the world recover its true story, theology must help the world enlarge its concept of freedom, linking freedom to the liberating power of the truth.

And this means reminding ourselves of the liberating power of doctrine.

It has been said thousands of times before, but it bears saying again: Too much of the contemporary theological debate is conducted through the essentially political and analytically sterile categories of "liberal" and "conservative" approaches to doctrine. These are, we must insist, wholly inappropriate categories for thinking through ancient and complex religious traditions. No one asks whether the Dalai Lama is a "liberal" or a "conservative" Buddhist. Why? Because we instinctively understand that these are the wrong categories to apply to a subtle, learned man and the complex religious tradition he represents. The same self-denying ordinance should be applied to contemporary Christian life and the nature of Christian doctrine.

The issue here is not simply one of semantic hygiene. Theology parsed according to these defective criteria—theology that asks whether a given position is "liberal" and "conservative"—distorts the very thing it tries to grasp, for it misses the relationship between tradition and innovation, the static and the dynamic, in the life of the Church. What can seem static in the Great Tradition of Christianity in fact reflects the Church's internal dynamism and creates the impetus for the unfolding of new, dynamic elements in Christian life. What can seem dead tradition is in fact the engine of development and innovation. Consider three examples.

The first is Holy Scripture. The canon of Scripture is fixed. But the fact that the Church does not add new books to the canon does not make Scripture a dead letter. Rather, the canon ensures that what is truly the Word of God can be received freshly and in its integrity by every generation of believers, inviting them to a deeper faith through the mediation of the Bible.

Then there is the Church's sacramental system. The sacraments are not simply traditional rituals, performed because previous generations performed them before us. Rather, the sacraments enable each new generation of Christians to experience the great mysteries of faith—the life, death, and Resurrection of the Lord—anew. Every day, the sacraments remind every generation of Christians that just on the far side of the ordinary—water, salt, and oil; bread and wine; marital love and fidelity—lies the extraordinary reality of a God who so loved the world he created that he entered that world, in his Son, to redirect the world's history back toward its true destiny, which is eternal life within the light and love of the Trinity.

Finally, there is the matter of authority. The Church does not have structures of pastoral authority in order to impede human creativity. Rather, authority in the Church exists to ensure that Christians, including theologians, do not settle for mediocrity. Authority in the Church is meant to help all of us hold ourselves accountable to the one supreme criterion of faith, the living Christ. This is the great service that pastoral authority does for theology. Theologians should acknowledge it as such.[1]

All of which means that one of theology's tasks in the twenty-first century will be to retrieve and renew the concept of *tradition*. In the distinctively Christian understanding of the term, "tradition," which from its Latin root, *traditio*, means "handing on," begins inside the very life of God the Holy Trinity.[2] That "handing on"—that radical self-giving that mysteriously enhances both giver and receiver—took flesh in the life of Christ and continues in the Church through the gift of the Holy Spirit. A venerable formula distinguishes between tradition, the living faith of the dead, and traditionalism, the dead faith of the living. In the theological creativity of John Paul II—in his groundbreaking Theology of the Body, in his social doctrine, in his concept of the Marian Church of disciples that makes possible and makes sense of the Petrine Church of jurisdiction and office, in his analysis of the life issues crucial for the human future—we may see at work innovative and compelling teaching, rooted in tradition, reminding the world of the story it has too often forgotten and creating the foundations for a springtime of evangelization.

Thus, the first lesson theology might well learn from John Paul is that theology must grasp, welcome, and convey to our contemporaries the liberating power of doctrine. Doctrine is not excess baggage weighing us down on our journey of faith. Doctrine is the vehicle that enables the journey to take place.

The second lesson for theology from Pope John Paul II is that theologians must learn once again to *do theology on their knees*, not simply at their desks or in their libraries.

During his fourteen years as archbishop of Kraków, Karol Wojtyła did his intellectual work in the chapel of his residence, at a table set up before the Blessed Sacrament. It was a habit he brought with him to Rome. For more than two decades, John Paul II did much of his intellectual work in the chapel of the papal apartment. That is where he crafted his homilies, his audience addresses, his magisterium. That, he believed, is where theology is best done, for theology, in the fullest sense of the term, is another way to "practice the presence": the presence of the living God.

Given the different circumstances in which theologians work, not every theologian can do theology before the Blessed Sacrament. But theologians can always think and write, self-consciously, in the presence of the Lord. If theologians are to do this, though, theologians must recognize another ancient truth—namely, that theology does not take a neutral standpoint, looking at the Church and its tradition from "outside," as if examining a specimen through a window. Theology, in the proper vocational sense of the term, is always done within the community of faith. And while theology may have multiple audiences, including the world of secular scholarship, theology's primary audience must always be the community of believers, the Church. Otherwise, theology ceases to be theology and becomes a form of religious studies. Religious studies, to be sure, have their own integrity and importance, and there is much that theology can learn from that discipline. But the work of religious studies must not be confused with the vocation of the theologian.

To do theology "on our knees," to "practice the presence" while doing theology, does not mean abandoning critical intelligence. Rather, it means grasping again, as the Doctors of the Church did, that true theology proceeds in a dialectic between critical intelligence and a reverent reception of the Great Tradition. The resolution of that dialectic, under grace, is wisdom.

To participate in this dialectic requires, of course, that theologians must understand the tradition before they begin analyzing it. In an important address to the faculty and students of the Pontifical Gregorian University on December 15, 1979, John Paul II enthusiastically welcomed theology's new dialogue with contemporary science and modern philosophy, arguing that the signature phrase of his pontificate—"Be not afraid!"—applied to what he termed "the great movements of contemporary thought."[3] Whatever deepens our understanding of the "whole truth" about humanity and its world, deepens our understanding of Christ, the redeemer of the world, he suggested.[4] Yet genuine theological development in dialogue with modernity had to be based on a "responsible assimilation of the patrimony" of Christian wisdom.[5] A good theological education, he implied, does not begin with critically dismantling the tradition. It begins with learning the tradition. That is a lesson for every twenty-first-century theologian.

To insist on this ongoing, prayerful dialogue with the Lord as essential to the theologian's task is more than a methodological consideration. Our times have given us too many examples of what happens when the dialectic between critical intelligence and a reverent, prayerful reception of tradition breaks down, and the tradition is regarded as simply another item in the theologian's tool kit, of no greater importance than any other. One of the most frightening of those examples is that of the *Deutsche Christen*, those German Christians who sold the birthright of the Great Tradition for the lethal mess of pottage that was Nazi ideology. As a *Deutsche Christen* pastor once put it, "For us, what Jesus said is not decisive. And Church councils, too, err and have erred. We gladly let ourselves be labeled heretics for this knowledge, for it has always been heretics that have saved the Church's life." In plain fact, of course, it was not the *Deutsche Christen* who "saved" the Church during the Third Reich, but theologically astute witnesses like Dietrich Bonhoeffer, who exemplified the dialectic of the Great Tradition and critical, contemporary intelligence. And if that suggests that part of the theologian's vocation must always be the risk of martyrdom, of giving full and public witness to the truths of the faith however uncomfortable they may be, then that, too, is something to reflect upon as we ponder the vocation of the theologian.

The third thing theology can learn from Pope John Paul II is that *theology today must be ecumenical in its sensibility.* I use the word "ecumenical" here in several senses.

Theologians must practice what the great Russian Orthodox theologian, Father Georges Florovsky, once called the "ecumenism of time." The conversation of theology today must include, as honored partners, the master theologians of the past. For truth is not confined by the boundaries of chronology, and there is much to be learned today from those who have practiced the vocation of theology in the past, including the very distant past. As the Second Vatican Council understood well, *aggiornamento*, "updating," must always proceed from *ressourcement*, a return to the sources of Christian wisdom in Scripture, the Fathers, and the medieval masters. The ecumenism of time promotes a truly open theological conversation that is safeguarded from the cult of the contemporary.

Catholic theologians today must practice ecumenical theology in the specific sense of theological dialogue with Christians of other churches and ecclesial communities. In doing so, Catholic theology not only learns from the wisdom of other Christian traditions, important as that is. Catholic theology in critical dialogue with other Christian communions gives ever more ample visible form to the *unity* that Christ bequeathed to his Church and does so by a deeper mutual penetration of the *truth* which Christ also left his Church.

As Pope John Paul II demonstrated time and again, especially in his epic pilgrimage to the Holy Land, twenty-first-century Catholic theology must also take account of its roots in the Old Testament; of Christianity's common moral border with the Jewish people; and of Christianity's divinely mandated engagement with living Judaism, the people of the covenant.

And Catholic theologians must be in active conversation with followers of other great world religions, in the confidence that all truths point to the one Truth, who is God. The world doubts that the most deeply held convictions of human beings can be put into genuine conversation; the world suspects that the encounter between those convictions can only lead to conflict. Theology in the twenty-first century must demonstrate how a commitment to the truth is also and always a commitment to an open, respectful conversation with others. In doing so, Catholic theology will be doing far more than observing the academic proprieties; it will be helping the world recover a crucial lost part of its story.

Finally, John Paul II teaches us that *the theological vocation is a vocation to holiness*. True theology, the Pope told the Gregorian University in 1979, is an encounter with Christ, and genuine theological teaching is a way to "convey to the young a living experience of him."[6] Theology does not, in other words, exist for itself; it exists for the Church and for the "formation of Christians."[7] That, the Pope continued, was why theologians should do their "work for truth courageously and openly, free of every prejudice and pinching narrowness of mind."[8] What we ought to love, the Pope concluded, is not our own skills, formidable as they may or may not be, but what Saint Thomas Aquinas called the "excellence of truth."[9] That is the path to sanctity for the theologian, who shares in the universal call to holiness and who is charged with the responsibility of helping lead others to holiness.

In reminding the Church of the liberating nature of doctrine, twenty-first-century Catholic theologians will both serve the household of faith and enable the modern world—and whatever is coming after the "modern world"—to understand that genuine freedom is always ordered to truth and finds its fulfillment in genuine human flourishing.

In doing their work "kneeling," the theologians of the twenty-first century will emulate the Master who came not to be served but to serve, and will remind the world that self-giving, not self-assertion, is the royal road to human happiness.

In pursuing the ecumenism of time, the Christian ecumenical dialogue, the essential conversation with living Judaism, and the encounter with the other great world religions, the Catholic theologians of the twenty-first century will remind that world that tolerance means the engagement of differences in respectful dialogue, not the avoidance of differences or the acceptance of a public arena shorn of religiously grounded moral convictions.

And in pursuing the theologian's vocation as a means to holiness, the theologians of the twenty-first century will sanctify both the Church and the world. The world may have forgotten its story. But it remains, nonetheless, a world that, in the words of Gerard Manley Hopkins, is "charged with the grandeur of God"[10]—a world that is yearning for the truth that theologians are uniquely positioned to offer it.

May Catholic theologians be messengers and servants of that truth.

CHRISTIAN HUMANISM VS. INHUMAN HUMANISM

University of Dallas, Irving, Texas, May 14, 2000

Dear Graduates:

In 1996, I wrote in a column that the University of Dallas was the best Catholic college in America. I'm told that this caused a little controversy elsewhere. Well, being no stranger to controversy, let me say it again: This university is a shining jewel in the crown of higher education in the United States. It is a leader in the reform of the American academy. And it is a model of Catholic higher education for the future. An ancient Chinese proverb has it that "there is great confusion under heaven and the situation is normal." At a time of great confusions in American colleges and universities, the University of Dallas has held firm to four classic convictions that are the foundation of our civilization:

Here, we believe that there are truths built into the world and into human beings.

Here, we believe that we can know those truths.

Here, we believe that, in knowing those truths, we come to understand our obligations.

Here, we believe that in meeting those obligations, we experience our true fulfillment as human beings, in the joy that is the fruit of our spiritual lives.

It is now up to you to bring those truths to the families you will form, the vocations you will pursue, the country you will help lead—and to a world that, as ever, needs truth in order to live freedom, nobly.

How can we imagine the world in which you will live out the education you have received here? You may remember the old story that, as they were leaving the Garden of Eden, Adam turned to Eve and said, "Well, my dear, we live in a time of transition." Everyone here today—graduates, parents, grandparents (perhaps even great-grandparents!)—has lived through transitions so rapid, and so momentous in their implications, that it takes a special effort of remembrance to understand the range and depth of the change we have experienced in just three generations.

During the lifetimes of those present here today, humanity has plumbed the depths of the natural world in both macrocosm and microcosm. We have split the atom, we have looked through the Hubble Space Telescope into the first moments of creation, and we are mapping the human genome. We have broken free of our planet and begun the exploration of space. Once-worthless materials like silicon have become sources of unprecedented wealth. And those tiny silicon chips have fueled a communications revolution that is changing world civilization (and our daily lives) as profoundly as the invention of agriculture, the invention of the printing press, and the Industrial Revolution once did.

The past century has also seen two world wars, a Cold War, the rise and fall of political systems of unparalleled brutality, the greatest persecution of Christians in the history of the Church—and the worldwide expansion of the cause of freedom, which Pope John Paul II described at the United Nations in 1995 as "one of the great dynamics of human history."[1]

How are we to read the signs of *these* times? What do they portend for the world in which you will live your adult lives and fulfill your vocations?

Some things, on the surface of the future, seem reasonably clear. As a group, you will likely live longer, travel more widely, and enjoy more leisure time and material prosperity than any generation of human beings before you. Some of you may go to Mars; others of you will almost certainly visit the moon. One or another of you may discover a cure for cancer or solve the riddle of the common cold. One or another of you may found a new religious community; others may help revitalize a venerable order of priests or nuns. Still others will lead lives that may never make it into bibliographies or history books but will be remembered with affection and esteem by children and grandchildren, neighbors, friends, and colleagues.

But all of you will live in a world in which the ancient temptation to steal fire from the gods and remanufacture the human condition is re-emerging in technological form. Raising your families, living your vocations, and fulfilling the responsibilities of citizenship in that kind of world will pose questions for you that have been posed to no other generation of human beings in history. Living your freedom—living the virtues that make for human excellence—in this brave new world will be a profound challenge. And that challenge is, at bottom, religious in nature.

Let me try to describe its essential character by borrowing from one of the most learned men of your grandparents' generation, the French Jesuit theologian Henri de Lubac.

Fifty years ago, during the Second World War, Father de Lubac tried to parse the singular terrors of the twentieth century. What, he asked, had produced communism, Nazism, and that gross utilitarianism that reduces human beings to objects for manipulation? De Lubac was a man who believed that ideas have consequences. And his answer was that the evils of the twentieth century were the products, in one way or another, of something genuinely new in human affairs—something he called "atheistic humanism."[2]

Atheism was, of course, nothing new; the village atheist and the radically skeptical intellectual were familiar figures in the human drama. But *atheistic* humanism was a genuine *novum*, something really new. This was not the skepticism of individuals. This was atheism with a developed ideology, a worldview, a program for remaking the world. And its prophets—Auguste Comte, Ludwig Feuerbach, Karl Marx, Friedrich Nietszche—all taught that the God of the Bible was an enemy of human dignity.

This, de Lubac argued, was a great reversal. For the ancient world had experienced biblical religion as liberation—a liberation from the whimsies of Fate. If God had created the world and the men and women who inhabited it, and if each human being had a direct link to the Creator through worship and prayer, then men and women were no longer the playthings of countless gods, spirits, and demons who played games with our lives. The biblical God was neither a willful tyrant nor a remote abstraction. He was not a cosmic watchmaker, content to create the world and then leave it to its own devices. The God of Abraham, Isaac, Jacob, and Jesus had entered history and had become our companion on the pilgrimage of life. To be in communion with this God was to be liberated from Fate, liberated for freedom, liberated for human excellence.

But what Judaism and Christianity proposed as liberation, atheistic humanism called bondage. Getting rid of God, it was argued, was the precondition to human despair. This was atheistic *humanism*, on the march in the name of human liberation. And this new thing, de Lubac proposed, was at heart of the crisis of the modern world.

Moreover, this new idea had demonstrated that it had the gravest consequences. Brought into history by the great tyrants of the mid-twentieth century, it had also proven something on which we should all reflect for the rest of our lives. It is not true, de Lubac suggested, that human beings cannot organize the world without God. What atheistic humanism had proven was that, without God, we could only organize the world against each other. Exclusive, ultramundane humanism, de Lubac concluded, is inevitably inhuman humanism, even if it imagines itself to be motivated by the highest intentions.[3]

But what, you may ask, does this have to do with the twenty-first century? Lenin, Stalin, Hitler, and the rest of that sordid lot were defeated by the generation of your grandparents and parents. Isn't de Lubac's analysis, insightful as it may have been in 1942, a bit outdated today? I think not. And here is why.

I believe that historians of the future will remember the decryption of DNA and the mapping of the human genome as the decisive scientific fact—indeed, the decisive *human* fact—of these times. The completion of the Human Genome Project within a matter of years will hold out the prospect of extending lives by early-detection techniques and precisely designed vaccines, and ultimately correcting the genetic defects that lead to sickle cell anemia, Huntington's disease, and various cancers. These are welcome prospects.

But at the same time, the new genetically based technologies will give us the means to remanufacture the human condition by remanufacturing human beings. And in this power, unprecedented in history, lies a world of temptation. If we do not, as a civilization, resist those temptations, the world will suffer the kind of dehumanization that was once imagined only by novelists. Today, though, it is no longer a question of whether we are in Aldous Huxley's "brave new world."[4] When the British government establishes a "Human Fertilisation and Embryology Authority" (so reminiscent of Huxley's "Central London Hatchery and Conditioning Centre"), we are clearly living in the "brave new world" already. The question is what we—what you—are going to do about that fact.

What are we to do about a revolution in biotechnology that is moving with such rapidity that what was once unthinkable—like cloning—becomes a two-day news story, followed by a week of jokes on late-night television?

What are we to say to those who promise an unlimited future for humanity if only we permit them to conduct experiments with the most vulnerable members of the human community today?

How are we to guide the development and deployment of the new genetic knowledge and the new biotechnologies so that they contribute to genuine human flourishing rather than create a world of stunted humanity, a world of souls without longing, without passion, without striving, without suffering, without surprises or desire—in a word, a world without love?

Responding wisely to that revolution will be, for you, what meeting the challenge of the Second World War was for your grandparents and what responding to the threat of the Soviet empire was for your parents. Indeed, the challenge will arguably be greater, for unlike your grandparents and parents, you will not be asked to meet the threat of what is indisputably evil; you will be challenged to use this new knowledge, these new goods, so that they do not produce evils.

How will you respond?

What have you been given here that will help you respond, prudently and effectively, to the challenge of the brave new world and its temptations?

How will you take the new knowledge that is reshaping the human world and direct it toward opportunities for genuine human flourishing?

One possible response to the biotechnological revolution is to retreat into enclaves—bunkers—leaving the brave new world to sort out its own affairs and trying to maintain small communities of integrity. Perhaps it may come to that, in time. But that time is not yet here.

The response to atheistic humanism in this new form—a scientific hubris that regards our genotype as the essence of ourselves, and that plans, as some scientists frankly admit in private, nothing less than the eugenic remaking of virtually immortal human beings—must be *Christian* humanism—a humanism rooted in the biblical image of human beings as made in the image and likeness of God; a humanism formed in the model of Christ the redeemer, the model of true humanity; a humanism in which knowledge is disciplined by the moral truths that were inscribed in human beings by our Creator. Over against an atheistic humanism in which human beings are the creators and arbiters of life, standing in eugenic judgment on others' worthiness to live or die and promising salvation through genetic engineering, we must posit the humanism of biblical religion, in which God is the Creator of life and in which life is always a miracle, never a habit. In the face of the temptations of the brave new world, in which our humanity is reduced to a fortuitous mixture of proteins and the soul is thought a matter of chemistry, we must defend the grandeur and nobility of our imperfect but redeemable human condition, with its God-given capacities for sacrifice, effort, courage, and love.

You, the members of the Class of 2000, are in a distinctive position to advance the cause of that genuine humanism, because you have been immersed in its great tradition here at the University of Dallas.

For here we understand, with G. K. Chesterton, that man is not merely an evolution but rather a revolution.

Here we understand that something new, something unprecedented, something of inestimable and irreducible worth entered the natural world when human beings walked onstage.

All those long hours of study as you sought to master the great books of Western civilization; the time that many of you spent in Rome; the late-night arguments in the dorms and apartments and those endless exams and papers—all of this has equipped you to be the agents of a new reformation, a reformation of our culture, through which the dramatic advance of science can be put to truly human purposes.

For as Pope John Paul II has reminded us for more than two decades, culture is the engine of history over the long haul. The answers to the temptations of the "brave new world" will not come primarily through law, although that is no reason to abandon our commitment to the legal protection of all human life from conception until natural death. But given the rapidity of biotechnological change, the globalization of knowledge, and the sluggishness of the political process, there are limits to what law can do in the world we are now entering.

If we are to master the new biotechnologies rather than their mastering us, we must rebuild a culture capable of cherishing human life as inherently precious rather than instrumentally useful.

We must refashion a culture which recognizes that human dignity is not something the powerful ascribe to those they favor, but a truth built into us.

We must reclaim a culture in which suffering is understood to be ennobling, a culture which realizes that the only truly humanizing immortality is the eternal life of communion with the God who created us, redeemed us, and calls us home.

These are awesome responsibilities. Many of those present here today have helped prepare you to face these challenges, and I hope you take the opportunity to thank them: your parents and grandparents; your professors, and the staff and administration of this university; your pastors and your friends. In making it possible for you to receive the kind of education you have received here, they have not simply made it possible for you to earn a diploma, as important as that is; they have also bestowed upon you a great trust.

When you look at those diplomas, think of them as marking a beginning, not an end. Remember all the human capital that has been invested in you. And take some time, in the future, to be as generous to others as your benefactors have been to you.

Seven weeks ago, in the Holy Land, I watched the greatest exponent of Christian humanism in our time, Pope John Paul II, go on pilgrimage to the places that were the stage on which the great drama of human history reached its climax. And it seemed to me that there was something fitting about the fact that the Pope, who had wanted to visit the holy places for decades, was only able to do so as an old man, fulfilling his mission amidst physical difficulties. For it was precisely in that way that he reminded the world of the truth the holy places embody: that we find our fulfillment as human beings, not in self-assertion, but in radical self-giving. That is the message of Bethlehem and Nazareth, the Mount of Beatitudes and the Upper Room, Calvary and the Holy Sepulcher. And that is the truth on which you, the members of the Class of 2000, can build a world worthy of human beings.

You have been equipped for this great task by your years here. I am confident that you can do the great things that are expected of you—indeed, that will be demanded of you. You are capable of moral greatness, and heroism will be demanded of you. No doubt you will fail from time to time. Remember that the answer to failure is not to lower the bar of expectation, but to get up, make amends, and try again, always keeping the bar set high. Don't settle for less than the spiritual and moral grandeur of which you are capable.

And remember, as you walk along the pilgrimage of life, that you have never met, spoken, argued, or played with a "mere mortal."[5] Everyone you will meet along the pathways of life is a person with an inalienable dignity, an infinite value, and an eternal destiny.

That, dear graduates, is the great lesson of the education you have received. And with it, you can build a civilization of love.

NO ORDINARY PEOPLE

Franciscan University of Steubenville, Steubenville, Ohio, May 8, 2004

Dear Graduates:

Commencements are solemn occasions. But for the Christian imbued with the joy of the Gospel, occasions like this cannot be moments of dour solemnity. So let me begin with a true story.

Shortly after Pope John Paul II had left our country in 1995 after visiting New York, Brooklyn, and Baltimore, I was at dinner with the Holy Father in Rome. He asked me how I thought his American pilgrimage had gone. I replied, "Holy Father, I have a friend and colleague who's a leading figure in the Southern Baptist Convention. He's also from East Texas. Shortly after you left our country, he called me and said, 'Down where Ah come from, we say, "You folks have fahn'ly got yo'selves a Pope who knows how to pope"'." The polyglot pope was utterly baffled—until I explained that in East Texan, which is a dialect of Texan, which is a dialect of Standard English, "pope" is both a noun and a verb. At which point, the 263rd successor to Saint Peter dissolved in laughter.

For more than twenty-five years now, we have all been privileged to live at the same historical moment as John Paul II. Most of you graduating today have no memory of any other pope. Those of us whose memories go back much farther know that no pope in our lifetimes—perhaps no pope in centuries—has left such an imprint on history. But even that, I suggest, does not take the full measure of the man whom future generations may well know as "John Paul the Great." Perhaps baseball helps.

In one of the most compelling baseball books ever written, *The Boys of Summer*, Roger Kahn described the legendary Jackie Robinson in these terms: "Like a few, very few athletes ... [Jackie]

Robinson did not merely play at center stage. He *was* center stage; and wherever he walked, center stage moved with him."[1]

In the same way, Pope John Paul II has not simply left an imprint on history. He *is* history, and wherever he goes—whether that be to Poland in 1979, Nicaragua in 1983, Chile in 1987, Denver in 1993, or the Holy Land in 2000—history moves with him. And history is changed because of his presence.

How does this happen? Not simply because of a winsome personality—although he surely has that. And not just because of an acute mind—although he certainly has that too. No, John Paul II's impact on history—his singular capacity to *be* history, to embody the history of his times as only one other man, Winston Churchill, did during the last century—is the result of his faith, his convictions, and his commitments.

In a word, his impact on history is a result of his discipleship.

Are there lessons to be learned from that discipleship for you who will shape the twenty-first century? I think so. Let me suggest three such lessons, as a graduation present to you on this landmark day.

John Paul II lives an intense sense of vocation that has implications for all of us. In the Catholic Church today we still use the word "vocation" as if it applies primarily, or even solely, to priests and nuns. The Pope, who knows the crucial importance of the ordained priesthood and consecrated religious life in the Church, disagrees. In his mind, and according to the teaching of the Second Vatican Council, every baptized Christian has a vocation: a singular, unique place in the cosmic drama of God's creative and redemptive purposes.

Each one of us, the Pope believes, is an actor in a drama with eternal consequences. And each one of us has a distinctive role to play in that drama.

It is interesting to remember that John Paul II, as a young man, struggled—*really* struggled—to discern his vocation, his unique place in God's scheme of things. He was intensely attracted to the theater. He had the normal social life of a young man of his time, including serious friendships with both young women and young men. When he began his university studies, he certainly intended to live his life as a committed Christian, but he thought he would do that as a layman: an actor or writer or director in the theater, perhaps later a professor of language. It was only after an intense period of reflection and prayer that he came to a different understanding: that God had chosen him for the priesthood, and that to that being-chosen there could only be one answer.

How very different the history of our times would have been, had young Karol Wojtyła not taken seriously the question of where and how God wanted him to "play" within the drama of history.

That is the kind of seriousness of purpose that all of us can learn from John Paul II. Many of you will enter the world of work after this graduation; others of you will continue your studies. No matter what you will be doing tomorrow, or next week, or next September, however, there is a lesson for you in the life of John Paul II: Don't think of your life simply as a "career." Think of your life as a vocation.

God has something unique in mind for each of you. There is something singular that each of you brings to the making of history. Think of your lives in those terms, and you'll never fall prey to the most deadening of temptations: the temptation of boredom.

In the second place, we can learn something from the Pope's conviction that life is dramatic. When John Paul thinks of "the human drama," he's not thinking only in grand, sweeping, historical terms. He's thinking very individually, very concretely.

In *Novo Millennia Ineunte* (Entering the New Millennium), his apostolic letter closing the Great Jubilee of 2000, the Holy Father reflected on his experience of standing in the window of the papal apartment during the jubilee year, watching long lines of pilgrims, day after day, waiting their turn to go through the Holy Door of St. Peter's. Each one of those lives, the Pope wrote, represented a unique encounter with Christ, a unique story—a unique drama.

Each of us, John Paul teaches, lives a life that is structured like a drama. Why? Because each one of us lives, every day, in the gap between the person I am today and the person I ought to be. That is a dramatic situation. Closing that gap—becoming more the person I ought to be—is the drama of daily life.

Those of you who have visited London know that, on the Underground, the London subway, there are endless signs admonishing riders to "MIND THE GAP"—the space between the subway car and the edge of the platform. As I suggested to a group of priests in London recently, minding the gap is in fact the story of all our lives, not just our lives on the subway. And we are not simply to "mind" the gap; in cooperation with God's grace, we are to close the "gap" between who we are today and who we really ought to be. That's what it means to grow as a human being. That's what it means to become an adult—and then to keep on growing.

This profound conviction about the drama of every human life is what allowed John Paul II to say, in Fatima, on May 13, 1982—one year to the day after he was shot down in his front yard, St. Peter's Square—"In the designs of Providence, there are no mere coincidences." Nothing is just "coincidental." Everything counts. *Everyone* counts. In John Paul II's dramatic understanding of our lives, every person we meet, every situation in which we find ourselves, is an encounter or scene in the drama of life: the great, cosmic, divinely authored drama in which our individual lives are playing, and the unique drama that is each one of us.

So, the second lesson we learn from John Paul II is to "mind the gap": to live our lives fully and intensely, because each of us is capable by grace of spiritual and moral grandeur. Each of you is capable of spiritual and moral greatness. Some of you will go on to do great things, as the world measures "greatness." But all of you are capable of greatness in the most noble, the most deeply human sense of the term; you can be the person of moral conviction and purpose and goodness that you were made to be—the person that you must be, if you're to fulfill your human and Christian destiny.

Finally, let me suggest that there is a profound lesson for the members of this graduating class in John Paul II's age, and indeed in his physical difficulties of recent years.

This may sound peculiar. You are young. He is old. You are vigorous. He, once a great sportsman—a daredevil skier, a man who could hike for hours on end, a kayaker and hockey player—now leads the Church from a wheelchair. The Pope often treats his infirmities with the medicine of humor. A few months after he had had his not-altogether-successful hip-replacement surgery, I asked him, "Holy Father, how are you feeling?" "Neck down, not so good," he immediately shot back. But it's not simply his ability to laugh at his difficulties that commends John Paul, in his old age, to you who are young.

In a culture that tempts us to think of people as disposable when they become burdensome, or troubling, or inconvenient, John Paul II is teaching us—not just with words, but by a powerful example—that there are no "disposable" people. Human beings are not problems to be solved—or, in the case of the inconvenient unborn or the burdensome elderly, problems to be dismissed through the technological fixes of abortion or euthanasia.

Every human life is of consequence. Every human life has inherent, built-in, inextinguishable dignity. Every human life has infinite value. That is what John Paul II teaches us when he walks, in pain, in the footsteps of Jesus and Saint Paul, in the Holy Land, in Damascus, in Greece. That is the truth he embodies when he returns insults with affection, when he acts on the belief that even those most filled with hate can become, once again, capable of decency.

There are no "ordinary" people: That is the third great lesson to be drawn from the life of John Paul II. As C.S. Lewis once wrote, "Nations, cultures, arts civilizations—these are mortal.... But it is immortals whom we joke with, work with, [and] marry"[2]—men and women made for an immortal destiny. To realize that—to look at the persons sitting next to you and recognize them as fellow creatures destined for glory—does not mean we are to be constantly solemn. As Lewis put it, "We must play. But our merriment must be of that kind (and it is, in fact, the very merriest kind) which exists between people who have, from the outset, taken each other seriously—no flippancy, no superiority, no presumption. And our charity must be a real and costly love, with deep feeling for the sins in spite of which we love the sinner—no mere tolerance or indulgence which parodies love as flippancy parodies merriment. Next to the Blessed Sacrament itself, your neighbor is the holiest object presented to your senses."[3]

To live that truth is to live life at its most bracingly, engagingly, thrillingly human.

To live that truth is to live life as the adventure that God intended it to be from the beginning.

To live that truth is to become the kind of person who can be happy living with God forever.

That is the kind of love for which your Catholic education has prepared you. For that is what Catholic higher education is for: the preparation of vocationally serious men and women for whom faith and reason meet in one foundational conviction—that every human life is, by definition, extraordinary. That is the conviction on which this college can and must build its future.

In living out that conviction by preparing men and women whose competence is enhanced by their character, the Catholic colleges and universities of the United States perform an immense public service. For our freedom depends, in the final analysis, on the content of our character as a people.

Only a people of character will be able to understand that, in public terms, freedom is not a matter of doing what we like, but of having the right to do what we ought.

Only a people of character will be able to build community out of the materials of diversity.

Only a people of character will know how to deploy the explosion of knowledge in the life sciences so that the biotechnologies of the future serve the ends of genuine healing, rather than leading us into a brave new world of stunted humanity.

Only a people of character will be able to defend freedom in the world by defending the human rights of all, especially the first civil right of religious freedom.

By preparing those kinds of citizens, Catholic colleges and universities today are defending the truth that Thomas Jefferson inscribed in the birth certificate of American independence: that our freedom rests on self-evident moral truths about human beings, our origins, and our destiny.

Congratulations on your graduation. Permit me a last suggestion: Take a moment, on this happy day, to thank those who have brought you to this moment of celebration and transition—your parents and grandparents, your teachers, and the administrators of this college. And in thanking them, make a quiet promise to yourself that you will be as generous with others as these men and women have been with you.

In the years before you, think back sometimes, perhaps often, on what it meant to have earned your baccalaureate degree at a time when a Christian giant—John Paul II—walked the earth. And learn from him the truth that he has preached: that each of you, because of the grace of God in Christ, is an extraordinary person with a destiny greater than your imagining.

Godspeed on your journey.

MAKING YOUR SOUL

Mount St. Mary's University, Emmitsburg, Maryland, May 10, 2009

Dear Graduates:

Thank you for honoring me with the invitation to address you today. And thank you for honoring my work with the degree, Doctor of Divinity. As was just mentioned, I received my undergraduate education in philosophy at the Liberal Arts College of St. Mary's Seminary and University in Baltimore. So, if I may borrow from President Kennedy on Harvard and Yale, I now have an abundance of riches: a St. Mary's education and a Mount St. Mary's degree. So I thank you.

It has been one of the privileges of my life to have spent more than two and a half decades chronicling the achievements, and explicating the thought, of a great man: Pope John Paul II. He was, certainly, a great man. Part of his greatness lay in the fact that he had a very firm grip on his own fallibility. In September 1997, the Italian Bishops' Conference hosted a national Eucharistic Congress in Bologna. John Paul II was helicoptered up there on a Sunday night to give the closing address. A staffer at the bishops' conference had gotten the bright idea that Bob Dylan would be a good set-up act for the Pope. So, perhaps a half hour before the Holy Father appeared, Dylan came out on stage before hundreds of thousands of Italians, floppy hat, guitar, harmonica, and so forth, and did a few songs, ending with his signature composition, "Blowin' in the Wind." The Pope came out and, demonstrating his remarkable capacity to seize an opportunity, discarded his prepared text and immediately began talking about the Holy Spirit "blowin' in the wind" of the modern world, and about Jesus Christ as the one road that all of us must walk down, for "Christ, who said 'I am the way' ... is the road of truth, the way of life." It was a remarkable performance. Three days later, I was at lunch in the papal apartment, and before I could even get seated after grace, John Paul II fixed me with that look across the table and said, "Who eeze Bob DEE-lahn?"

We are now a month shy of the thirtieth anniversary of another moment when John Paul II rose to an occasion—this time, in a way that changed the course of history. For next month marks the thirtieth anniversary of what I have come to call the "Nine Days of John Paul II": June 2 through June 10, 1979, the nine days of the late Pope's first pilgrimage to his Polish homeland, during which he ignited a revolution of conscience—a moral revolution—that played a crucial role in the collapse of communist tyranny and in the liberation of the Slavic peoples of central and eastern Europe.

How did he do it? He did it in ways that should resonate with graduates of this university, which is itself the bearer of a distinguished history marked by the labors of saints and other great witnesses to the power of Catholic conviction, and which has now committed itself to four distinguishing characteristics that explain the role John Paul II played in the decade-long drama that led to the demise of European communism.

John Paul II did it through *faith*: faith in the power of the truth to cut through the communist culture of the lie.

He did it through *discovery*: By putting a life spent probing the truth about the dignity of the human person to work in liberating men and women from the shackles of hopelessness that bound them, he empowered his people to imagine a new, nobler, more human future for themselves, their children, and their country.

He did it through *leadership*: the kind of priestly and episcopal leadership that for two millennia has taught the people of the Church that, as Saint Paul put it to the Galatians, it is "for freedom that Christ has set [us] free" (5:1).

And he did it through *community*: for by replanting the seeds of civil society in a Poland wracked by forty years of totalitarian oppression, John Paul II laid the foundations for a new type of resistance community—a community of solidarity that proved stronger than tanks, truncheons, fire hoses, and the other weapons of communist repression.

But, you may say, all of this was done by a great man—so what does that have to do with me? To which I would reply, all of this was done by a man who, when he was your age, never imagined that he would be pope, never imagined that he would become perhaps the pivotal figure of the second half of the twentieth century, never imagined that the world would recognize his greatness and the Church his heroic virtue.

He was, in a word, much like you.

And that suggests to me that each of you can also do great things with your lives.

Some of you will do great things as the world measures greatness. Some of you will do great things as the Church measures greatness, joining the ranks of the great figures who have walked here on Mary's mountain: Saint Elizabeth Ann Seton; Bishop John Dubois; Archbishop John Hughes; Bishop James Edward Walsh of the Class of 1910, a living martyr for ten years in a Chinese communist prison. Who knows, perhaps one of you will even top Jim Phelan's remarkable record as a basketball coach. But each of you can do great things in the one, essential way that Karol Wojtyła, John Paul II, did great things. You can do the greatest thing of which human beings are capable: You can conform yourself to the will of God for your life.

Many of you will enter the world of work after this graduation; others of you will continue your studies. No matter what you will be doing tomorrow, or next week, or next September, there is a lesson for you in the life of John Paul II: Don't think of your life simply as a "career." Think of your life as a vocation.

God has something unique in mind for each of you. There is something singular that each of you brings to the making of history. Think of your lives in those terms, and you'll never fall prey to that most deadening of temptations: the temptation of boredom.

That is the kind of life—a life of high adventure in the greatest of adventures, the making of your soul—for which Mount St. Mary's has prepared you. For that is the entire purpose of Catholic higher education, rightly understood—Catholic higher education exists to form vocationally serious men and women in whom faith and reason support a transforming conviction: the conviction that every human life is, by definition, extraordinary. That is the conviction on which this university was founded. That is the conviction on which this university can and must build its future.

In living out that conviction by preparing men and women whose intellectual competence is deepened by their character, the Catholic colleges and universities of the United States perform an immense public service. For, in the final analysis, our freedom depends on the content of our character as a people. That is how Dr. Martin Luther King, Jr., asked that his children be judged. That is how we should all wish to be judged. For character counts, both for the happiness of each of our lives and for the future of America.

By preparing citizens of character, Catholic colleges and universities today are defending the claim inscribed on the birth certificate of American independence: that our freedom rests on self-evident moral truths about human beings, our origins, and our destiny.

These tasks are ever more urgent today, for we live in a culture that is deeply confused about what freedom means and deeply conflicted about how freedom is to be lived. In the most famous oration in American history, delivered just a few miles from here at the cemetery in Gettysburg, President Lincoln, whose bicentenary we mark this year, called on the Americans of his day to give "this nation, under God ... a new birth of freedom." That must be your task, too.

The freedoms we cherish in the United States have been put in jeopardy by many threats over the 233 years of our independence. Freedom was put in jeopardy by the institution of slavery, America's original sin. Freedom was jeopardized by ethnic and religious prejudice. Freedom in this century was threatened by a great depression, by fascism, Nazism, and communism. Freedom in your own lifetimes has been threatened by the rise of jihadism, which claims that the murder of innocents is pleasing to God. Defending freedom in the past drew deeply on our nation's virtue capital. Defending freedom today also requires that we be a people of virtue.

And what does virtue require of us?

Virtue requires us to acknowledge, and to defend, the first principle of justice, according to which innocent human life has an inalienable dignity and value that must be recognized by law. Never flag, never fail, never weary in defense of the right to life. Never give up on the great civil rights issues of our time—the life issues.

Virtue requires us to recognize that the temptation of Prometheus remains with us, and that there are things that we can do, from a scientific point of view, that we must not do, from a moral and humanistic point of view.

Virtue requires us to defend and promote the cause of freedom, rather than retreating into a bunker of hemispheric isolation and an iPod world of self-absorption.

Virtue requires us to live as John Paul II challenged the young people of the world to live: by never, ever settling for anything less than the spiritual and moral greatness of which, with God's grace, you are capable. Never, ever settle for less than that.

The virtues that are the foundation of this American experiment in ordered liberty are known from both faith and reason. In spending these past years on Mary's mountain, you have been immersed in both—in both faith and reason. As you walk off the mountain today, take both faith and reason with you. Nurture them in your mind, heart, and soul. Living your lives vocationally—living your lives as the gift to others that your own life is to you—you can give America a new birth of freedom.

And the confessors, the martyrs, and all the other saints who once walked here, on Mary's mountain in the Catoctins, will be cheering you on, all the way.

Godspeed on your journey.

DEFENDING RELIGIOUS FREEDOM IN FULL
A Generation's Challenge

Benedictine College, Atchison, Kansas, May 12, 2012

Dear Graduates:

Thank you for inviting me to join you on this great day.

It has been one of the great graces of my professional life to have been given the opportunity to work regularly with young men and women of intelligence, wit, and character—*after* their parents had done the heavy lifting. So a special word of thanks, today, to the parents of today's graduates—and the grandparents, and the other family members—who have helped bring you, the Class of 2012, to this pivotal moment in your lives.

Today is, by its nature—and I think at Benedictine College we can still speak of the "nature" of things—a day of celebration, a day of remembrance, and a day of thanksgiving. Permit me to take a few minutes to suggest that you consider it a day of challenge as well: a challenge that might lead to a certain kind of vocational commitment.

We share, today, a unique and critical moment in the history of the Catholic Church in the United States. At the time of the American Revolution, Catholics accounted for less than one percent of the population of the thirteen colonies—a tiny population clustered primarily in my native Maryland and a few Pennsylvania counties. Yet within a few decades of the Founding, the great tides of European immigration that began to wash onto the shores of the new nation—those "huddled masses yearning to breathe free," as they are memorialized on the Statue of Liberty—brought millions of Catholics to the New World: at first, Irish and Germans; later, Italians, Poles, Czechs, Slovaks, Ruthenians, and the many others who wove their lives, their traditions, and their aspirations into the rich tapestry of American democracy. Those nineteenth-century immigrants felt the sting of anti-Catholic prejudice, even anti-Catholic violence. But notwithstanding that bigotry, Catholics have, I believe, almost always felt at home in these United States.

We have felt at home because we have thrived here; with the exception of immigrant Jews, no religious group has prospered more in America than the Catholic community. Yet Catholic "at-homeness" in the United States has had a deeper philosophical and moral texture. One of the great Catholic students of American democracy, Father John Courtney Murray, described that side of the Catholic experience of America in these terms over a half century ago, in *We Hold These Truths: Catholic Reflections on the American Proposition*:

> Catholic participation in the American consensus has been full and free, unreserved and unembarrassed, because the contents of this consensus—the ethical and political principles drawn from the tradition of natural law—approve themselves to the Catholic intelligence and conscience. Where this kind of language is talked, the Catholic joins the conversation with complete ease. It is his language. The ideas expressed are native to his universe of discourse. Even the accent, being American, suits his tongue.[1]

In this second decade of the third millennium, there are many grave questions being debated in America: the question of the legal protection of innocent human life from conception until natural death; the question of long-term strategy and morally worthy tactics in the war against Islamist jihadism; the question of how we attend to the sick and how we manage immigration; the question of fitting public policy ends to fiscal means; the question of building an appropriate regulatory structure around the biotech revolution so that the new genetic knowledge leads to genuine human flourishing rather than to a stunted and manufactured humanity; the question of the health of American civil society and of the American national character—the list goes on and on. The very question of what should be on "the public policy agenda," and what ought to be left to the private and independent sectors, is being as vigorously contested in our country today as at any time since the Great Depression and the New Deal. Yet amidst all this churning, the gravest question for our public *culture* is whether what Father Murray called the "American consensus"—that ensemble of "ethical and political principles drawn from the tradition of natural law"—still holds.

There are reasons to be concerned.

In October 2009, the nation's political newspaper of record, the *Washington Post*, ran an editorial condemning what it termed the "extremist views" of a candidate for attorney general of Virginia who had suggested that the natural moral law was still a useful guide to public policy. The *Post*, determined to nail down the claim that homosexual orientation is the equivalent of race for purposes of U.S. civil rights law, deplored this as "a retrofit [of] the old language of racism, bias, and intolerance in a new context." Yet the *Post*'s own claim was, to adopt its language, "extremist." For it suggested that the label "bigot" ought to be applied to notable historical personalities who had appealed to the natural moral law in causes the *Post* would presumably regard as admirable: figures such as Thomas Jefferson, staking America's claim to independent nationhood on "self-evident" moral truths derived from "the laws of nature"; or Martin Luther King, Jr., arguing in his "Letter from Birmingham Jail" that "an unjust law is a human law that is not rooted in eternal law and natural law";[2] or Pope John Paul II, who, at the United Nations in 1995, suggested that the truths of the natural moral law—"the moral logic which is built into human life,"[3] as he put it—could serve as a universal "grammar" enabling cross-cultural dialogue.

Appeals to the natural moral law we can know by reason underwrote the American civil rights revolution. Appeals to that same natural moral law underwrite the pro-life movement, the successor to the civil rights movement. And appeals to the natural moral law have underwritten U.S. international human rights policy for the past thirty years—until, that is, December 2009, when the Secretary of State of the United States, in a speech at Georgetown University, emptied the concept of religious freedom of everything save the "freedom to worship" while asserting, in a catalogue of what she claimed were fundamental international human rights, that people "must be free ... to love in the way they choose,"[4] which "choice" must, presumably, be protected by international human rights covenants and national and local civil rights laws.

This speech, as things turned out, was one harbinger of an assault on religious freedom that continues to this day—an assault that imagines "religious freedom" to be a kind of "privacy right" to certain leisure-time activities, but nothing more than that. This dramatic misconception of religious freedom was evident in the Obama administration's attempt to rewrite federal employment law by dissolving the "ministerial exemption" that had long protected the integrity of religious institutions. It was evident in the administration's refusal to continue funding the U.S. bishops' efforts to help women who had been victims of sex-trafficking (because the Church refused to provide abortion as part of that work). And it has been most dramatically evident in the HHS mandate that requires all employers (including religious institutions with moral objections and private-sector employers with religiously informed moral objections) to facilitate the provision of contraceptives, sterilizations, and abortifacient drugs like Plan B and Ella to their employees.

All of this suggests that one of the great challenges of your generation will be to rise to the defense of religious freedom in full. And, indeed, what could be a more apt challenge for the graduates of a college named in honor of the saint whose inspired vision and evangelical vigor preserved the civilization of the classical world when it was in danger of being lost? What better challenge for the graduates of Benedictine College, named for one of the patrons of Europe, whose life's work saved the West as a civilizational enterprise built from the fruitful interaction of Jerusalem, Athens, and Rome?

For the defense of religious freedom in full which you must mount must be both cultural—in the sense of arguments winsomely and persuasively made—and political, in that you must drive the sharp edge of truth into the sometimes-hard soil of public policy.

What is this "religious freedom in full" that you must defend and advance?

It surely includes freedom of worship, but it must include more than that; the Kingdom of Saudi Arabia is content with freedom of worship, so long as the Christian worship in question takes place behind closed doors in the American embassy compound in Riyadh. Religious conviction is community-forming, and communities formed by religious conviction must be free, as communities and not simply as individuals, to make arguments and bring influence to bear in public life. If religiously informed moral argument is banned from the American public square, then the public square has become, not only naked, but undemocratic and intolerant. If, on the other hand, religiously informed moral argument is welcome in public life, then we have the possibility of rebuilding, not a sacred public square (a goal the Catholic Church rejected at the Second Vatican Council), but a civil public square, in which tolerance is rightly understood as differences engaged within a bond of civility formed by a mutual commitment to reason.

It is a matter of both political common sense and democratic etiquette that Catholics in public life should make our arguments in ways that our fellow citizens, who may not share our theological premises, can engage and understand—which is to say, in our particular case, that Catholics should bring to bear in public life the moral truths we hold through arguments framed by the grammar and vocabulary of the natural moral law. That is what John Paul II did at the United Nations in 1979 and 1995. That is what Benedict XVI did at the U.N. in 2008 and in the German *Bundestag* in 2011. That is what the bishops of the United States, and lay Catholics in their millions, have done over the past four decades in defense of life. And if there are some who consider such appeals to the natural moral law a form of tarted-up bigotry, well, we shall simply have to inform them, politely but firmly, that they are mistaken—and then demonstrate why.

Religious freedom in full also means that communities of religious conviction and conscience must be free to conduct the works of charity in ways that reflect their conscientious convictions. This is neither the time nor the place to discuss the problems that have been posed by tying so much of Catholic social service work and Catholic health care to government funding—save, perhaps, to note that these problems did not exist before the Supreme Court erected a spurious "right to abortion" as the right-that-trumps-all-other-rights, and before courts and legislatures decided that it was within the state's competence to redefine marriage and to compel others to accept that redefinition through the use of coercive state power. What can be said in this context, and what must be said, is that the rights of Catholic physicians, nurses, and other health care professionals are not second-class rights that can be trumped by other rights-claims; and any state that fails to acknowledge those rights of conscience has done grave damage to religious freedom rightly understood. The same can and must be said about any state that drives the Catholic Church out of certain forms of social service because the Church refuses to concede that the state has the competence to declare as "marriage" relationships that are manifestly not marriages.

Dear graduates, your defense of religious freedom is going to require the skills of reasoning and argument that you acquired here at Benedictine College. It is going to require that some of you accept the risk and challenge of public service in elective office. And it is going to require all of you to support those who take, as their vocation, the defense and promotion of religious freedom in full.

This will be the work of a lifetime. But it must begin sooner rather than later, for the threats to religious freedom among us are great, and many of them are deeply embedded in postmodern American culture. This work will not be without cost. Some of you may suffer various forms of martyrdom in taking up this cause: the martyrdom of ridicule, of being labeled "intolerant" and "bigoted"; the martyrdom of career paths blocked and promotions denied because of your adherence to the moral truth of things; the martyrdom of political defeat, or a judicial case well-argued but lost. Fidelity to the truth can have its costs. Yet as John Paul II taught young people all over the world, those costs are worth paying because the truth sets us free in the deepest sense of human liberation. Thomas More, patron saint of Catholics in public life, was never more a free man than when he bent his neck to the executioner's axe in free adherence to the truth.

Let us pray that it does not come to that for any of you, or indeed for any of us. But let us also be clear on the stakes for which your generation is playing, which are nothing less than the long-term integrity of American democracy. So, be the culture-forming heirs of Saint Benedict that your education here has prepared you to be. Be the champions of religious freedom in full. In doing that, you will give America a new birth of freedom—freedom tethered to truth and ordered to goodness, freedom that sets us free in the noblest sense of human liberation.

Godspeed on your journey.

THE TRUTHS ABOUT TRUTH

Ukrainian Catholic University, L'viv, Ukraine, July 6, 2013

Dear Graduates:

Thank you for inviting me to share this happy day with you.

The Ukrainian Greek Catholic Church has had a special place in my heart for almost thirty years, since the late Professor Bohdan Bociurkiw—the great historian of the UGCC under Stalinist persecution—and I spent a year together in Washington as fellows of the Woodrow Wilson International Center for Scholars. There, Dr. Bociurkiw gave me a personal tutorial in Ukrainian history and extensive lessons in the dramatic, heroic story of the Greek Catholic Church in Ukraine. Later, Dr. Bociurkiw helped me draft the 1988 *Appeal for Religious Freedom in the Soviet Union*, which was signed by virtually every major Christian religious leader in America to honor the millennium of Christianity among the Eastern Slavs. The *Appeal* was presented to President Ronald Reagan in the White House and helped shaped his historic speech at the Danilov Monastery in Moscow on May 30, 1988—and thus I hope the *Appeal* had some effect in helping liberate the Ukrainian Greek Catholic Church in the last years of the Soviet Union.

Later, in my work on the biography of Pope John Paul II, I came to what I hope is a deeper understanding of the history of the Ukrainian Greek Catholic Church in Ukraine and its importance for the future of the world Church—and I tried to bring that understanding to the world through the two volumes of my John Paul II biography, which you have been so kind as to translate into your language.

And so, if I may make my own the words of John Paul II on his visit to Ukraine in 2001, "I greet a land which has known suffering and repression, while preserving a love of freedom which no one has ever managed to repress." I come to you today as a friend, a fellow Catholic, and an author who has borne witness to your modern history as a Church of confessor and martyrs, a history of fidelity and courage that I hold in the highest esteem.

It is from that history, I believe, that you will draw the strength and courage to build a free and virtuous society in the Ukraine of the future. Through their witness, the confessors and martyrs of the Ukrainian Greek Catholic Church planted in your country seeds of integrity, seeds of courage, and seeds of compassion that can, with your help, bring forth a rich harvest in shaping the free and virtuous Ukraine of the future. The example of these confessors and martyrs is history's gift to you; building a society that lives freedom in truth is your task for the future.

You face great challenges in building that future: challenges posed by the long-term cultural effects of the communist deconstruction of the human person and by the communist destruction of culture and society; challenges posed by the temptations of a postmodern Western culture that is rich in material prosperity but impoverished in the things of the spirit. In meeting those challenges, you have been given a precious instrument by this university: the gift of the truth—the truth we know by both revelation and reason; the truth that comes to us from both Jerusalem and Athens; the truth that sets us free in the deepest meaning of liberation.

You may, and if you will permit me, you should thank your teachers for this gift of the truth. In the Western world, the arts of teaching have too often been degraded into a subset of the arts of entertainment—when they're not debased into a subset of the arts of career advancement. As today's graduates have learned, perhaps not without some struggle, good teaching challenges us, even confronts us, as good teach ers invite us to learn and embrace what is true and good and beautiful, so that the true, the good, and the beautiful shape the contours of our life's pilgrimage.

Thus on this day when we rightly applaud our graduates, let us take a moment to applaud good teachers.

Building the free and virtuous society in the Ukraine of the twenty-first century will require courage. For the legacy of the past that shapes the Ukraine of the present is not only the noble legacy of the confessors and martyrs. That legacy also includes a weakened grasp on the true, the good, and the beautiful, a weakness that expresses itself in social fragmentation, a weak civic culture, corruption in public life, and a lack of trust among people. Building the free and virtuous society in the Ukraine of the twenty-first century is thus not only a matter of building a robust free economy and a stable democracy; it requires rebuilding civil society and civic culture, a task for which this university is uniquely equipped and to which it has courageously and creatively dedicated itself.

How should you, the Class of 2013, approach the challenge of building a free and virtuous Ukraine that history and God's providence have put before you?

How, in your role as citizens, will you bring moral truths to bear on politics, in business, in the formation of culture?

How, in your role as parents, will you instill in the next generation an understanding of, and a deep appreciation for, the fact that there are deep truths built into the world and into us? That freedom is not mere willfulness? That life is not just the pursuit of pleasure? That nobility and compassion and justice are the true measure of a life well lived?

For those of you who choose the sacred ministry or consecrated religious life, how will you live the vows of your ordination or consecration in such a way that you are agents of the New Evangelization, inviting others into friendship with the Lord Jesus Christ and into the communion of disciples in mission that is the Church?

How will you live lives of fidelity to your vocation, in whatever vocation you embrace, in a world that often tells you that fidelity is a great nonsense?

As you learn, often through hard experience, how to play the challenging role that history has set before you—the role of being the lead generation in an evangelical Catholicism that is a culture-forming counterculture—keep in mind some of the essentials that the good teaching you have been given here has helped you to make your own. Keep in mind what brave men like the Czech dissidents Václav Havel and Václav Benda taught the world during the last years of the Cold War: that even amidst severe difficulties, it is possible to "live in the truth," and that living in the truth is the greatest of human adventures. Keep in mind that John Paul II, when asked what he judged to be the most important word in the Holy Scriptures, immediately responded, "Truth."

And keep in mind what the Catholic intellectual and cultural tradition in which you have been immersed here at the Ukrainian

Catholic University has taught you about the truth: that truth is *accessible;* that truth is *symphonic;* and that truth is *liberating.*

Truth is accessible. There are many ironies in history, and one of the greatest ironies that we have witnessed in our time is that the Catholic Church, charged by many leaders of the eighteenth-century continental European Enlightenment with being an enemy of reason, has become the world's premier institutional defender of the capacity of human reason to grasp the truth of things. Two centuries after Voltaire urged his compatriots to "crush" the "infamy" that was the Church in order to liberate human reason, the Catholic Church stands before a world awash in skepticism and says, with John Paul II in the 1998 encyclical *Fides et Ratio,* "Yes, we can get to the truth through the arts of reason. Yes, we can know the deep truths that are embedded in the world and in us."[1] A century after the proponents of what Father Henri de Lubac, S.J., called "atheistic humanism" declared that the God of the Bible was the enemy of human maturation and liberation, believers in the God of the Bible, inspired by the Bishop of Rome, unleashed a revolution of conscience that eventually brought down the greatest tyranny in history, the Soviet empire.

Postmodern Western culture in the West teaches that there is only "your truth" and "my truth." Graduates of the Ukrainian Catholic University know that that is not true. And in giving your country a new birth of freedom ordered to goodness, you must insist, calmly and reasonably, that there is not simply "your truth" and "my truth", that there is actually something properly called "*the* truth," which we can access, if imperfectly and incompletely, through reason—a reason that, Catholics would insist, is amplified by revelation, even as our understanding of revelation is purified by reason.

This is not an abstract point, a matter of settling an intellectual debate. For if there is only *your* truth and *my* truth and neither one of us recognizes anything as *the* truth, then against what horizon of judgment, or by what standard, will we settle our differences when your truth comes into conflict with my truth? There isn't any such horizon or standard. So, either you will impose your power on me, or I will impose my power on you. Nietzsche, mad prophet of postmodernity, saw this coming; Joseph Ratzinger prophetically labeled it the "dictatorship of relativism," the day before his election as Pope Benedict XVI;[2] Pope Francis has described a world without a firm grasp on moral truth as a world without peace because "everyone is his own criterion."[3]

The free and virtuous Ukraine of the future cannot be built on a foundation of skepticism and cynicism about truth. It will therefore be your role, graduates of the Class of 2013, to form a civic culture around the conviction that truth is accessible.

Truth is symphonic. Fragmentation and disintegration are among the chief characteristics of European intellectual life today: Everything is in bits and pieces; nothing fits together; there is no "frame" in which the parts can be composed into a whole. Little wonder that cynicism, skepticism, and irony are prominent features in twenty-first-century Western culture. In the face of all that, the Catholic intellectual tradition insists that fragmentation is not all there is. The Catholic intellectual tradition tells us that there is a symphony of truth, in which the various instruments by which we apprehend what is true and good and beautiful play together melodiously.

And that which forms the fragments of intellectual stone into a mosaic of symphonic truth is love: the love which is the basis of the unity of the Church; the ecclesial love, itself an expression of Trinitarian love, in which the world may recognize the unity for which it yearns, but which it never finds on its own.

Truth is liberating. There are many sorrows in what the great Marian hymn, the *Salve, Regina*, calls *hac lacrimarum valle* (this valley of tears); the people of Ukraine have surely borne more than their share of sorrow over time. But perhaps the characteristic sorrow of twenty-first-century life in Europe—a sorrow that strikes the well-taught Catholic as a true sadness, a self-inflicted wound—is the sorrow that comes from self-absorption: the sorrow we find in the childish sandbox in which the object of worship is the Imperial Self, the god called "Me, Myself, and I." The well-taught Catholic invites others, both those within the household of the faith and those outside it, to reject self-absorption and narcissism and to breathe the bracing, invigorating, liberating air of a life lived in conformity with those truths that are built into reality and into us.

For all genuine human liberation is freedom *in*, and freedom *for*, the truth of who we are and the truth of what our eternal destiny is. All genuine human liberation flows from making our lives into the gift for others that life itself is to each of us. If you, the graduates of the Ukrainian Catholic University, can embody that Law of the Gift in your own lives, even a cynical world will wonder, "How can you live that way?" Then you can explain: "I live that way through the grace of God in Christ." And in that way, through the example of lives lived honorably, nobly, and compassionately, you can help liberate your country from the chains of the past, build a future of freedom ordered to goodness, and become agents of the New Evangelization.

We believe, as Catholics, that God has a unique vocation in mind for each of us. And so each graduate of this university must, with the help of the truths you have made your own here, face the challenge of vocational discernment—of discerning, through the help of grace, that unique *something* that God has had in mind for you from all eternity. You are not alone in meeting that challenge. For you can undertake that discernment through the prism of the truth, the goodness, and the beauty you have encountered here at the Ukrainian Catholic University. And you can do so in the calm confidence that the drama of each of our individual lives is "playing" within the cosmic drama that has the God of Israel and the Father of our Lord Jesus Christ as its producer, director, scriptwriter, and protagonist.

And there is still more to encourage you on your way, to help you in your vocational discernment, and to strengthen you in your task as citizens called to build the free and virtuous Ukraine of the future. For by grace, through faith, we have seen the ultimate truth of what God intends for humanity: We have seen that truth and that future in the Resurrection we celebrate at Easter. Because of that—and however challenging the times in which we live and the circumstances in which we find ourselves—we know that, in the end, the human story is not a cosmic tragedy, but a divine comedy. And we know that between now and the drama's climax, we are called to live in the pentecostal joy that comes from the fire of divine love.

That is the faith, the hope, and the love that inspired Andrey Sheptytsky and Josyf Slipyj and that gave them the courage to persevere—the courage and perseverance that are the foundation on which this university, of which both these great men dreamed, has been built. Their lives, lived in the truth, proved that, over time, the truth can change what seems unchangeable, and that love, stronger than fear, can bend the curve of history toward freedom and justice.

May their noble and holy examples inspire you, the graduates of the Ukrainian Catholic University, to accept the challenge of twenty-first-century history, and to use the truths you have made your own here into the tools by which to build a civic culture of freedom ordered to goodness in Ukraine.

God bless you and keep you on your journey.

AGENTS OF THE NEW EVANGELIZATION

University of Dallas, Irving, Texas, May 18, 2014

Dear Graduates:

Three weeks ago, the Church recognized the heroic virtues of the two "bookend" popes of the Second Vatican Council, as Pope Francis, before a million pilgrims in and around St. Peter's Square, solemnly declared Pope John XXIII and Pope John Paul II to be saints. Pope Saint John XXIII is the first bookend of Vatican II: the pope who had the inspiration to summon the twenty-first general council in the history of the Church, and the courage and wisdom to see the Council through its difficult first period in 1962. Pope Saint John Paul II is the second bookend of Vatican II because it was he, working in close harness with the man who would become his papal successor, Joseph Ratzinger, who gave Vatican II an authoritative interpretation through his remarkable magisterium.

Our two new saints are not random or accidental bookends, however. They're a matched set of bookends, because both popes shared a vision of the Council's purpose and a hope for the Council's impact.

John XXIII wanted Vatican II to be a new experience of Pentecost for the world Church—a new encounter with the fire of the Holy Spirit that would enliven Christian witness at the end of the twentieth century, offering the world the medicine of the divine mercy through which we experience the Truth who is the Triune God. John Paul II, on the day after his election as pope, said that the "full implementation" of Vatican II would be the program of his pontificate, a pledge he fulfilled over more than a quarter of a century. And in doing so, John Paul II led the Church into that new experience of Pentecost for which John XXIII hoped and prayed, through the Great Jubilee of 2000.

In closing the Great Jubilee on January 6, 2001, with the apostolic letter *Novo Millennio Ineunte* (which, for any non-UD graduates present, I will translate as "Entering the New Millennium"), John Paul II urged the Church of the twenty-first century and the new millennium to leave the comfortable but shallow waters of institutional-maintenance Catholicism and to "put out into the deep" (Lk 5:4) of late modernity[1]—to rediscover the evangelical and missionary passion that seized the first Christian community and led them into mission, once the Holy Spirit had given them the words with which to explain what they had "seen and heard" (1 Jn 1:1) in their encounters with the Risen Lord.[2]

The graduates of the University of Dallas are singularly well prepared to be the agents of this "New Evangelization," as John Paul II called the grand strategy of the twenty-first-century Church that John XXIII had the courage to envision. For in the challenging cultural circumstances in which twenty-first-century Christians must witness to the Gospel and offer men and women the possibility of friendship with Jesus Christ, there is no better preparation for being a Church permanently in mission than the classic Catholic liberal arts education for which the University of Dallas is known and respected throughout the world.[3]

Here, through that classic Catholic liberal arts education, you have learned the ecumenism of time, drinking deeply from those wells of wisdom that are fed by streams of knowledge and insight drawn from the great minds and spirits of the past.

Here, you have learned that "tradition" is neither a synonym for dullness nor the enemy of human progress; for here you have learned that "tradition," as the great Chesterton noted, is "the democracy of the dead,"[4] the willingness to think that those who came before us—Homer and Virgil, Augustine and Aquinas, Dante and Milton and Shakespeare—may have important things to teach us.

Here, you have learned that the tradition of the West is built on the three pillars of Jerusalem, Athens, and Rome: biblical religion, which teaches us that life is a pilgrimage in which we are called to follow the God of Israel and the Church on the path he is taking through history; the Greek faith in reason's ability to get at the truth of things that is embedded in the world and in us; the Roman conviction that the rule of law is superior to the rule of brute force.

Each of those pillars is under assault throughout the Western world today. In the nineteenth century, what Henri de Lubac called "atheistic humanism"[5] jettisoned the God of the Bible and declared that Western high culture would henceforth be a God-free zone. In the twentieth century, the deconstruction of the humanities in an aggressively secular academy led, not to liberated minds, but to minds chained in the prisons of uncertainty, skepticism, irony, and cynicism. In the twenty-first century, and as a result of what happened in the nineteenth and twentieth centuries, the "dictatorship of relativism" prophetically analyzed by Benedict XVI now threatens the rule of law from Anchorage to Kyiv and at all points in between.

So, you have your work cut out for you, and that work is nothing less than the exhilarating, challenging, and sometimes dangerous task of giving the West a new birth of freedom rightly understood—freedom tethered to moral truth and ordered to goodness; freedom lived nobly rather than selfishly; freedom lived for the common good in solidarity with other pilgrims through history.

And if, in the years and decades ahead, that task of cultural renewal seems daunting, perhaps even impossible, remember that Saint John Paul II believed that you could do it—that your generation could lead the world into what he called, at the United Nations in 1995, a "new springtime of the human spirit."

John Paul II's confidence in young people was a happy by-product of his early years in the priesthood—when he was a university chaplain in Kraków in the late 1940s and early 1950s, in a country choking on the acrid fumes of Stalinism after being beaten for over five years by the lethal scourges of German National Socialism. With the young men and women he met at the Kraków Polytechnic, the Kraków Academy of Music, the Kraków Academy of Fine Arts, and other institutions of higher learning in that beautiful city, young Father Karol Wojtyła formed remarkable networks of friendship and solidarity that lasted for more than half a century. The lay friends Father Wojtyła made in those years remained among his closest friends until his death in 2005. And as he helped form his young friends into mature Christian men and women, preparing them for the vocation of marriage or helping them discern vocations to the priesthood or religious life, they helped form him into one of the most dynamic priests, and later one of the most dynamic bishops, of the Church.

In those networks of friendship, Wojtyła came to understand something that the Second Vatican Council would later put at the center of its reflection on the Church: what the Council called, twenty years or so after Wojtyła and his young friends lived it, the "universal call to holiness." The Church, Wojtyła and his young friends came to understand, exists for holiness—for enlivening and empowering what the grace of God makes possible in all of our lives. Sanctity is not a matter for the sanctuary alone; sanctity is every Christian's human and baptismal destiny.

The networks of friendship Father Karol Wojtyła created with young people—young people very much like you—were zones of freedom and zones of truth in a world of tyranny and lies. Here, Wojtyła's young friends met the great minds and spirits of Western civilization—just as you have done at the University of Dallas. Here, in these zones of truth and freedom, Wojtyła's young friends learned compassion and charity and the dignity of every human life, at all stages of life and in all conditions of life—just as you have done at the University of Dallas. Here, in the free space for free conversation created by the openness of Father Karol Wojtyła, the man who would become pope, Wojtyła's young friends learned to live their lives, not simply as a matter of "career," but as a matter of *vocation*, discerning that unique *something* that God has in mind for every human life—just as you have begun to do at the University of Dallas.

In this remarkable story of friendship, we can see the beginnings of some of the great things for which the pontificate of John Paul II would become noted: World Youth Days; the Theology of the Body; the call to the laity to convert the world; the dialogues between science and religion, and between the humanities and religion; even the Great Jubilee of 2000. And in exploring those early years in the priestly life of Saint John Paul II, I think we find answers to a question I have been asked dozens of times: Why was John Paul II such a magnet for the young?

The answer to that question can't be celebrity goofiness, of the sort to which we're all unhappily accustomed in this cultural moment; celebrities never did what John Paul II did with young people, and in any event, in the last, difficult years of his life, the bent and crippled John Paul II didn't look like any "celebrity." Yet the magnetism remained, and in the days before he died, thousands of young people from all over the world came to St. Peter's Square to keep vigil outside the Pope's window, to help him in his dying as he had helped them in their living.

Why? I think there are two reasons why John Paul II was a magnet for the young.

The first was his transparent honesty. There was no falseness in the man, no hedging, none of the ambiguity that is often a postmodern mask hiding deep confusion. He did not ask young people to do anything he had not done. He did not ask young people to bear any burden he had not borne. He simply asked them to let him, and the Church, accompany them on the pathways of life, in moments of failure as well as moments of success, so that those pathways might eventually become a pilgrim's progress toward sanctity.

And the second reason why John Paul II was a magnet for the young was his challenge. Unlike twenty-first-century popular culture, John Paul II did not pander to young people. He challenged young people, because he knew, from his experiences with his young friends in Kraków, that young people want to be summoned to live lives of heroism—that young adulthood is a time to dream great dreams, to imagine how things ought to be, and to bend heroic efforts to fixing what is broken in our own lives and in society.

Above all, John Paul II's challenge to young people was a challenge to claim, and own, and live their human dignity. In a host of variations on one great theme, John Paul II said the same thing to millions of young people in Rome, Buenos Aires, Compostela, Częstochowa, Denver, Paris, and Toronto: *Never, ever settle for anything less than the spiritual and moral grandeur that the grace of God makes possible in your lives.* Never settle for less than that. You will fail, as we all do; but that is no reason to lower the bar of expectation. Get up, dust yourself off, seek forgiveness and reconciliation, and try again. But never, ever settle for anything less than the spiritual and moral greatness that is available to you, and of which you are capable by God's grace. Don't ever settle for less than that.

If the generation of which this Class of 2014 is a part is going to meet the challenge of giving America, and the West, a new birth of freedom, it will do so because it becomes a generation of saints: well-educated, thoughtful, and articulate saints; compassionate and merciful saints; saints for the new millennium who refuse to surrender to the tyranny of low expectations, personal and public; saints in the image of the young Pole who never imagined himself pope, but whom the Church and the world now know as Pope Saint John Paul II.

He is now more than an image to ponder, an example to emulate. He is your powerful intercessor. And Saint John Paul II will not fail to support you as you go out, today, from this great university to the ends of the earth, contemporary witnesses to the ancient and enduring truths you have made your own here.

Godspeed on your journey.

MORE THAN STARDUST

Franciscan Missionaries of Our Lady University, Baton Rouge, Louisiana, May 22, 2017

Dear Graduates:

Thank you for the invitation to be with you in Baton Rouge today. I love this part of America, and it is always a pleasure to come here—even if it usually costs me extra time on the treadmill when I return home. And thank you for inviting me to share this wonderful occasion with you. My warmest congratulations go to the Class of 2017.

Speakers at commencements are notorious for offering advice—usually unsolicited, often off-the-mark, and typically unremembered. Perhaps the finest example of a public personality whose advice was to the point—if not always followed—was Conrad Hilton, founder of the enormous hotel chain that bears his name. Mr. Hilton was being interviewed on national television many years ago and was asked what one thing he would most like the viewers to remember, given his vast experience of humanity. Conrad Hilton looked the camera in the eye and without missing a beat told his fellow Americans, "Please—put the shower curtain *inside* the tub." Sage counsel, that. But let me offer today's graduates today another piece of wisdom, from a very different source: Pope Pius XI.

As the shadows of fascist, Nazi, and communist totalitarianism lengthened across Europe in the late 1930s and a terrible war threatened, Pius XI commended this thought to the Catholic Church: "Let us thank God that he makes us live among the present problems. It is no longer permitted to anyone to be mediocre."[1]

Dear graduates, those words could well have been addressed to each of you, across the decades that separate us from Pius XI. For their summons to excellence captures the essence of the education—the Franciscan and Catholic education—you have received here at this university. And they embody the challenge you face as you take what you have learned here out into the world, especially into the world of health care and healing.

Here, you have been taught that the patients you will serve are men and women with an inherent dignity and value that demands your respect and calls forth your compassion.

Here, you have been taught that "health care" is far more than an "industry" or a "sector" of the American economy—rather, health care is a vocation, a calling, a way to live your life as a gift to others, as each of your lives was and is a gift to you.

Here, in this remarkable part of America, you have seen the national aspiration to liberty and justice for all embodied in a unique culture that could teach the rest of America something about civility, harmony, and solidarity—even as, perhaps, this unique culture could learn a few things from other parts of the country about keeping cholesterol under control!

Here, you have not only been educated, important as that is; you have been *formed*. You have been formed in a Franciscan spirit of reverence for life, and you have been formed in a spirit of Franciscan responsibility for creation and for creation's most noble creature, the human person—the man or woman made in the image and likeness of God and destined for beatitude and glory.

Here, you have been taught and formed in the convictions that we are not just congealed stardust and that humanity is not just a happy accident of cosmic biochemical processes.

Remember that. For those convictions are essential to your future work as healers, a work that should touch hearts and souls as well as bodies. The advance of medical science in the lifetimes of everyone present here today has been breathtaking. Yet those amazing advances in the science of healing have not always been complemented by parallel advances in wisdom about the ways in which the new technological capabilities we possess should be deployed.

The health care profession needs a soul as well as a mind. You can be that soul. This university can be that soul by offering its students the wisdom of theology, philosophy, and the liberal arts as well as scientific knowledge and professional skills.

To carry this school's diploma is to carry a great responsibility. The future of Franciscan health care, which has played such an important role in our national life, is being entrusted to you. In the decades ahead, you will be the face of this Franciscan ministry to society.

In the decades ahead, you will bring the spirit of Saint Francis and Saint Clare to an American health care system that is in danger of dehumanization, even as its technical wonders multiply exponentially.

In the decades ahead, you must, in the Franciscan spirit, help form the conscience, as well as the soul, of the profession of healing in the United States.

The life of faith and professional life cannot be siloed, as if they were two aspects of our lives that never intersect. A genuinely Catholic and Franciscan faith will shape every facet of your lives—your souls, your minds, your families, your professional work. America is too full of silos today. The education you have received here, the hard work you have done here, the sacrifices you and your families have made so that you could be here and learn here and be formed here—all of these have prepared you to be men and women who break out of the silos that divide us: men and women who demonstrate to others that the greatest satisfaction in life comes from making our lives into a gift for others.

Thank you for letting me share this day with you. Always put that shower curtain inside the tub! But above all, please remember the words of Pope Pius XI—"It is no longer permitted to anyone to be mediocre."

LAWYERING AS A VOCATION

Ave Maria School of Law, Naples, Florida, May 12, 2018

Dear Graduates:

Thank you for inviting me to share this commencement with you.

Today is a day for celebration. It's also a day for reflection, as one moment in our graduates' lives ends and a new chapter begins. So, permit me to reflect briefly with you on the meaning of law, on law and the renewal of American democracy, and on the practice of law as a vocation.

Last month, our nation marked the fiftieth anniversary of the death of the Reverend Dr. Martin Luther King, Jr. Like other martyrs over the centuries, Dr. King was not a perfect man; but he died a martyr in the cause of justice and reconciliation, and in defense of the noble ideas that are the moral bedrock of our country. Dr. King is best remembered today for his stirring speech at the Lincoln Memorial on August 28, 1963. There, he bore witness to his "dream" that, one day, his children would be judged by the content of their character and not by the color of their skin. That speech, like Lincoln's second inaugural address—another stirring, biblically inspired oration delivered by another imperfect man who was a martyr for the causes of justice and reconciliation—is now part of America's cultural patrimony. Yet Dr. King made an equally important contribution to our national heritage in a letter he wrote to fellow clergymen from a jail cell in Birmingham, Alabama, four months before he spoke at the Lincoln Memorial.

Dr. King and his colleagues in the Southern Christian Leadership Conference had been criticized by some local Alabama clergy for the program of nonviolent demonstrations they were leading, protesting segregation statutes in Birmingham—at that time, quite probably the most segregated city in the United States. His critics were particularly concerned about the civil rights demonstrators' willingness to break local laws intended to enforce segregation and to muffle or prevent protests against it. King's response—the response of a Baptist minister—was thoroughly Catholic and bears repeating today:

> One may well ask, "How can you advocate breaking some laws and obeying others?" The answer lies in the fact that there are two types of laws: just and unjust. I would be the first to advocate obeying just laws. One has not only a legal but moral responsibility to obey just laws. Conversely, one has a moral responsibility to disobey unjust laws. I would agree with St. Augustine that "an unjust law is no law at all."
>
> Now, what is the difference between the two? How does one determine whether a law is just or unjust? A just law is a man-made code that squares with the moral law or law of God. An unjust law is a code that is out of harmony with the moral law. To put it in the terms of St. Thomas Aquinas: An unjust law is a human law that is not rooted in eternal law and natural law.[1]

Eighty years before Dr. King wrote his "Letter from Birmingham Jail," Pope Leo XIII made precisely the same argument in several encyclicals that laid the intellectual foundations of modern Catholic social doctrine. Pope Leo, like Dr. King, took his concept of law from Thomas Aquinas. In doing so, he challenged the legal positivism of his day—and ours—according to which "law" is simply whatever the law says it is: period, full stop. Leo XIII and Dr. King, drawing on the insights of Saint Thomas, understood that this legal positivism empties law of moral content, detaches it from reason, and treats law as merely an expression of human willfulness.

Leo XIII offered the world a nobler concept of law; a true law, he proposed, has three characteristics: A true law is a rule mandated by reason; a true law is enacted by a properly constituted authority; and a true law serves the common good of society. The modern political tradition that begins with Thomas Hobbes thinks of law as sheer coercion. Leo XIII, with Thomas Aquinas, disagreed. To their minds, true law is authoritative *prescription*, grounded in reason. True law reflects moral judgment, and its power comes from its moral persuasiveness. Law, rightly understood, appeals to conscience—to that often-fragile but nonetheless real human instinct for the good and the true—not just to fear.[2]

What does this have to do with our American situation today? Everything.

In the twenty-first-century United States, the law is too often understood as a codification of willfulness rather than a precept of reason, as freedom is too often understood to be a matter of unbridled choice—or as the famous moral philosopher Frank Sinatra would put it, freedom is "I did it *my* way." This false concept of freedom and the false concept of law that goes with it are at the root of our Supreme Court's mistaken decisions on abortion and marriage in *Roe v. Wade*, *Casey v. Planned Parenthood*, *Windsor v. United States*, and *Obergefell v. Hodges*. And beneath those false ideas of freedom and law lies another error that is putting our democracy in jeopardy: the idea that there is only your truth and my truth, but nothing properly describable as *the* truth.

What happens, though, if "your truth" and "my truth" collide and there is no standard of judgment—call it "*the* truth"—by which we can settle our differences? What happens is that you impose your power on me, or I impose my power on you—sometimes through cultural bullying and shaming, but more often these days through the distortion of the law.

That imposition—that power play—is what Cardinal Joseph Ratzinger called, in April 2005, the "dictatorship of relativism."[3] It is alive and well throughout the Western world today, eating away at the moral and cultural foundations of democracy. It is one cause of the current turmoil in the European Union. It is eroding religious freedom and freedom of conscience in Canada. And it is a primary cause of the turbulence of twenty-first-century American public life.

If we're disturbed, as we should be, by the condition of American politics today, we should look beneath the headlines, the soundbites, and the twitter feeds and ponder the state of our public moral culture. We are where we are, not by accident but because the ideas of freedom and law that shape our public life have become severely distorted. The moral and cultural foundations of our republic need, not just shoring up, but deep and fundamental renewal. That is a task for generations, but it must begin now—and that task must engage each of you, the Class of 2018 of Ave Maria School of Law.

You will engage that task in different ways. Some of you will do it through honorable legal practice. Some of you will do it in academic life. Some of you will do it through public service, in elective or appointive office. Perhaps some of you will do it as judges. But whatever your station in legal life, you will help give America a new birth of freedom rightly understood if you remember the noble idea of law that animated Saint Thomas Aquinas, Pope Leo XIII, and Dr. Martin Luther King, Jr.; if, as citizens and legislators, you help reconnect our laws to the moral law, and if, in all walks of legal life, you think of your legal work as a vocation, not simply a career.

The men and women who bend the curve of history in a more humane direction live vocationally. That's true of the great figures I've mentioned here. These towering human personalities understood, each in his own way, that every human being has a God-given vocation: a unique place, and a singular responsibility, in the divine plan of history. Discerning that vocation can take time and may involve false starts. Living that vocation can be costly. But living vocationally—constantly asking yourself, "Am I doing what I *ought* to be doing now?"—is the most exhilarating way to spend out one's life. It's also the most spiritually enriching. Living vocationally may, on occasion, cost you a sleepless night. But living vocationally guarantees that you will never have a boring day.

In the Gospels of Matthew and Luke, Jesus rebukes Satan with the reminder that "man shall not live by bread alone" (Mt 4:4; Lk 4:4). Nor is a noble and spiritually rich life lived by fame alone, or wealth alone, or power alone, or pleasure alone—and certainly not by billable hours alone. Each of you graduates has before you, not just a legal career, but a legal *vocation*. If, in your practice of law, you help remind the American legal profession that black-letter law and the moral law must be in active, ongoing conversation with each other, so that the laws that govern us reflect the moral truths written into the human heart and into the human condition, you will be living vocationally. You will be helping rebuild the foundations of American democracy. And you will be vindicating the kind of legal education you received at Ave Maria School of Law.

Congratulations on your graduation. Best wishes for your work. And Godspeed on your journey.

YOUR OWN WESTERPLATTE

St. Thomas More Academy, Raleigh, North Carolina, May 25, 2024

Thank you for inviting me to share this day with you.

Some things in life can never be too short. Visits to the dentist and lines at Chick-fil-A come immediately to mind. So do presidential State of the Union addresses and New York Yankees winning streaks. Those of you pursuing scientific studies in college will soon learn that an organic chemistry class can never, *ever* be too short.

I think this Can't-Be-Too-Short rule also applies to commencement addresses. This day is about you, our graduates, not about me. So as your patron, Saint Thomas More, said on the scaffold, just before his execution, "I shall be brief."

Jerzy Stuhr, a renowned Polish actor, found himself in Rome in the 1990s and was invited to dinner in the papal apartment by Pope John Paul II—who, as you know, had been an actor as a young man. After they were seated, the Pope looked across the table at his guest and said, "Pan Jerzy, what brings you to Rome?" To which Mr. Stuhr replied, "Your Holiness, I am playing in *Forefathers' Eve*"—one of the most famous dramas in Polish literature, and a play so emotionally charged with patriotic energy that its public performance was banned in the Russian parts of partitioned Poland in the nineteenth century.

Hearing this, John Paul got very excited and recited whole chunks of the play (in which he had once acted) from memory. Then he asked, one veteran actor to another, "So, Pan Jerzy, what role do you take?" Mr. Stuhr looked a bit sheepish, and then replied, "Your Holiness, I regret to report that I am Satan"—who is indeed a character in the play. The Pope was silent for a moment; the pontifical eyebrow went up, and then John Paul said, "Well, none of us gets to choose our roles, do we?"

That might have been a bit of papal whimsy from a man who didn't imagine being a priest, much less a pope, when he was your age. But I think John Paul II was also making a different, and deeper, point: one that another saint, Saint John Henry Newman, made in 1848 when he wrote this prayer, which is well worth pondering on this commencement day, or indeed any other day:

> God has created me to do Him some definite service. He has committed some work to me which He has not committed to another. I have my mission. I may never know it in this life, but I shall be told it in the next. Somehow I am necessary for His purposes, as necessary in my place as an archangel in his....
>
> I am a link in a chain, a bond of connection between persons. He has not created me for naught. I shall do good; I shall do His work. I shall be an angel of peace, a preacher of truth in my own place ... if I do but keep His commandments....
>
> Therefore, I will trust Him; whatever I am, I can never be thrown away. If I am in sickness, my sickness may serve Him, in perplexity, my perplexity may serve Him. If I am in sorrow, my sorrow may serve Him. He does nothing in vain. He knows what He is about. He may take away my friends. He may throw me among strangers. He may make me feel desolate, make my spirits sink, hide my future from me. Still, He knows what He is about.[1]

Amen. He knows what he is about.

As you, our graduates, have learned here at St. Thomas More Academy, each of you is an idea in the mind of God. That means, to continue the dramatic metaphor, that each of you has a specific role to play in the long arc of the human drama. That drama, Christians and Catholics believe, is not some lucky accident in which random, cosmic biochemical forces fortuitously conjured up *us* over the course of fifteen billion years or so. We know that we have not come from nowhere; we know that we are going somewhere; and we know that there is purpose in the great cosmos.

Each of us lives a personal drama. And each of our personal dramas "plays" within a greater drama. That greater drama is one in which there are eight acts: Creation, Fall, Promise, Prophecy, Incarnation, Redemption, Sanctification—and finally, at the end of the drama, the Wedding Feast of the Lamb in the Kingdom of Heaven.

It will take some time for each of you to discern just what your unique role in that great drama is. Your roles may change over the course of your lives. You may be called on to play multiple roles at a given moment. But if you live your lives asking one question—"What is God asking of me *now*?"—you will discover that, while your lives may be challenging, they will never be dull or boring.

Living into the future according to that one great question—"What is God asking of me *now*?—is the greatest of adventures. And it will prepare you for the greatest, most tremendous adventure of all, which is eternal life in the light and love of God the Holy Trinity.

As you begin the next phase of this great adventure, let me offer you another story from the life of Saint John Paul II, which speaks to the challenges before you—and to the help that is always available in meeting those challenges.

Westerplatte is a narrow peninsula framing the Bay of Gdańsk in the northwest of Poland. There, one of the first battles of World War II in Europe was fought. At a quarter to five in the morning on September 1, 1939, the German battleship *Schleswig-Holstein* opened fire on the small Polish garrison at Westerplatte, expecting that the vastly outnumbered and outgunned Poles would run up a white flag. That, to put it mildly, was a misimpression. The Poles—mostly youngsters your age or slightly older, with no combat experience—not only resisted the offshore bombardment; they repelled amphibious assaults by German marines, suffering serious casualties in the process. The Polish garrison finally surrendered on September 7. But they had so impressed the aggressors that the German commander allowed the Polish officer leading the Westerplatte garrison to keep his ceremonial sword.

Addressing a vast throng of young Poles at Westerplatte in 1987, John Paul II, speaking slowly and forcefully in his beautiful, sonorous Polish, invoked the memory of the heroes of Westerplatte, while explaining how those young Polish soldiers were relevant to young people of every time and place. Here's what the Pope said:

> Here in this place, at Westerplatte, in September 1939, a group of young Poles, soldiers under the command of Major Henryk Sucharski, resisted with noble obstinacy, engaging in an unequal struggle against the invader. A heroic struggle.

> They remained in the nation's memory as an eloquent symbol. It is necessary for this symbol to continue to speak, for it to be a challenge ... to new generations....
>
> Each of you, young friends, will also find your own "Westerplatte." ... [T]asks you must assume and fulfill. A just cause, for which one cannot but fight. Some duty, some obligation, from which one cannot shrink, from which it is not possible to desert. Finally—a certain order of truths and values that one must "maintain" and "defend": within oneself and beyond oneself.... At such a moment (and such moments are many, they are not just a few exceptions) ... remember ... [that] Christ is passing by and he says, "Follow me." Do not forsake him.[2]

Dear graduates of the Class of 2024 of St. Thomas More Academy: If you carry one thing of what I have said here into the future, let it be this: Remember that, in both your joys and your challenges, Christ is passing by and saying, "Follow me." Remembering that, you will never be alone.

Remembering that, you will be empowered to live, not without fear, but beyond fear.

Remembering that, you will, in time, discover the singular adventure that God has in mind for each of you: the adventure and the mission that will be your unique path to happiness, and ultimately to holiness and beatitude.

Thank you for allowing me to share these thoughts with you today, and Godspeed on your journey.

TWENTIETH-CENTURY WITNESS AND TWENTY-FIRST-CENTURY MISSION
Eastern Catholics and the Universal Church

Cathedral of the Immaculate Conception, Philadelphia, Pennsylvania, June 2, 2019

It is a distinct honor and a great personal pleasure to be invited to participate in the ceremonies marking the enthronement of His Grace, Borys Gudziak, as Archeparch and Metropolitan of Philadelphia. Metropolitan Borys and I met more than thirty years ago in circumstances that seemed quite random then, but which I think we have both come to regard as providential, as the friendship begun at the reception following the baptism of a mutual friend's child has grown, and as we have worked together in a variety of venues and ways for Christ and his one Church. To cite just one personal memory: I had the pleasure of giving an inscribed copy of then-Father Gudziak's book, *Crisis and Reform: The Kyivan Metropolitanate, the Patriarchate of Constantinople, and the Genesis of the Union of Brest*, to Pope John Paul II over dinner one night in 1999; and I am quite sure that that great saint, a voracious reader with a deep love for Ukraine, started reading it later that evening.

I am also deeply touched that the Ukrainian Greek Catholic Archeparchy of Philadelphia should have invited me, a Latin-Rite Catholic, to participate in this week of festivities by speaking on "Twentieth-Century Witness and Twenty-First-Century Mission: Eastern Catholic Churches and the Universal Church." My presence here is a sign of the fraternity and solidarity that characterize the one, holy, catholic, and apostolic Church, which now breathes freely with both

---

This is a different kind of "commencement" address—in this case, inaugurating the celebrations at which Borys Gudziak was enthroned as Archeparch of Philadelphia for Ukrainian Greek Catholics.

its Latin and Greek lungs. And who knows? It may also be a sign of reconciliation, such that Philadelphians have forgiven me, a native Baltimorean, for the thumping my Orioles laid on your Phillies in the 1983 World Series.

When we think of the witness of Eastern Catholics in the twentieth century, and particularly of the witness of the Ukrainian Greek Catholic Church, our minds naturally turn first to the great men and women who held firm to the Catholic and apostolic faith during the starvations and slaughters of the mid-twentieth century, and during the communist persecution that followed. We think of the New Ukrainian Martyrs beatified by John Paul II during his pastoral pilgrimage to Ukraine in 2001; we think of the many martyrs whose names are not in the Church's liturgical calendar, but who nonetheless "washed their robes and made them white in the blood of the Lamb" (Rev 7:14) and now reign with him forever. We think of the Venerable Andrey Sheptytsky, and pray that his beatification is not long delayed. We remember the Servant of God Josyf Slipyj, whose witness in the Gulag inspired novelist Morris West to create a fictional—and perhaps even prophetic—Ukrainian pope in *The Shoes of the Fisherman*. In my commencement address at the Ukrainian Catholic University in 2013, I challenged the graduates to be faithful to the martyrs whose sacrifice laid the foundation on which UCU was built. That challenge applies equally to all Ukrainian Greek Catholics wherever they live, in Ukraine or in the diaspora, just as it applies to every Catholic, whatever rite they practice.

It was the first great Christian thinker to write in Latin, the late second- and early third-century North African theologian Tertullian, who, in his *Apologeticus*, wrote, "*Plures efficimur, quoties metimur a vobis; semen est sanguis christianorum* (Whenever you mow us down, we multiply; the blood of Christians is seed)." And while many Catholics, East and West, on all continents, bore witness in the twentieth century to the truth of Tertullian's maxim that the blood of martyrs is the seed of the Church, the Greek Catholic Church of Ukraine bore a particularly impressive witness.

In thinking of the Ukrainian Greek Catholic Church's witness in the twentieth century, though, we should remember more than blood and martyrs; we should think of a Church that became a safe deposit box of national identity, memory, and culture when malign forces sought to erase the very idea of "Ukraine" from the world's vocabulary. We remember how Borys Gudziak and an intrepid band of brothers and sisters realized the dreams of Andrey Sheptytsky and Josyf Slipyj and built a great Catholic center of higher learning in Ukraine—a university that would deepen and broaden the culture that Sheptytsky in particular did so much to both preserve and nourish.

The Ukrainian Greek Catholic Church of the twentieth century was not only a Church that taught the world Church how to die nobly; it also taught the world Church how to live as a culture-forming counterculture, bringing new life to physically devastated lands and healing morally devastated populations, demonstrating the power of the Gospel to make whole again what had been so badly broken by evil incarnate. And so we also remember with gratitude a man who embodied that capacity of the Church to be an agent of cultural renewal in a singular way: His Beatitude Cardinal Lubomyr Husar, whose work and witness in the independent Ukraine that emerged from under the rubble of Soviet communism made him the most revered and respected leader in the country.

The relationship between Eastern Catholics and the world Church has not always been an easy one: even in these United States, where the unique Greek Catholic way of being Catholic was not always welcomed by some in the dominant Latin-Rite Church. We thank God that those days are over, that the Church is once again breathing with both its Eastern and Western lungs, and that we can learn from each other and enrich each other's experience of being the Body of Christ. What, then, are the particular gifts that Eastern Catholics bring to the universal Church in the twenty-first century? Permit me to suggest six.

The first is *the gift of adoration.* The great interior disloyalty of the modern world (as Romano Guardini put it) is its failure to worship truly because of its conviction that humanity is self-sufficient. Yet a world without true worship—the worship of that which is worthy of worship—is a claustrophobic world: a world without windows, doors, or skylights; a world that becomes suffocating; a world that, sooner or later, becomes nihilistic. And on the way to nihilism, a world without true worship substitutes false gods for the one true God, in order to satisfy the innate, built-in human desire to worship. We have just recalled the bloodlands of eastern Europe, including the Holodomor and the massacres of the Holocaust committed on Ukrainian soil; one and all, those slaughters were the result of the worship of false gods.

That is why the adoration-centered liturgy celebrated by the Eastern Catholic Churches is so important for the world Church, and indeed for the world. As a Latin-Rite Catholic, I am a firm believer in the liturgical reforms of the Second Vatican Council, properly implemented. But that implementation has been, as you know, uneven at best, and its unevenness almost always involves a loss of the necessity of adoration. So, there is much that Latin-Rite Catholicism can learn from the Eastern Catholic Churches as we continue the reform of the liturgical reform in the West.

The primary truth we Latin-Rite Catholics can learn from our Eastern brethren is that the liturgy is a celebration of the presence of the living Christ among us—a foretaste of the Wedding Feast of the Lamb in the New Jerusalem, as described by Saint John in the last chapters of the Book of Revelation. Eastern Catholics also remind the rest of the world Church that Catholic worship is explicitly Trinitarian. Indeed, scholars of the first Christian centuries tell us that it was the invocation of the thrice-holy God in the primitive liturgy that led over time to the development of the Church's Trinitarian theology and doctrine; thus the omnipresence of the Trinity in Eastern Catholic worship invites the entire world Church to enter more deeply into the self-giving love and mutual receptivity of Father, Son, and Holy Spirit. Finally, Eastern Catholic worship reminds the world Church that our liturgical life places us in a new and different time zone. Or as patristics scholar Robert Louis Wilken puts in *The Spirit of Early Christian Thought*, "Liturgy is always in the present tense,"[1] but this is a different kind of "present." In the liturgy, and especially in its Eucharistic remembrance of the Last Supper and the Passion of the Lord, "the past becomes a present presence that opens a new future."[2]

The second gift the Eastern Catholic Churches offer the rest of the world Church is *the gift of iconography*. And by this, I do not mean simply the beautiful icons that now adorn many Latin-Rite Catholic churches and homes. I mean that your Church, in its icons, offers the world Church a powerful reminder that, as Dr. Wilken put it, "the way to God passes through things that can be seen and touched."[3] This is, of course, at the very foundation of the faith. In Acts 10:41, Peter describes the first witnesses to the Resurrection—that history-shattering event at which the Kingdom of God became manifest in the world and its story—as those "who ate and drank with him after he rose from the dead." But it is a truth of which we need constant reminding today.

For we live in a Gnostic culture, in which everything is plastic and malleable, subject to change by human will—even our embodiedness as men and women. Despite (or perhaps because of) the materialism of the postmodern West, our culture is one that in fact denies any significance to the material givenness of things—and that denial poses a very sharp challenge to Catholics, for whom material things (like water at baptism, bread and wine in the Eucharist, the oil of confirmation, marital love and fidelity) are the means by which God's own life, the life of grace, flows into the world. Icons can help us all meet the challenge of this new Gnosticism, reminding us as they do that what lies between this world and the world of divine life and grace is not a fixed border, and still less a wall, but something like a membrane, through which nutrients flow from the Source of life to us.

Icons are also a gift to the world Church from Eastern Christian traditions because their beauty opens up the possibility that a world that has lost touch with the true and the good might get a grip on truth and goodness again. As the Swiss theologian Hans Urs von Balthasar reminded the world Church, the transcendental of beauty can be a path back to the true and the good. When we see something beautiful, we know that it's, well, beautiful; it's not "maybe beautiful." And we know that that beauty is good: It's not "good for me," or "good for you," but *good*, period. In nurturing the arts of Christian iconography, then, the Eastern Catholic Churches do essential service to a confused postmodern culture, as beauty invites an exploration of the permanence of truth and goodness in the order of things.

The Eastern Catholic Churches also do us all a service by what I might call *the gift of "theosis."* Less than forty-eight hours from now, Latin-Rite Catholics will get an annual shock from the Office of Readings in the Liturgy of the Hours, where they will read this from Saint Basil the Great's *Treatise on the Holy Spirit*: "Through the Spirit we become citizens of heaven, we are admitted to the company of the angels, we enter into eternal happiness and abide in God. Through the Spirit we acquire a likeness to God; indeed, we attain what is beyond our most sublime aspirations—we become God."[4] And here, in the work of a fourth-century Cappadocian bishop, is the definitive rebuttal of the false charges laid by those nineteenth-century atheistic humanists who declared the God of the Bible the enemy of human maturation and sought to throw the God of the Bible out of history in the name of human liberation.

The hard fact, which confronts us daily, is that the degraded humanism of our time—which has been deeply influenced by nineteenth-century thinkers like Comte, Feuerbach, Marx, and Nietzsche (while rarely rising to their level of intellectual sophistication)—has dumbed down the very idea of the human. On this view, each of us is simply a twitching bundle of desires; all of those desires are equal; the achievement of those desires is the full meaning of happiness and fulfillment; and the role of the state is to clear the path to the satisfaction of our desires. But there is nothing mature here, nothing noble, nothing truly human. This is infantilism, and when it becomes cultural common wisdom, it leads to any number of horrors—including, to take a local Philadelphia example, Kermit Gosnell and his slaughterhouse of the innocent unborn.

In challenging this dumbed-down, degraded, and ultimately lethal concept of the human person, the Catholic Church must always recall the teaching of the Second Vatican Council in paragraph 22 of the Pastoral Constitution on the Church in the Modern World: On the holy face of Christ, we meet both the Father of mercies and the truth about our humanity.[5] Jesus Christ, crucified and risen, reveals the full dignity and eternal destiny of the human person—and in affirming Jesus as Lord, as in celebrating the Solemnity of his Ascension, we affirm that this human stuff of which we are made now lives within the life of the Trinity, within the life of God.

We are made for glory, not simply for transient satisfaction. We are made for God, and God has so entered into our lives through the sacraments that we can, with Saint Basil the Great, speak about our being divinized. By reminding the world Church of the great theme of "theosis" among the Eastern Fathers, the Ukrainian Greek Catholic Church and the other Eastern Catholic Churches help the world Church lift postmodern humanity out of the playpen of self-absorption, as Catholicism calls the twenty-first century to live in the truth that we are far, far greater than we think—not because of our merits, but because of our redemption.

And then there is *the gift of converting culture.* Despite the burdens of the office, John Paul II had some fun being pope, and I think he rarely had more fun than when he named Saints Cyril and Methodius the co-patrons of Europe along with Saint Benedict. That gesture was yet another way of John Paul reminding the world Church that the Christian East had much to teach the Christian West—in this particular case, about the inculturation of the Gospel. That the brothers from Thessaloniki initiated the process that led to what we now know as Old Church Slavonic was not only a shrewd tactical move in evangelizing the Slavic peoples; it was a culture-shaping initiative that displayed the Church's capacity to preserve and develop what is best in a people's heritage. It was also a demonstration of the true catholicity or universality of the Church, which until then had imagined there to be only three languages suitable for the things of God: Hebrew, Latin, and Greek. When Pope Nicholas I received the Slavic Scriptures from Cyril and Methodius and placed them on the altar of the Basilica of Saint Mary Major in Rome, Catholicism took a giant step toward being more fully "catholic." And an essential link between the "two lungs" of what we would eventually know as the civilization of Europe was forged.

This mission of healing and converting culture has been continued in our time by the foundation of an institution to which I have already referred, the Ukrainian Catholic University—an institution of higher learning explicitly dedicated to the healing of a culture of mistrust and corruption caused by the totalitarian disasters of the twentieth century. UCU is not a credential mill, although the credentials it grants its students are perhaps the most respected in the country. It is not just a place for punching one's ticket to a well-paying job. It is a genuine community, where students and faculty together are building the kind of culture of truth, goodness, and honesty that can sustain a free and prosperous Ukraine in the future. Cyril and Methodius would, I'm sure, be pleased. So would Andrey Sheptytsky and Josyf Slipyj, as the world Church looks to the Ukrainian Catholic University for a model of what a genuinely Catholic university can be, and to the Greek Catholic Church of Ukraine for an example of what it means to be a public Church, a culture-forming Church, that is, not a partisan Church.

And fifth, there is *the gift of the Holy Spirit.* That must sound a little odd, as we know that the Spirit was given to the entire Church.

But it is no secret that Latin-Rite Catholicism tends to be, de facto if not doctrinally, binitarian, celebrating the gift of the Holy Spirit at Pentecost—and then largely forgetting the Spirit for another year. Western theology's focus on the will may have played a part in this tacit forgetting that it is only in the Spirit that we can say "Jesus is Lord." But as Saint Gregory of Nyssa put it, there is no part of Christian faith that is "not covered by the Holy Spirit. That is why the confession of the Son's Lordship is made in the Holy Spirit by those who receive him, the Spirit coming ... to all those who approach the Son in faith."[6]

Saint Thomas Aquinas taught Latin-Rite Christianity that, for God to end the world, God would not have to do something; God would have to stop doing something. That sustaining creativity of God is the Holy Spirit, and the *Catechism of the Catholic Church* cites the Byzantine liturgy, the Troparion of Morning Prayer for Sundays of the second mode, to make the point: "It belongs to the Holy Spirit to rule, sanctify, and animate creation, for he is God, consubstantial with the Father and the Son.... Power over life pertains to the Spirit, for being God he preserves creation in the Father through the Son."[7]

The Holy Spirit is also the bond of unity within the Church—a bond that, whatever its expressions in human solidarity and friendship, is, in essence, divine, because it is a work of grace. The Eastern Catholic Churches' intense consciousness of the Holy Spirit thus reminds the rest of the world Church that the Church is not of our making but of God's, and that when we make the Church in our own image and by our own lights, we make a mess—or worse.

And while this list of gifts could be extended, let me conclude by citing *the gift of the Fathers* as a great Eastern Catholic patrimony that is crucial in the ongoing reform of the world Church. Western Christianity suffers today from "presentitis," too often misconstruing Vatican II's call to discern the "signs of the times" as a summons to imitate contemporary culture and accommodate to its mores. Eastern Christianity, by contrast, lives, worships, and thinks in a spiritual world in which Athanasius and John Chrysostom, Gregory Nazianzen and Basil, Gregory of Nyssa and Maximos the Confessor are vibrant, living presences, not books on a library shelf. From these great Eastern teachers of the Church, the entire world Church of the twenty-first century can learn the skills of expository preaching: preaching that begins with the conviction that the Word of God, the Logos, lives in the Word of God, the Holy Scriptures; preaching that invites the People of God to see the world through a biblical lens. And that kind of seeing is essential to curing the self-absorbed myopia of postmodernity and the moral astigmatism that defines wrongs as rights.

Eastern Catholicism's immersion in the Fathers also teaches the world Church to practice the ecumenism of time, giving a voice in the current deliberations of the Church to those who have gone before, and whose theology and preaching have passed the test of time in proving their spiritual fecundity. At a moment when too much of the Church in the West imagines that theology began anew some two hundred years ago—or even some fifty years ago—such that what went before is of only antiquarian interest, the gift of the Fathers is a precious offering from the Eastern Catholic Churches to all of Catholicism, even as that patristic heritage is the foundation on which the theological development of the Ukrainian Greek Catholic Church and other Eastern Catholic communities unfolds.

Finally, what of the future?

I believe the basic challenge facing the Archeparchy of Philadelphia and the Eastern Catholic Churches throughout the United States is identical to the challenge faced by the Archdiocese of Philadelphia and the rest of Latin-Rite Catholicism in this land: the challenge of living what John Paul II called the New Evangelization.

Living the New Evangelization begins with recognizing that the days when Catholic faith was transmitted by ethnic or cultural heritage are over in the West, including the United States. Thirty years from now, perhaps twenty, no one living the life of a Latin-Rite Catholic in America is going to answer the question, "Why are you a Catholic?" by answering, "Because my great-grandmother was born in County Cork." Or the south of Bavaria. Or Palermo. Or Guadalajara. Or Kraków. Or Lisieux. Or in rural Portugal or Spain. Similarly, no Ukrainian Greek Catholic of the mid-twenty-first century is going to be able to answer the question, "Why are you a Catholic?" by reference to their Ukrainian grandparents or great-grandparents, their suffering, and their faith. Those days are over.

Why? Because we live in a culture that is not neutral to the faith but hostile to the faith. And because that is the cultural air that surrounds us and which we cannot help inhaling, Catholicism by osmosis—Catholicism conveyed by ethnic or cultural inheritance,

"DNA Catholicism," if you will—is finished. The Catholicism of the future, whether it draws its liturgy, spirituality, and polity from the Christian West or the Christian East, will be a Catholicism that is deliberately chosen and embraced, not a Catholicism that is inherited. And Catholicism will only be chosen and embraced when it is offered and proposed.

That means that this Archeparchy and its suffragans, like the Archdiocese of Philadelphia and the entire Latin-Rite Church throughout the United States, must become, once again, a missionary enterprise: a Church in which everyone understands himself or herself to be a missionary disciple who was given the Great Commission at baptism; a Church in which every one of those missionary disciples understands that he or she is entering "mission territory" every day—at home, at work, in the neighborhood, in our lives as citizens, and in our lives as consumers.

This "evangelical" way of being Catholic is that to which the Second Vatican Council, as authoritatively interpreted by John Paul II and Benedict XVI, summoned the world Church. It is the Church that has heard John Paul II's call, when closing the Great Jubilee of 2000, to "put out into the deep" (Lk 5:4)[8]: to leave the shallow and brackish waters of institutional maintenance and sail into the often-turbulent waters of the postmodern world for a great catch. It is the Church that has heeded the call of Pope Francis to missionary discipleship in *Evangelii Gaudium*. The Ukrainian Greek Catholic Church brings to that global enterprise all the modern experience and all the ancient gifts I've outlined here; it also offers the world Church a living example of the truth that the only Catholicism that can attract twenty-first-century men and women to friendship with the Lord Jesus Christ and incorporation into his Body, the Church, is Catholicism in full.

Those who kept the Ukrainian Greek Catholic Church alive in Ukraine when it was the largest illegal and underground religious community in the world did not do so by preaching or practicing "Catholic Lite." They may have been deprived of their churches and schools; but no one could take the full symphony of Catholic truth away from them. That symphony empowered the heroic sacrifice that has re-created the Church in Ukraine, and that should inspire the Ukrainian Greek Catholic Church of this Archeparchy and its suffragans.

Perhaps the greatest challenge you will face as a Church of the New Evangelization is the challenge of inspiring young people to embrace friendship with the Lord Jesus, who is the answer to the question that is every human life. Happily, in the new Metropolitan of Philadelphia and in the Major-Archbishop of Kyiv-Halyč, His Beatitude Sviatoslav Shevchuk, you have been blessed with shepherds and leaders with long experience of forming living and vibrant Christian communities among young people, often under very difficult material circumstances.

Here in the United States, of course, the issue is not material resources; it is vision and will. The Venerable Andrey Sheptytsky and the Servant of God Josyf Slipyj were men of vision and will. Through their intercession, and inspired by their example, the Ukrainian Greek Catholic Church of Philadelphia and its sister Churches throughout the United States can be a true light to the nations, setting the world ablaze with the fire of the Spirit, healing a wounded culture, and offering twenty-first-century humanity a noble vision of human possibility that leads to genuine beatitude through friendship with Jesus Christ, the Risen Lord and King of the Universe. Glory be to him forever.

Part Two

UNIVERSITY LECTURES

Catholic Matters

IRONIES OF MODERN CATHOLIC HISTORY
The Church and Pluralism

Boston University, Boston, Massachusetts, April 11, 2015

In considering how the Catholic Church has wrestled with the challenges posed by modernity and pluralism over the past two centuries, it will be helpful at the outset to clarify some terms.

By "Catholic Church," I mean here the teaching authority of Catholicism as embodied in the Bishop of Rome as universal pastor of the Church—and, at one significant moment, the bishops of the Church gathered in ecumenical council with and under the Bishop of Rome. This by no means exhausts what "the Catholic Church" means. But given the unique authority structure of Catholicism, this definition provides a useful (and manageable) focus for considering the complex set of relationships with which we are wrestling.

By "modernity," I mean what I take it all of us mean: societies characterized by the decline of aristocracy (inherited power and wealth); the desacralization of power by the sharp differentiation of religious and political authority and the dominance of the latter in the public sphere; mass education; social mobility; popular participation in government; the rationalization and bureaucratization of virtually every aspect of life; great improvements in nutrition and medicine, with a concomitant rise in life expectancy; and the vast expansion of the leisure time available to everyone—societies in which the scientific method provides the primary paradigm for human knowledge, neither faith nor religious "knowledge" is taken for granted, and tensions exist (to one degree or another) between believers (individually and corporately) and the ambient public culture.

By "pluralism," I will accept, at least at the outset, Peter Berger's concept of the coexistence of different worldviews and value systems in the same society.[1] This is a largely descriptive definition (although "coexistence," which is not easy, hints at something more than mere description). Later, I shall suggest a more normative concept of "pluralism" that I hope will be helpful in analyzing the questions involved in understanding religion-and-modernity.

The Catholic Church's wrestling with the profound changes through which humanity has passed since the rise of the scientific method, the triumph of the Industrial Revolution, and the overthrow of traditional political orders has evolved over time. Although the story is more complex than typically rendered by historians with a secularist cast of mind, it is not too much of an exaggeration to suggest that Catholicism-and-modernity began with a papal preview of Nancy Reagan's antidrug campaign: "Just say no." This was followed by a period of exploration and a search for a reasonable accommodation with modernity, which caused considerable internal ecclesiastical quarreling (and elbow-throwing) before the accommodationist forces prevailed; their triumph reached a high-water mark at the Second Vatican Council, whose Pastoral Constitution on the Church and the Modern World not only embraced modernity but celebrated crucial aspects of it. Then, as modernity gave way to postmodernity, two popes of genius began to articulate a deep critique of modernity "from within," as distinguished from the earlier critique "from without." Now, as the Church enters its third millennium, Catholicism has squarely faced the fact that, however its relationship to postmodernity and the contest of worldviews within it evolves, the Catholic future depends on proclamation and evangelization—that is, the Church's future, like religious conviction itself, can no longer be a taken-for-granted thing, but has to be effected.

Let me explore each of these phases in turn, albeit with far more brevity and concision that the complexities of the historical record would warrant in a more extended study.

Gregory XVI and Pius IX: Catholicism against Modernity

The problem of Catholicism-and-modernity can be subdivided along several lines of analysis: the Church's relationship to the passing of the traditional political order and the rise of new forms of government; the Church's relationship to the passing of the traditional cultural order and the displacement of metaphysics at the heart of the Western intellectual project; the Church's relationship to the passing of traditional society and the rise of new forms of community, including new forms of economic life. But however we subdivide the question, the overall problem of Catholicism-and-modernity in the nineteenth century was inextricably bound up with the fact that the pope was a sovereign head of state: The pope ruled the Papal States, which at various moments meant that the pope was politically sovereign over as much as one-third of the Italian peninsula. Cultural and intellectual modernity certainly challenged the then-regnant forms of Catholic intellectual life; social modernity, in the form of the "social question," eventually compelled an entirely new Catholic appraisal of modern economic life and its impacts on society. But it was the challenge of political modernity that was the immediate and urgent question for Popes Gregory XVI (1831–1846) and Pius IX (1846–1878), because political modernity threatened the very existence of the papacy as they understood it—and by threatening the papacy as they understood it, political modernity threatened the Catholic Church as they understood it.

The Holy See—the embodiment of the ministry of the Bishop of Rome as universal pastor of the Catholic Church—had been recognized for centuries as having juridical, and thus diplomatic, personality; the Holy See exchanged embassies and other forms of diplomatic representation with other sovereign actors long before the modern state existed.[2] As subsequent history proved, the Holy See could exercise its unique form of sovereignty—and thus the pope could maintain his essential independence from all earthly sovereignties—from a tiny parcel of land. Yet that was not how Gregory XVI and Pius IX saw things. The origin of the Papal States in the Donation of Pepin, the ratification of that donation by Charlemagne, and the complex history of the Papal States within the shifting alliances of European politics need not detain us. The point is that both Gregory XVI and Pius IX saw in political modernity a threat, first to their authority within the Papal States, and later to the existence of the Papal States themselves: a threat they understood to be fraught with implications beyond those touching their position within Italy.

There were other issues at play here, of course. The Catholic Church of the nineteenth century (and the first half of the twentieth, for that matter) paid very little heed to the Anglosphere, and to the ways in which the English and Scottish Enlightenments led to forms of modernity that were not identical to those that emerged from the French or Continental Enlightenment.[3] Thus from the point of view of Gregory XVI and Pius IX, "the Enlightenment" primarily meant the French Revolution, which meant the Civil Constitution of the Clergy, which meant the subordination of the Church to the French regime, which meant the Terror, the suppression of the Vendée, the martyrdoms memorialized in Poulenc's *Dialogues of the Carmelites*, and all the rest of that bloody business. "Enlightenment" also meant the kidnapping of Pius VI and his death while under arrest by French revolutionary troops, and the kidnapping and detainment at Fontainebleau of his successor, Pius VII: a broad-minded man who might have brokered a new Catholic dialogue with modernity had he not been constantly badgered (and worse) by Napoleon.

Nor was the Church's experience in France unique, for throughout continental Europe, the formation of the modern nation-state was typically undertaken against the Catholic Church (a pattern first set in Tudor England in the sixteenth century[4]). Here, two principal examples were the Italian *Risorgimento*, a deeply anti-clerical affair, and the Bismarckian *Kulturkampf*, an attack on the Church that went (iron-fisted) hand-in-glove with the Iron Chancellor's assembly of the Second Reich and his early management of the new imperial Germany.[5] And as if that were not enough, there was the Catholic experience of "enlightened" monarchy in the Habsburg lands (where Emperor Joseph tried to turn the Church into a "department of the police," as he famously put it); there were recurrent anti-clerical agitations in Spain and Portugal; and the 1834 Articles of Baden attempted to divide Swiss Catholics from the authority of Rome. Above all, and always lurking in the background, there was the threat to the Papal States. That threat was realized, in the worst form papal nightmares could imagine, in the 1870 absorption of Rome into the Kingdom of Italy, after which Pius IX withdrew inside the Leonine Wall and declared himself the "Prisoner of the Vatican"—and not a small amount of elite public opinion throughout Europe thought the papacy and the Catholic Church were finished as a force in human affairs.

Gregory XVI's stance toward modernity was that of an unblushing and candid reactionary. To be sure, he was not monochromatic: He had genuine artistic and intellectual interests; he was the pope who condemned slavery and the slave trade; he insisted on fostering a native clergy and building native hierarchies in Africa, Asia, and Latin America, thus ringing the changes on colonialism and its claims to ecclesiastical as well as political hegemony. Yet convinced as he was that the modern liberal political order was grounded in a religious indifferentism that, more often than not, took the form of hostility to faith, he condemned the efforts of French Catholics like Lamennais, Lacordaire, and Montalembert to find a rapprochement with the new liberal politics. And he denounced freedom of conscience and the press, and Church-state separation, in the 1832 encyclical *Mirari Vos* and the 1834 encyclical *Singulari Nos*—which, at that point, represented the high-water mark of the Catholic rejection of political modernity and the institutional pluralism (especially on matters of Church and state) built into it.

J. N. D. Kelly does not exaggerate when he writes that that Gregory XVI left his successor a "grievous legacy."[6] That successor, Pius IX, initially attempted something of a course reversal, introducing administrative and legislative reforms in the Papal States and making positive gestures toward resurgent Italian nationalism. But the experience of the revolutions of 1848, when he was temporarily driven out of Rome, turned him toward the rejectionist stance of Gregory XVI, after which the pontiff mocked as "Pio No-No" set his teeth against further reform in his own domain and stoutly (if futilely) resisted Cavour and the forces of Italian unification.[7] In the order of ideas, this papal rejectionism reached a new plateau in 1864 with the encyclical *Quanta Cura* and its attached "Syllabus of Errors": a root-and-branch rejection of modernity in virtually all its forms, which ended with the famous condemnation of the notion that the Roman Pontiff "can or should reconcile himself to, or agree with, progress, liberalism, and modern civilization."

Yet even amidst this robust rejectionism, Pius IX paradoxically set in motion dynamics that would lead to the modernization of the papacy itself. He was immensely popular. As his political authority diminished, his spiritual authority increased exponentially, hinting at forms of political and diplomatic influence he could not imagine, but which others of his successors deployed. And while it would not be right to give him full marks or sole credit for this, the fact is that European Catholicism during his lengthy pontificate (the longest in reliably recorded papal history) was renewed and regenerated, not least in reaction to the political antipathies that Pius IX aroused and against which he contended so fruitlessly, both in terms of his own political position and that of many of his bishops (many of whom, in Bismarck's Germany, were in jail or in exile when Pius IX died in 1878).

From Leo XIII through Pius XII: Catholicism Exploring Modernity

On February 20, 1878, less than two weeks after the death of Pius IX, Gioacchino Vincenzo Pecci was elected pope as a place keeper; then sixty-eight, it was thought that he would keep the Chair of Peter warm for a few years—the cardinals evidently did not want to repeat the previous, three-decades-long pontificate. Taking the regnal name Leo XIII, he proceeded to confound the expectations of those who elected him by enjoying the second-longest reign in reliably recorded papal history (until topped by John Paul II). More to the point, he took, at the outset of his pontificate, a bold, grand-strategic decision that is nicely captured in his funerary monument, to the left of the high altar in the Basilica of St. John Lateran. In that sculpture, Leo is not depicted in one typical papal funerary pose, lying "asleep" on his back with his hands piously folded on his chest (as is his thirteenth-century predecessor, Innocent III, who rests to the right of the high altar). Rather, Leo XIII is depicted standing, the tiara on his head, his right foot thrust forward, and his right hand raised and extended in what has the appearance of a gesture of invitation—as if he were saying to modernity, "We have a proposal to make; we have something to talk about."

Leo XIII's grand strategic decision was to eschew both the rejectionism of his two immediate predecessors and the supine accommodation to modernity characteristic of a lot of nineteenth-century liberal Protestantism, and to substitute for these two impossible strategies (as he thought of them) a third option: a Catholic engagement with modernity conducted with explicitly Catholic tools, newly sharpened for the task.[8] The Leonine Revolution he created took several forms, the effects of which are still being felt in world Catholicism today.

It was Leo XIII who energized modern Catholic intellectual life with the 1879 encyclical *Aeterni Patris*, which mandated a close study of Thomas Aquinas in the original texts (i.e., unfiltered by centuries of commentators); Thomas' brilliant and orthodox appropriation of the New Learning of his day (especially the rediscovered philosophy of Aristotle) suggested to Leo that Aquinas was an especially apt guide for Catholic intellectuals seeking a critical engagement with modern science, modern philosophy, and modern theology. Moreover, Leo named as cardinal in 1879 John Henry Newman, one of nineteenth-century Catholicism's most imaginative thinkers; that Leo would go out of his way to honor a man whose distinctive style and theological method could not be fit into any one methodological box suggested that Leo, for all that he was a dedicated Thomist, was also something of a pluralist in terms of intellectual method.

It was Leo XIII who opened the Vatican Secret Archives to qualified researchers of all faiths (and no faith), thereby inaugurating the modern Catholic study of Catholic history—which led to the inevitable discovery that the Church did, indeed, change and develop over time, the claims of antimodern rejectionists notwithstanding.

It was Leo XIII who launched the first modern Vatican Observatory and supported studies in astronomy and other natural sciences at the Vatican, thus beginning a rapprochement between Catholicism and modern science.

It was Leo XIII who initiated the modern Catholic study of the Bible (an enterprise already into its dissecting/deconstructive phase in liberal Protestantism) by supporting the creation of the École Biblique in Jerusalem in 1890, issuing the encyclical *Providentissimus Deus* in 1893 (on the new higher criticism of the Bible), and founding the Pontifical Biblical Commission in 1902.

It was Leo XIII who, with the 1891 encyclical *Rerum Novarum*, became the founding father of modern Catholic social doctrine: that distinctive Catholic philosophical and theological reflection on society, economy, culture, and polity under the conditions of modernity that has continued to this day.[9]

And it was Leo XIII who, in his 1895 letter to the Catholic bishops of the United States, *Longinqua Oceani*, taught that the liberal American political arrangement—the constitutional separation of the institutions of Church and state—*tolerari potest* (could be tolerated), thus opening the door to what would become, in time, the Catholic human rights revolution, the Catholic defense of religious freedom for all, and the Catholic role in what Samuel Huntington dubbed the "Third Wave" of democratic revolutions.[10]

Leo XIII died in 1903 at age ninety-three, and it is no distortion of the record to suggest that the next five and a half decades of Catholic history were a contest, sometimes bitter, over the Leonine Revolution and its attempt to engage modernity with distinctively Catholic tools. Leo's opponents generally won the day during the pontificate of Pius X (1903–1914), but the Leonine party had its innings again during the pontificate of Benedict XV (1914–1922). Benedict's successor, Pius XI (1922–1939), extended Leo's Catholic social doctrine, and his 1931 encyclical *Quadragesimo Anno*, with its principle of "subsidiarity," underscored the importance of the plural institutions of civil society, both in themselves and as a barrier against the totalitarian temptation toward which political modernity seemed to be succumbing in that low decade, the 1930s. His successor, the much-maligned Pius XII (1939–1958), actively fostered Christian Democratic parties in postwar Europe and, in his teachings on Catholic worship, the Bible, and the nature of the Church as the "Mystical Body of Christ" (rather than as the *societas perfecta* beloved by Catholic antimodern rejectionists) helped prepare the theological foundations for the Second Vatican Council (in whose documents his magisterium would be the second most frequently cited source, after the Bible).

Thus was the stage set, by Leo XIII and the battle over his legacy, for the next phase of the drama of Catholicism-and-modernity.

Vatican II—The Catholic Embrace of Modernity

Leo's fifth successor, John XXIII, was elected on October 28, 1958, as another elderly placeholder—and in this case, the expectations of the conclave were met by a short pontificate of some four and a half years. But like Leo, John XXIII took a bold strategic decision at the outset of his papacy, announcing on January 25, 1959, that he intended to summon the twenty-first ecumenical council in the history of the Church, which would be known formally as the Second Ecumenical Council of the Vatican and informally as Vatican II. In a wide-ranging ecclesiastical career prior to his election as successor to Pius XII, Angelo Giuseppe Roncalli had experienced no small amount of the ecclesiastical air turbulence generated by the Leonine Revolution and the sometimes-harsh reactions to it from antimodern Catholic rejectionists. But while he was a man of quite traditional piety, Roncalli was also a trained and accomplished historian; and nunciatures in Bulgaria, Turkey, Greece, and France had given him a good understanding of the turmoil of the mid-twentieth century. Thus he understood that the dynamics of engagement with modernity that Leo had set in motion had somehow to be gathered together and focused, so that the Church might approach the third millennium of Christian history with renewed energy and a positive program, capable of responding to cultural, social, political, and economic circumstances that had changed vastly during his lifetime.

John XXIII only lived to see the first session of his Council, held in the fall of 1962, before dying in June 1963. But his example and leadership set a tone for the Council that lasted throughout its four years of annual fall sessions.[11] By the time the Council met for its fourth and final period in the fall of 1965, the party of rejectionism—the party that traced its ancestry to those who had resisted the Leonine Revolution—had been decisively rejected; and the Council was prepared to consider, and then pass, its most distinctive document, the Pastoral Constitution on the Church in the Modern World, known by the first words of its Latin text as *Gaudium et Spes*.

Unlike other Vatican II documents—indeed, unlike any previous conciliar document—*Gaudium et Spes* was an invitation to conversation—or, in the favorite trope of the day, to "dialogue." In the Pastoral Constitution, the Church sought, not passive and obedient students, but active conversation partners with divergent and different worldviews. Thus, *Gaudium et Spes* was an unprecedented attempt to meet "the modern world" on the modern world's own terms, accepting ungrudgingly the dramatic cultural, social, economic, and political changes that had characterized the past two centuries of human history and finding in those changes far more light than darkness.

Yet for all that it seemed to presage a new moment in the old drama of Catholicism-and-modernity, *Gaudium et Spes* seems, in the retrospect of fifty years, a remarkably timebound document.

The Pastoral Constitution suggested, for example, that the two great challenges to biblical religion in the modern world were Marxism and

Sartrean existentialism, neither of which has, to put it gently, a lot of traction today. The document recognized that women's roles had changed under the conditions of modernity; but it seems, in retrospect, oblivious to the tidal wave of ideological feminism that was about to wash over the Western world. The Pastoral Constitution noted the impact of the splitting of the atom; but it had virtually nothing to say about the two other world-changing scientific developments of the modern world: the unraveling of the DNA double helix (and the new genetics it made possible) and the invention of the oral contraceptive pill.

Gaudium et Spes sympathetically explored the modern crisis of faith and suggested, correctly, that the Church's own failures had to be taken into full account when measuring the advances of agnosticism and atheism. But most strikingly for our purposes, there is not the slightest hint in the Pastoral Constitution that the world just might become *more* religious under the conditions of late modernity, and that revitalized religious conviction could play a determinative role in world politics. In other words, if Vatican II in its embrace of modernity did not imagine designer babies, gene therapy, Betty Friedan, Gloria Steinem, and Europe's demographic winter, neither did it imagine the Solidarity movement, the Moral Majority, the entrepreneurial Protestantism of Latin America, the house churches of China, or, in a less admirable vein, Osama bin Laden and Abu Bakr al-Baghdadi.[12]

Neither did the Fathers of Vatican II imagine that, in the Church's European heartland, the greatest challenge to the religious worldview would not be atheism (of either the Marxist or Sartrean variant), but massive religious indifference: what David Bentley Hart has usefully described as "metaphysical boredom."[13] *Gaudium et Spes* anticipated with seeming relish a new, respectful conversation between belief and unbelief; the Pastoral Constitution completely failed to anticipate the yawn of indifference with which such proposals for dialogue would be received in the high culture of western Europe within a few years after *Gaudium et Spes* was published. This failure to anticipate the thick fog of religious indifference that would characterize Europe after 1968 is one of the most striking features of the Pastoral Constitution, read in the retrospect of a half century. And it suggests that the Council Fathers embraced modernity just on the cusp of its turn into postmodernity, in which the "truth" the Council Fathers sought to explore in dialogue with nonbelievers of good will would be held to be either a chimera or a cultural (or class-based) construct.

This can be put in another, parallel way: *Gaudium et Spes* affirmed what one of its subsections styled the "autonomy of earthly affairs," and acknowledged that the methods proper to the modern scientific exploration of nature are "at once the claim of modern man and the desire of the Creator."[14] But while the Pastoral Constitution did caution that, "once God is forgotten, the creature is lost sight of as well,"[15] the Council Fathers did not seem to anticipate (save in its communist form) what Charles Taylor has dubbed "exclusivist humanism": an aggressive secularism that denies, not merely revelation, but even transcendent moral reference points for the ordering of social life. Thus, while the Pastoral Constitution usefully distinguished the three interlocking sectors of a modern society—the cultural, the economic, and the political—it did not wrestle at any length with the ways in which the deterioration of the cultural sphere under the impacts of epistemological skepticism, moral relativism, and metaphysical nihilism could do grave damage to both free economics and free politics; that analytic task would be left to one of the contributors to the drafting of *Gaudium et Spes*, the Polish professor-bishop Karol Wojtyła, when he became Pope John Paul II.

Vatican II sought to "solve" the problem of Catholicism-and-modernity through an embrace of pluralism that ran parallel to the American Jesuit scholar John Courtney Murray's normative description of "pluralism" as creeds intelligibly in conflict.[16] Plurality—difference—had been written into the script of history, Murray wrote; indeed, it seemed to have been written into history by the Creator, so it was fruitless to bang one's head (or miter) against the fact of difference in the vain search for a uniformity of worldview, a monism, imagined to have characterized the premodern world. The real task, Murray suggested, was to transform the social fact of plurality (meaning difference) into the social accomplishment of plural*ism*: an orderly conversation about the common good in all its aspects, made possible by commonly shared moral reference points that could be known by reason. That, too, seemed Vatican II's hope: that the Church could make its proper contribution to the human conversation about the human future, as one interlocutor among a plurality of interlocutors, made into a community of conversation by a common commitment to a stable intellectual and moral framework for debate and dialogue.

Yet it is precisely that stable framework that postmodernity—which at best can concede "your truth" and "my truth" but nothing properly describable as "the Truth"—seems determined to deny. Thus it might be said that Catholicism, at Vatican II, embraced modernity and pluralism just as modernity was beginning to decompose into postmodernity, and just as the pluralism of contrasting worldviews in a mutually enriching encounter with each other was being deconstructed back into mere plurality. The stage was thereby set for the contributions of two men who had had significant impact on the deliberations of Vatican II, but who had come to understand that its reading of the "signs of the times" was shallow.

John Paul II and Benedict XVI: An Internal Critique of Modernity

In terms of the questions of Catholicism-and-modernity and Catholicism-and-pluralism, the pontificates of John Paul II (1978–2005) and Benedict XVI (2005–2013) should be considered as a single moment of intellectual engagement with the cultural crisis of late modernity and the emergence of a postmodern world that is both robustly religious and deeply conflicted about both its luxuriant plurality and the meaning of pluralism. Gregory XVI and Pius IX had mounted a critique of modernity from the outside, so to speak; John Paul II and Benedict XVI, both modern intellectuals with distinguished pre-papal academic careers, offered a critique of late modernity and the emerging postmodern world from "within": a critique that began not with rejection, but with a broad acceptance of the accomplishments of modernity, before turning to a critique of what both popes perceived as the danger of the late modern/postmodern world's self-deconstruction into incoherence.

That internal line of critique was developed in several notable intellectual exercises: Among these may be cited John Paul II's encyclicals *Centesimus Annus* (1991), *Veritatis Splendor* (1993), and *Evangelium Vitae* (1995), and his apostolic letter *Ecclesia in Europa* (2003); and Benedict XVI's September addresses to the University of Regensburg in 2006, at the Collège des Bernardins in Paris in 2008, at Westminster Hall in London in 2010, and in the German Bundestag in 2011.[17] This extensive body of material can best be brought into focus through the prism of a drama that unfolded in the last years of John Paul II.

In 2003, a new constitutional treaty was being drafted for the about-to-be expanded European Union; and while the Euro-constitution was a very lengthy affair indeed, the most rhetorically violent arguments over its drafting and ratification had to do with whether a single word would appear in its preamble: In listing the sources of its twenty-first-century commitments to civility, tolerance, human rights, democracy, and the rule of law, would the framework document of the new "Europe" cite Christianity—or, more broadly, the biblical tradition? For the draft constitution's text had assiduously ignored Christianity, finding the cultural roots of the new Europe's commitments to democratic values and norms in the classical tradition, the Enlightenment, and modern thought.[18] But amidst the maelstrom of controversy over this question (which the international constitutional scholar J. H. H. Weiler, himself an Orthodox Jew, described as a by-product of European "Christophobia"[19]), the issue that engaged John Paul II and Benedict XVI was given concise formulation in a widely translated and published op-ed article by two paladins of European postmodern thought: Jürgen Habermas and Jacques Derrida, who argued that the New Europe must be "neutral between worldviews."

That, it seemed to both John Paul II and Benedict XVI, utterly begged the question, How could there be genuine pluralism "creeds intelligibly in conflict"—if there were no normative framework of agreed reference points to guide the conversation? Here was Richard John Neuhaus' "naked public square"[20] raised to a first principle of constitutional order and made into the official European public ideology. How any of this comported with "pluralism" was quite unclear; indeed, the Habermas/Derrida proposal seemed to flatten out the landscape of the late modern and postmodern world, forcing the rich plurality of European worldviews onto a Procrustean bed that seemed constructed from Charles Taylor's "exclusive humanism." Indeed, the Habermas/Derrida proposal amounted to a bizarre, hyper-secularized form of the old altar-and-throne alliances of the days of absolutism:

state-sanctioned monism, in which both E.U. and national law enforced an extreme, monochromatic *laïcite*—putatively in the name of social comity; in fact, in the name of epistemological skepticism.

Put another way, the architects of the E.U. naked public square seemed to imagine that democracy and the free economy—those distinctive expressions of modernity in the spheres of political and economic life—were machines that could run by themselves, were the apparatus of governance, production, and exchange properly designed. John Paul II, in *Centesimus Annus*, had explained in some detail why that was impossible. Yes, the machinery was important, and modernity had done a good job of building political and economic systems for self-governance, and for productivity and prosperity. But it takes a certain kind of people, he argued, living certain virtues, to make the machinery of the free economy and the free society work so that the net result is human flourishing. The formation of those virtues, and the mature, modern men and women who lived them in a public atmosphere of civility and tolerance, was the task of the third part of the triad of the free society—the moral-cultural sector. And it was the vitality of that sector (often described as "civil society") that would tell the tale on the vitality of democracy and the free economy—and that would make possible a genuine pluralism, understood as "creeds intelligibly in conflict."

Benedict XVI deepened the Catholic engagement with, and critique of, late modernity and postmodernity in four important lectures. The first, delivered at his old university, Regensburg, in September 2006, frankly recognized the accomplishments of modernity in distinguishing religious and political authority in society and in defending religious freedom and freedom of conscience as fundamental human rights.[21] At Regensburg, the former professor Joseph Ratzinger also celebrated what he termed the providential encounter of biblical wisdom with Greek philosophy while affirming that human reason was a reflection of the Λόγος, the divine reason. He also acknowledged that faith must be purified by reason lest faith become superstition and suggested that faith unpurified by reason was one cause of the religiously legitimated violence that was rocking the early twenty-first-century world.

If the Regensburg Lecture was a reminder that, in the Catholic view of things, faith must be reasonable, Benedict XVI's lecture at the Collège des Bernardins in Paris, in September 2008, reversed the polarities and cautioned against a too-narrow understanding of reason, suggesting that positivism was the "capitulation of reason" and that a culture that deliberately cut itself off from the things of the spirit would become dull and eventually dehumanizing.[22]

In an address at Westminster Hall in September 2010, the German pope who had previously thanked the British people for winning the Battle of Britain in 1940 reminded his audience of parliamentarians and other distinguished Britons (gathered in the very place where Thomas More had been found guilty and condemned to death) that law descends into tyranny when positive law is detached from the moral law that provides a kind of grammar for intelligible public discourse in a plural world.[23] The Pope reiterated that theme in a different key a year later when, addressing the German Bundestag in September 2011, he reminded his listeners of Augustine's fifth-century question—"Without justice, what else is the state but a great band of robbers?"—and explicitly linked the lesson embedded in that question to the German experience of power divorced from right under National Socialism.[24] Then, while speaking near the ruins of the *Führerbunker* from which the world had, in his lifetime, been driven to "the edge of the abyss,"[25] he returned to a theme he had previously articulated in Paris and suggested that a public intellectual climate dominated by positivism was a bunker of the human spirit in which the new Europe risked suffocating, should that positivism snuff out the robust dialogue of worldviews that could, as Murray might have put it, turn the mere fact of plurality into the social accomplishment of pluralism.

Immediately prior to his election as pope, Cardinal Joseph Ratzinger had preached a sermon to his fellow cardinals at the Mass *Pro Eligendo Romano Pontifice* (For the Election of the Roman Pontiff), during which he warned against a rising "dictatorship of relativism" throughout the Western world: the use of coercive state power to impose on all of society a way of life determined by the postmodern canons of epistemological skepticism and moral relativism—the use of coercive state power, in other words, to eliminate the robust dialogue of worldviews in the public square in the name of a "tolerance" prepared to tolerate everything but normative worldviews, whether religiously or rationally derived.[26] That warning, when read alongside the substantive analyses of the crisis of late modernity and emerging postmodernity articulated by John Paul II and Benedict XVI, suggests that, after two centuries of wrestling with modernity and its attendant plurality of worldviews, the Catholic Church found itself in the paradoxical position of defending modernity and genuine pluralism against the coercive efforts of postmodernity to flatten out the dialogue of worldviews in the name of a state-sanctioned monologue.

There are, as one sociological wit used to say, many ironies in the fire.

Catholicism in Postmodernity: The Recovery of the Evangelical Imperative

This brief sketch of the broad outlines of Catholicism-and-modernity from the point of view of papal teaching has necessarily skipped over many fascinating examples of what was happening on the ground, so to speak, while the drama of this papal wrestling with modernity and its attendant pluralism unfolded. I have barely hinted at the liberal Catholic opposition to the antimodern rejectionism of Gregory XVI and Pius IX, an opposition involving such considerable figures as von Ketteler, Döllinger, and Acton. I have not explored how the American experience of Catholicism—the experience of a vibrant and growing Church under the conditions of political modernity—posed an important challenge to the Eurocentric papal understanding of Catholicism-and-modernity, conditioned as it was by the experience of what Owen Chadwick called in his Gifford Lectures the "secularization of the European mind."[27] I have not mentioned the temptation among some Catholic antimodern rejectionists to find in fascism an antidote to modernity and its discontents: a blindness that resulted in both the sinister (the celebration of the early Third Reich as the spiritual answer to Weimar's clash of worldviews by the abbot of the Benedictine Abbey of Maria Laach) and the bizarre (the "knight-monks" of Vichy France who imagined themselves training new cadres of a Catholic elite for a new France "beyond" modernity, secularism, *laïcite*, and pluralism).[28] As for the present, while Catholicism has experienced the withering away of religious conviction predicted by classic secularization theory in what once seemed such impregnable Catholic redoubts as Spain, Portugal, Ireland, and Québec, contemporary Catholicism has also experienced the empirical falsification of the classic secularization hypothesis through its explosive growth in Africa and its relatively robust position in the United States. And then there is the fascinating question of whether traditionally Catholic societies like Poland, Slovakia, and Lithuania—where the faith was preserved, almost as if in amber, through the pressures of life under communism—will, in the postcommunist world, follow the path trod by other European Catholic nations.

What can be said by way of conclusion is what living in a post-Feuerbachian world that has passed through the "fiery brook" of modernity means for the Catholic Church—it means that culturally "kept" religion has gone the way of legally established religion, and that the Church of the future must be a Church permanently in mission. Or to get down to specific cases, in the Catholicism of the future, no Catholic (or at least very few Catholics) will be able to say, "I am a Catholic because my great-grandmother was born in County Cork (or Cracow, or Guadalajara, or Munich, or Palermo, or the South End of Boston)." The Catholicism of the twenty-first century and the third millennium will be chosen, not inherited by ethnicity or absorbed by some other form of religious osmosis. And it will only be chosen because it has been proposed.

Thus the final paradox of the story of Catholicism, modernity, and pluralism: Through its encounter with modernity, Catholicism has rediscovered the evangelical or missionary imperative from which it began, two millennia ago.[29]

THE CATHOLIC UNIVERSITY OF THE TWENTY-FIRST CENTURY

FASTA University, Mar del Plata, Argentina, May 4, 2012

On August 15, 1990, Pope John Paul II signed the apostolic constitution *Ex Corde Ecclesiae* (From the Heart of the Church). While the constitution was intended in part to correct certain aberrations in Catholic higher learning that had developed in the post–Vatican II period, *Ex Corde Ecclesiae* is more fruitfully read as a proposal for the future: as the Magna Carta of Catholic higher education in the twenty-first century and the third millennium. For, like many other important documents in the magisterium of John Paul II, *Ex Corde Ecclesiae* was intended to prepare the Church of the third millennium for the springtime of evangelization—the New Evangelization—of which John Paul spoke with increasing urgency throughout his lengthy pontificate.

A Reverence for Higher Learning

Ex Corde Ecclesiae was written by a pope who had a deep and abiding reverence for higher learning.

That *pietas* first formed in Karol Wojtyła when he was an undergraduate student at the venerable Jagiellonian University in Kraków—an experience of university life that lasted but a year, for the Nazi occupation of Poland shut down central Europe's second oldest university in November 1939 and shipped 184 of its professors and other Kraków-based academics to the Sachsenhausen and Dachau concentration camps.

Wojtyła's reverence for university life deepened after the war, in the struggle to maintain a theological faculty within the Jagiellonian University during the first decade of Polish communism. That struggle would be lost when the theology faculty—the oldest component of the Jagiellonian—was shut down in 1954, an act of cultural vandalism that Wojtyła never forgot.

Yet communism was never able to completely crush Catholic higher learning in Poland. For the Catholic University of Lublin, the only Catholic college or university in the entire communist world, held tenaciously to its precarious independence. And it was there, as a lecturer and then professor in philosophical ethics, that Wojtyła's reverence for Catholic higher learning was consolidated. There, as his colleague Professor Stefan Swieżawski once put it, he took part in the intellectual life of "the only place between Berlin and Seoul where philosophy was free."[1] There, he learned in depth what he had intuited when the Jagiellonian University reconstituted itself as an underground institution during the Nazi occupation: A university can be an oasis of truth in a desert of mendacity and falsehood.

Indeed, John Paul II's reverence for university life was such that he maintained his connections to Lublin as pope, until the press of his papal responsibilities led him to cease guiding doctoral dissertations, as he had continued to do in the early months of his pontificate.

This long-standing reverence for the university and its unique role as a guardian of culture infuses *Ex Corde Ecclesiae*. There, John Paul II wrote that the Catholic institution of higher learning should be the repository or defender of "a kind of universal humanism ... dedicated to the [study] of all aspects of truth in their essential connection with the supreme Truth, who is God."[2] This "essential connection" was not, John Paul insisted, a burden or a barrier to free inquiry. On the contrary, for the Catholic Church, which was the mother of universities and which had given birth to those unique institutions from its very heart, had long taught that all true knowledge is a reflection of Christ the *Logos*, the Word through whom all that is came into being. And it is Christ the Lord, John Paul wrote in *Ex Corde Ecclesiae*, who "alone is capable of giving fully that Wisdom without which the future of the world would be in danger."[3]

The Present Danger

To understand fully John Paul II's vision of the Catholic university as the guardian of a "universal humanism," it is important to understand the nature of that "danger" to the human future as John Paul understood it.

During the Second Vatican Council, Karol Wojtyła began to sketch out his most comprehensive philosophical work, *Person and Act*, which would be published in 1969. His description of that project to Henri de Lubac, S.J., the distinguished French Jesuit theologian with whom he had worked at Vatican II in drafting the final text of what became *Gaudium et Spes*, the Pastoral Constitution on the Church in the Modern World, is instructive. Wojtyła wrote,

> I devote my very rare free moments to a work that is close to my heart and devoted to the metaphysical sense and mystery of the PERSON. It seems to me that the debate today is being played out at that level. The evil of our time consists in the first place in a kind of degradation, indeed in a pulverization, of the fundamental uniqueness of each human person. This evil is even much more of the metaphysical order than of the moral order. To this disintegration planned at time by atheistic ideologies, we must oppose, rather than sterile polemics, a kind of "recapitulation" of the inviolable mystery of the person.[4]

This theme—that the civilizational crisis of late modernity was a crisis in the very *idea* of the human person—had preoccupied Wojtyła for some time. Now, to be sure, this might have seemed a "natural" or obvious concern for a philosophically inclined survivor of the brutal Nazi occupation of Poland during World War II and the subsequent communist usurpation of Poland's liberties—a man who knew from hard experience that ideas have consequences, for good and for ill. Yet Wojtyła's insight into the nature of the crisis cut much deeper than his critique of the two mid-twentieth-century totalitarian systems.

Nazism had been crushed by force of arms, and communism, Wojtyła imagined, would eventually implode because of its own intellectual implausibility. No, the problem was deeper. Nazism and communism were two especially brutal expressions of "a kind of degradation, indeed ... a pulverization, of the fundamental uniqueness of each human person." But there were subtler and therefore more insidious forms of that same dehumanization at work in the culture of the West. And Wojtyła set out to analyze them with his graduate students at the Catholic University of Lublin, in the mid-1950s.

Thus in his graduate-level seminar in 1956–1957, Wojtyła and his students made a close reading of the philosophies of David Hume and Jeremy Bentham under the general rubric of an examination of "Norm and Happiness." The net effect of Hume's principled skepticism about the capacity of human beings to know the truth of anything with certainty, Wojtyła believed, was to drive a thick wedge between morality and reality, such that the moral life inevitably drifted off into a realm of radical subjectivity. And the result of that drift, in Bentham, was utilitarianism: Utility, not dignity, would be the measure of man and the measure of the good.[5]

Here, indeed, was a prescient philosophy professor. Just as Polish Stalinism was receding from its apogee after the crisis of worker unrest in 1956, Wojtyła and his students, in a small Catholic university in an obscure part of Poland, looked more than thirty years into the future—a future no one else seemed capable of imagining, given the choking cultural smog of communist life—and began to scout the intellectual terrain of the *next* struggle for the human future: the struggle to defend intellectually the inalienable dignity and infinite value of every human life from conception until natural death. Even as the communist plague continued, Wojtyła and his students, in "the only place between Berlin and Seoul where philosophy was free," were reading British philosophers relatively unknown in Poland and analyzing the threat to the human future that would be posed if their thought were to be embodied in society, politics, and economics.

Here was university life "on the edge" in a most impressive way: not only "the edge" of resistance to communist bullying, but "the edge" of seeing beyond the limits of the present to the line of battle on which the war for the truth—the war for the human future—would be fought decades later.

Ideas and Their Consequences

Thirty years before the fall of communism, then, Karol Wojtyła began to see that if a successful defense of the "metaphysical sense and mystery" of the human person were not mounted and then embodied in the institutions of society and culture, the results would be terrible indeed: Bad ideas would have awful consequences. And the result would not be George Orwell's totalitarian dystopia, described in the novel *1984*; the result would be the soft-totalitarian dystopia of manufactured and genetically manipulated humanity described in the other great mid-twentieth-century dystopian novel, Aldous Huxley's *Brave New World*.

Huxley, it must be admitted, was not a very distinguished novelist; no one reads *Brave New World* for its literary elegance, the depth of its characterizations, or the subtleties of its plot. But Aldous Huxley was a genius at seeing into the darker possibilities of a dystopian future created by a science unhinged from the "metaphysical sense and mystery" of the human person—a science that would be guided by a distorted morality derived from the collapse of metaphysics.

Thus, Huxley's genius was not just that, in the late 1920s, he foresaw the possibility of a new and dehumanizing biotechnology, three decades before the discovery of the double helix structure of DNA by James Watson, Francis Crick, and Rosalind Franklin made modern genetics possible. Huxley also saw how this new power, detached from the deep truths about the dignity of the human person—including those deep moral truths embedded in the world and in us, and accessible to reason—would inevitably lead to a culture of manufactured, chemically induced "happiness," manipulated socially by a seemingly benign but in fact totalitarian political system.

In that respect, the key passage in *Brave New World* is not that remarkably prescient opening chapter where Huxley describes the workings of the Central London Hatchery and Conditioning Centre. The key passage occurs a little over halfway through the novel, when one of the totalitarian World Controllers, a man named Mustapha Mond, is deciding whether a new academic paper can be published:

> "A New Theory of Biology" was the title of the paper which Mustapha Mond had just finished reading. He sat for some time, meditatively frowning, then picked up his pen and wrote across the title-page: "The author's mathematical treatment of the conception of purpose is novel and highly ingenious, but heretical and, so far as the present social order is concerned, dangerous and potentially subversive. Not to be published." He underlined the words. "The author will be kept under supervision. His transference to the Marine Biological Station at St. Helena may become necessary." A pity, he thought, as he signed his name. It was a masterly piece of work. But once you began admitting explanations in terms of purpose—well,

> you didn't know what the result might be. It was the sort of idea that might easily decondition the more unsettled minds among the higher castes—make them lose their faith in happiness as the Sovereign Good and take to believing, instead, that the goal was somewhere beyond, somewhere outside the present human sphere; that the purpose of life was not the maintenance of well-being, but some intensification and refining of consciousness, some enlargement of knowledge. Which was, the Controller reflected, quite possibly true. But not, in the present circumstances, admissible. He picked up his pen again, and under the words "Not to be published" drew a second line, thicker and blacker than the first; then sighed. "What fun it would be," he thought, "if one didn't have to think about happiness!"[6]

This, then, is the cultural—indeed civilizational—crisis to which Catholic higher education must respond, according to the vision of John Paul II and the teaching of *Ex Corde Ecclesiae*.

It is a crisis in metaphysics: a denial that there are deep and abiding truths built into the human condition.

It is a crisis in epistemology: collapse of confidence that human beings can know those truths with a degree of certainty.

It is a crisis in the moral life: for absent those deep truths as a stable framework for moral reflection, we are left with Jeremy Bentham and his dehumanizing calculus of utility.

And it is a crisis in social and political life: for the just society—the free and virtuous society envisioned by Catholic social doctrine—cannot be built on the shaky foundations of a utilitarian public ethic, in which the question, *Should* we do this? is effectively banned from public life, and the only publicly admissible question is, *Can* we do this?

The Countercultural Catholic University

If that is the challenge, then what should be the response?

The response must be for Catholic institutions of higher learning in the twenty-first century to be *countercultural*: to be part of the culture-forming counterculture that is the Catholic Church of the post–Vatican II period.

This new mode of being Catholic, which is being born in the Church today, is what we might call mission-centered Catholicism, a

Catholicism radically focused on the proclamation of the Gospel and the conversion of the world, in a New Evangelization for the third millennium of Christian mission.

It is the Catholicism that is being born from a century and a quarter of Catholic reform that began with the pontificate of Leo XIII and included the rediscovery of authentic Thomism as a Catholic way of thinking uniquely suited to the challenges of our time.

It is the Catholicism that was nurtured in the great Catholic intellectual renaissance of the mid-twentieth century, which set the intellectual foundations for the work of the Second Vatican Council.

It is the Catholicism that was described in outline by the Fathers of Vatican II, in the Council's sixteen documents—documents that have been given an authoritative interpretation by John Paul II and Benedict XVI, two men of genius who were also men of the Council.

This mission-centered Catholicism is slowly, and sometimes painfully, replacing the Counter-Reformation Catholicism that dominated the Church's life from the late sixteenth century through the mid-twentieth century. Counter-Reformation Catholicism, with its focus on simple catechetical instruction and popular, devotional piety, was an appropriate response to the challenges posed by the Reformation at the dawn of modernity. It was the Catholicism that brought the faith to the Americas, and that tens of millions of immigrants brought to the Western hemisphere. It was the Catholicism that set the foundations on which we build today.

But as John Paul II understood, the cultural circumstances in which the Gospel must be proclaimed in the twenty-first century had dramatically changed throughout the Western world. As late as the mid-twentieth century, Catholicism was often culturally transmitted; at the very least, the ambient public culture was not overtly hostile to the faith. That is no longer the case. Throughout the Western world, the dominant high culture regards biblical religion and its moral teachings as dehumanizing and irrational.

Thus, we can no longer rely on the ambient public culture to help transmit the faith and shape public life in a humane way commensurate with Christian values. The Church must become its own culture-forming counterculture, a counterculture in which Word and sacrament form believers who, by the quality of their lives, attract others to hear the truth of God and humanity proclaimed in the Gospel of

Jesus Christ: "the faith which was once delivered to all the saints" (Jude 1:3).

This is the culture-forming, countercultural Catholicism to which John Paul II summoned the Church at the end of the Great Jubilee of 2000, in the apostolic letter *Novo Millennio Ineunte* (Entering the New Millennium). There, John Paul urged the Church to leave the shallow waters of institutional maintenance and, like the first disciples on the Sea of Galilee, put out "into the deep" (Lk 5:4) for a catch[7]—in this case, the "catch" of deeply converted men and women: men and women who are converted in mind as well as in heart; men and women possessed by the truth of God in Christ, and thus able to propose that truth to others; men and women capable of defending that truth and its intellectual plausibility against the twenty-first-century cultured despisers of biblical religion.

What is the role of the Catholic institution of higher education in this new moment of Catholic history that is being born today?

Permit me to make a few suggestions by way of a sketch.

A Nobler Aspiration

The Catholic college or university of the twenty-first century will measure itself and its aspiration by criteria other than those typically found in Western institutions of higher learning. This emphatically does not mean a slackening of commitment to intellectual excellence. But it does mean locating intellectual excellence within the mission of the Church, which is the sanctification of the People of God and the conversion of the world. For as Pope Benedict XVI said to the leaders of Catholic higher education in the United States in April 2008, "Fostering personal intimacy with Jesus Christ and communal witness to his loving truth is indispensable to Catholic institutions of learning."[8] It might seem an obvious thing to say, even a truism. But that has not been the self-understanding of many Catholic colleges and universities since Vatican II, and it must become so again if these institutions are to participate in the deep reform of the Church that is measured by the twin criteria of truth and mission.

Or to put the matter bluntly, Catholic universities that do not require their students to take courses in Augustine and Aquinas, or to read and absorb *Lumen Gentium* and *Dei Verbum* (the Dogmatic Constitutions on the Church and on Divine Revelation of Vatican II), have not begun to grasp the unique nature and mission of a Catholic institution of higher education.

In that same 2008 address at the Catholic University of America, Benedict XVI located the Catholic college or university firmly within the evangelical mission of the Church:

> All the Church's activities stem from her awareness that she is the bearer of a message which has its origin in God himself: in his goodness and wisdom, God chose to reveal himself and to make known the hidden purpose of his will (cf. Eph 1:9; *Dei Verbum*, no. 2). God's desire to make himself known, and the innate desire of all human beings to know the truth, provide the context for human inquiry into the meaning of life. This unique encounter is sustained within our Christian community: the one who seeks the truth becomes the one who lives by faith (cf. *Fides et Ratio*, no. 31). It can be described as a move from "I" to "we", leading the individual to be numbered among God's people.[9]

Catholic higher education, in other words, rejects the postmodern subjectivism that speaks of "your truth" and "my truth," in the confidence that every search for truth, if true, eventually leads to *the* Truth, who is God the Holy Trinity. Human inquiry is thus not drudgery; inquiry, like the learning that is born from it, is an exercise of love, for our deeper penetration of the truth leads us deeper in the divine mystery of love. The Catholic search for truth in Catholic institutions of higher learning begins with a certain knowing—a knowing that *the* Truth has been given to us, in Christ, even before we begin our inquiry into the many truths of the world. In this way, Catholic higher education helps lead postmodern culture out of the sandbox of subjectivism and into the adult world of genuine inquiry and genuine learning.

Saving Cultural Memory

Catholic higher education in the twenty-first century will also help the Western world retain its cultural memory, which is in danger of being lost under the pressures of "relevance" and an overwrought worry about developing marketable skills. Those skills are important; but what is even more important (as the economic disasters of the early twenty-first century should have reminded the world) is the character of the people who deploy those skills in the world of work. And the West has devised no better way of forming the character of the young than by immersing young men and women in the classics of Western civilization, so that their lives become a practice of the ecumenism of time—and their journey through life is enriched by having, as partners along the way, Homer and Plato and Aristotle and Virgil; Augustine and Aquinas; Dante, Milton, and Shakespeare; and those moderns who were themselves steeped in the classic liberal learning of the West. The curriculum of Catholic colleges and universities that take seriously the New Evangelization and the teaching of *Ex Corde Ecclesiae* will thus lay heavy (and required) stress on an extensive encounter with the classics, including that classic of biblical religion, the Bible.

Crisis Engagement

At the intersection of forming Christian character and honing Christian intellects, the Catholic colleges of universities of the twenty-first century must prepare their students to grapple with the three facets of the civilizational crisis that is the dominant cultural fact of the Western world today: the metaphysical-epistemological crisis, the moral crisis, and the social crisis.

Catholic colleges and universities will address the metaphysical crisis by demonstrating the intimate relationship between faith and reason—which, as the encyclical *Fides et Ratio* teaches, are the "two wings" on which the human spirit reaches out and grasps the truth of things.[10] Catholic institutions of higher learning will not be paralyzed by skepticism; recognizing that there are limits to the reach of reason, Catholic colleges and universities will nonetheless conduct the intellectual life on the premise that human beings can know things with a high degree of certainty. Moreover, Catholic colleges and universities will challenge the hegemony of the scientific method as the sole epistemological paradigm of human knowing and will demonstrate to their students that there is real knowledge to be gained from an encounter with literature, with the arts, with speculative philosophical thought—and with revelation.

Catholic colleges and universities will address the moral crisis by steeping their students in the virtue ethics of authentic Thomism. Thus, they will foster what Father Servais Pinckaers, O.P., has described as "freedom for excellence,"[11] which consists in forming the habit of choosing the right thing, for the right reason, such that freedom is tethered to truth and ordered to genuine human flourishing. Catholic institutions of higher learning will thereby challenge the cultural hegemony of freedom misconstrued as a function of the will and will relocate the moral life within the ambit of human reason. This, in turn, will empower the students of Catholic institutions of higher education to be agents of reform in society, rebuilding a public understanding of the intimate relationship between freedom and virtue.

Catholic colleges and universities will address the social crisis by introducing their students to the riches of the social doctrine of the Church, as an intellectually serious option for building the free and virtuous societies of the future. This introduction to Catholic social thought will emphasize the Thomistic intellectual architecture of the social doctrine tradition as articulated by Leo XIII in *Rerum Novarum*,[12] Pius XI in *Quadragesimo Anno*,[13] and John Paul II in *Centesimus Annus*.[14] In doing so, it will stress the Church's role as the builder of the culture that makes free politics and free economics possible and will stress the importance of moral reason in tempering and guiding democracy and the free market.

Living the Life and Enlarging the Horizon

Curriculum, though, will not be the only distinctive marker of the mission-centered Catholic college or university in the twenty-first century and beyond. Mode of life on campus, regular availability of the sacraments, an active, catechetically engaged campus ministry, and ample opportunities to serve society will distinguish the Catholic institution of higher learning from its counterparts in the secular worlds of higher learning.

Mission-driven Catholic colleges and universities will sponsor study-abroad programs specifically aimed at deepening their students' appreciation of the Catholic cultures of the world, especially the Catholic cultures of Europe, where the first successful inculturation of the Gospel took place and where the architecture of Catholic intellectual life was originally developed.

Encountering Beauty

Mission-centered Catholic colleges and universities of the twenty-first century will bear witness, especially in their chapels, to the truth stressed by Hans Urs von Balthasar and Benedict XVI: that beauty is a privileged path to faith in the postmodern world and a means of opening up deeper reflections on the true and the good—and, ultimately, on the glory of the Lord.

Catholic higher education faced many challenges in the twentieth century, including the assaults mounted by radically secularist political systems. Today's challenge is, arguably, even greater. For the very notion of "truth" is held in contempt by much of early twenty-first-century high culture, and the public result of that cultural contempt, as Pope Benedict XVI warned, is the attempt to impose a dictatorship of relativism—an attempt that is well advanced in Europe, in parts of the Western hemisphere, and in international organizations. Thus, the difference the Catholic colleges and universities of the twenty-first century can and must make is to reaffirm the human capacity to know the truth of things. In knowing and being grasped by the Truth of the Trinitarian God, and in developing a genuine humanism that relates all truth to the divine Truth, twenty-first-century Catholic institutions of higher learning, taking seriously the teaching of *Ex Corde Ecclesiae* and the responsibilities of the New Evangelization, will make a unique contribution to securing the cultural foundations of liberty and justice for all.

ON BEAUTY
The Forgotten Transcendental in a Post-Cultural World

Jagiellonian University, Kraków, Poland, November 5, 2008

In October 1990, during a weeklong conference in Moscow with leaders of the Russian democratic opposition, I found myself with a few free hours. So an American colleague and I hired a young Russian who had stationed himself in our hotel lobby, evidently eager to practice his English, and asked him to take us to and around the Kremlin. The three Orthodox cathedrals within the Kremlin walls had just been restored in honor of the 1988 millennium of Christianity among the eastern Slavs; thanks to the restoration, we could admire a vast array of Byzantine frescoes in something close to their original splendor. At one point on our tour, we stopped before a very large and quite beautiful fresco of the Last Supper; the characters were conventionally arranged, and there was no mistaking the scene. After a minute or so, our young Russian friend turned to my colleague and me and said, in complete innocence, "Please tell me: who are those men, and what are they doing?"

It is easy today, as it was easy throughout the twentieth century, to mock the "socialist realism" of communist art and architecture. It takes no special moral insight to condemn communist censorship or to deplore communist persecution of some of central and eastern Europe's greatest composers, poets, and novelists. Those with eyes to see and ears to hear knew at the time that communist culture was built on a lie, and thus produced various forms of ugliness.

Yet that boy's sincere question brought home to me communism's aesthetic emptiness, and the human wreckage it caused, in a wrenching, powerful way. Here was an intelligent, sensitive young man who had been culturally lobotomized. He had grown to late adolescence in a world in which one might still recognize the outward manifestations of beauty, but without being able to connect beauty to truth and goodness. For sixty-three years, Marxism-Leninism in Russia had tried to destroy a world of culture and to deconstruct what it could not destroy. The result was a generation living in a world without culture, a post-cultural world.[1]

As the memory of European communism continues to fade into the past, we would do well, however, to consider our own situation. Are we, who live in free societies shaped by the centuries-long cultural interaction of Jerusalem, Athens, and Rome—biblical religion, Greek rationality, Roman law—sliding into a post-cultural phase of our own history? The atheism of indifference, married to epistemological skepticism and moral relativism, has produced in contemporary Europe and America a postmodernism in which there may be "your truth" and "my truth," but nothing recognized by the entire culture as "*the* truth." And that, I suggest, is yet another recipe for creating a post-cultural world. Communist cult and ritual distorted men's apprehension of the true, the good, and the beautiful because communist cult and ritual were ordered to a false god. Similarly, the postmodern cult of the imperial autonomous Self tends to produce a dehumanizing culture, manifestations of which can be found along a continuum running from Berlin's *Komische Oper* to Internet pornography.[2]

The late Aleksandr Solzhenitsyn, who battled heroically against the post-cultural depredations of communism, explored several of these issues in his 1970 Nobel Prize lecture:

> One day Dostoevsky threw out the enigmatic remark, "Beauty will save the world." What sort of a statement is that? For a long time I considered it mere words. How could that be possible? When in bloodthirsty history did beauty save anyone from anything? Ennobled, uplifted, yes?—but whom has it saved? ...
>
> So perhaps that ancient trinity of Truth, Goodness, and Beauty is not simply an empty, faded formula as we thought in the days of our self-confident, materialistic youth? If the tops of three trees converge, as the scholars maintained, but the too blatant, too direct stems of Truth and Goodness are crushed, cut down, not allowed through—then perhaps the fantastic, unpredictable, unexpected stems of Beauty will push through TO THAT VERY SAME PLACE, and in so doing will fulfil the work of all three?
>
> In that case Dostoevsky's remark, "Beauty will save the world", was not a careless phrase but a prophecy?[3]

Pope John Paul II, in whose blessed memory we gather in these days, was a man much concerned with the many ways in which the branches of the tree of Truth and the tree of Goodness had been cut back, and in some cases lopped off, during the twentieth century. He knew that philosophical and moral vandalism had produced the two great mid-century totalitarianisms; he had lived the consequences of that vandalism as a student, priest, and bishop. Because of that, his own intellectual project and his magisterium as Bishop of Rome were aimed in no small part at revitalizing the roots of the trees of Truth and Goodness so that their branches might reach upward again, giving shade to the fragile saplings of those free societies that were planted in the same human soil. But what about John Paul II and the tree of Beauty?

As pope, he wrote little on the subject in a formal way, with the exception of his *Letter to Artists*, to which I shall turn in a moment. Nonetheless, we can find traces of Dostoevsky's prophecy about the salvific power of beauty in several facets of John Paul II's pontificate.

His papal motto, *Totus Tuus*, echoes the patristic conviction that the Virgin Mary appears to us in beauty, both in her Immaculate Conception and in her Assumption: *Tota pulchra est, O Maria*, as an antiphon for First Vespers of the Immaculate Conception put it in the pre-conciliar breviary. And if Mary is the first of Christian disciples and the model of all discipleship (as John Paul taught on many occasions), then true discipleship and beauty are clearly related, both now and in the Kingdom into which Mary was assumed as queen.[4]

John Paul raised to the cardinalate Hans Urs von Balthasar, the Swiss theologian who, in a singular way, put the "lost transcendental," beauty, at the heart of Catholic theology and its reflection on the divine mystery. In doing so, Balthasar reminded the Church that the glory of the Lord, the beauty of the Lord, and Christ's lordship are all one reality (just as they are all contained in the one-word title of the first panel of Balthasar's theological triptych: *Herrlichkeit*).

John Paul took the purse given him by the College of Cardinals for his golden priestly anniversary and used it to decorate the Matilda Chapel of the apostolic palace, bringing the art of the Christian East into the administrative center of the Church of the West. The same ecumenical and aesthetic instinct led the Pope to put Andrei Rublev's famous Trinitarian icon at the center of his Great Jubilee celebration of God's self-revelation to Abraham.

And, against the counsel of some, he authorized the cleaning of Michelangelo's Sistine Chapel frescoes, thus allowing the men and women of the twenty-first century to experience the beauty that had been created five centuries before in the service of God, the Church, and culture. In his homily at the 1994 Mass marking the completed restoration of the *Last Judgment*, John Paul spoke of Michelangelo's unveiling of "an extraordinary Christ ... endowed with an ancient beauty," in which the Florentine genius expressed in his art Augustine's praise of that "Beauty, ever ancient, ever new" which he had long sought to embrace. The entire Sistine Chapel, John Paul continued, was "the sanctuary of the theology of the human body." By capturing "the beauty of man created by God as male and female," Michelangelo's frescoes conveyed "the hope of a world transfigured, the world inaugurated by the Risen Christ." Rightly understood, this testimony to the "beauty of man" is a confession of the beauty of the Creator, in whom truth, goodness, and beauty are one. Indeed, John Paul went so far as to describe art like that in the Sistine Chapel as "in a certain sense, like a sacrament of Christian life, since in it the mystery of the incarnation becomes present.... The mystery of the word made flesh is reflected in a way that is ever new"—and those who see are made glad by catching a visible glimpse of the invisible glory of the Lord, manifest in the creation.[5] The Pope returned to these themes in the second panel of his last poem, *Roman Triptych*.

In striking this sacramental note—the invisible made present through the visible—John Paul was reflecting the settled conviction of the Catholic Church on the sacramentality of the world and the reality of the Incarnation, the two key issues in the iconoclast controversy in which the Church was enmeshed from approximately A.D. 725 until 842. The stakes in that often unseemly theological and political brawl were high, for culture as well as for the Church. Here is John Paul's commentary in his *Letter to Artists*:

> There arose ... a bitter controversy known to history as the "iconoclast crisis". Sacred images, which were already widely used in Christian devotion, became the object of violent contention. The Council held at Nicaea in 787, which decreed the legitimacy of images and their veneration, was a historic event not just for the faith but for culture itself. The decisive argument to which the Bishops appealed in order

> to settle the controversy was the mystery of the Incarnation: if the Son of God had come into the world of visible realities—his humanity building a bridge between the visible and the invisible—then, by analogy, a representation of the mystery could be used, within the logic of signs, as a sensory evocation of the mystery. The icon is venerated not for its own sake, but points beyond to the subject which it represents.[6]

Put in a slightly different way, the resolution of the iconoclast controversy in favor of the iconophiles kept beauty and truth linked: Beauty can be a window into ultimate truth, the truth of God in Christ. Put yet another way, the use of icons and images in the Church—which Poland's devotion to the Black Madonna so powerfully embodies—protects the Church against the Gnostic temptation to deprecate creation and to deny the sacramentality of the world: to deny that the materials of the world—bread, wine, water; salt and oil; marital love and fidelity—can be the vehicles by which God's grace comes into human hearts. In vindicating the defenders of icons, the Church was defending the Christian claim that, in Christ, we can touch the truth of our salvation: once, in history; now, sacramentally. Even in its most abstract neo-Platonic vesture, Christianity is not simply a matter of ideas, even true ideas. Christianity is a matter of truths enfleshed: the truth that God became man; the truth that, through the Incarnation of Christ and the redemption wrought by his cross, human beings were offered the possibility of sanctification—which the Church of the East is so bold as to call *theosis*, divinization.

In his defense of the overpowering human beauty of the Sistine Chapel frescoes as art touched by the sacramental, John Paul II was a faithful son of the Second Vatican Council. On the Council's last day, December 8, 1965, the Solemnity of the Immaculate Conception, the Council Fathers issued a message to artists, which concluded with an affirmation, a caution, and a plea:

> This world in which we live needs beauty in order not to sink into despair. It is beauty, like truth, which brings joy to the heart of man and is that precious fruit which resists the wear and tear of time, which unites generations and makes them share things in admiration. And all of this is through your hands. May these hands be pure and disinterested. Remember that you are the guardians of beauty in the world.

May that suffice to free you from tastes that are passing and have no genuine value, to free you from the search after strange or unbecoming expressions. Be always and everywhere worthy of your ideals.[7]

It seems clear that the world of the arts has not always heeded the Council's admonition, and John Paul II's summons, to be guardians of beauty. In its "Message to Rulers," the Council Fathers urged that men of power "allow Christ to exercise His purifying action on society. Do not [they pleaded] crucify Him anew. This would be a sacrilege for He is the Son of God. This would be suicide for He is the Son of Man."[8] The same plea, and that same warning, could just as easily be addressed to those whose talents and vocations should make them the guardians of beauty. The degradation of art is a form of sacrilege, for it demeans the materials through which God makes himself sacramentally present to his people. The degradation of art is also suicide, cultural suicide, for it severs beauty from truth and goodness and leaves us adrift in a post-cultural world, cut off from the deepest wellsprings of our civilization. The result, in terms of philosophical anthropology, is that bizarre phenomenon once described by the American critic Allan Bloom as "debonair nihilism": not the soured, cramped nihilism of the early Sartre, but the kind of nihilism that anesthetizes itself with vulgar pleasures on the way to oblivion.

At the center of the philosophical anthropology of Karol Wojtyła is the truth he called "The Law of the Gift"—human flourishing comes through the free and authentic gift of self to others, not through the assertions of the imperial autonomous Self. We are, he taught in numerous variations on a single theme, to make ourselves into the gift for others that our lives are to us. None of us is the cause of our own existence; we exist as gift, and it is into that giftedness that we must grow. That means that each of us, as John Paul wrote in his *Letter to Artists*, is an artist, a craftsman: "Not all [of us] are called to be artists in the specific sense of the term," he wrote. "Yet, as Genesis has it, all men and women are entrusted with the task of crafting their own life: in a certain sense, they are to make of it a work of art, a masterpiece."[9]

Thus art that does not contribute to our living the Law of the Gift is art that is not living its true vocation. Art that does not enable us to experience beauty in its relationship to truth and goodness does not enable us to grow into the gifts for others that we are meant to be.

Art that does not reflect the native human openness to the transcendent is art that risks grinding us into the dust. Artists, like men of power, can crucify Christ anew.

In the Septuagint, the Greek translation of the Hebrew Bible that shaped a large part of the religious imagination of the early Christian Church, God sees that his creation is both good and beautiful—in fact, Greek includes a word that combines the two: *kalokagathia*, or beauty-goodness.[10] The beauty-goodness of the world reveals the beauty, goodness, and truth of the Creator, whose Spirit, John Paul writes, is the "mysterious Artist of the universe."[11] It may seem too late for the postmodern world of the twenty-first century to recognize the promptings of that "mysterious Artist," especially in a Europe suffering from a crisis of cultural morale and an inability to recognize the great goodness in its history. But then we recall again, with John Paul, Augustine's cry in the *Confessions*, "Late have I loved Thee, O Beauty ever ancient, ever new; late have I loved thee!"[12] And because of that memory, we may hope, with the great Bishop of Hippo, that it is not too late for our post-cultural world.

John Paul II understood, with an insight granted to few others, that the anthropological question—the Question of Man—is at the center of the human dilemma in late modernity. Resolving this question, he knew, meant rediscovering the beauty of the human: the kind of human beauty manifest in the Sistine Chapel; the kind of beauty manifest invisibly in character, in goodness, in those men and women who live in the truth. "Living in the truth" was the resistance strategy deployed, at considerable cost, by east central European human rights activists determined to challenge the communist culture of the lie—what Václav Havel eviscerated as a "world of appearances trying to pass for reality."[13] The reality that was lost in that communist structure of mendacity was the reality of man.

The post-cultural world of postmodernism is another world of appearances trying to pass for reality. In this case, the appearances may seem, at first glance, less threatening. But they are just as lethal. For the "appearance" of sophisticated skepticism and the "appearance" of moral relativism conceal the reality of man, who was created to embody, with God's grace, truth, goodness, and beauty. Reclaiming our grip on moral truth is essential if the free society is not to self-destruct. So is the reclamation of beauty. For it is in the experience of goodness and beauty that we come to learn the truth about man, and thus come to a resolution of the Question of Man that will sustain a true humanism.[14]

The distinguished French philosopher Rémi Brague suggested a provocative reading of modern history some years ago. The nineteenth century, he proposed, was the century of *good-and-evil*: The "social question," posed by the Industrial Revolution, the emergence of an urban working class, and the demise of traditional society dominated the landscape. The twentieth century, Brague argued, had been the century of *true-and-false*: totalitarian ideologies, built on perverse misunderstandings of the human person, defined the contest for the human future that drove history from 1917 until 1991.[15]

And the twenty-first century? Ours, Professor Brague suggested, will be the century of *being-or-nothingness*. A soured cynicism about the mystery and wonder of being stalks the postmodern, post-cultural world. A post-metaphysical world has shown itself to be a world skeptical of truth and uncertain of goodness; for a world blind to the transcendentals is a world in which we are locked into the prison of our own desires, passions, and "needs."[16]

Might it be that beauty, the "forgotten transcendental," is the means by which the "mysterious Artist of the universe," the Holy Spirit, inspires artists and all men and women of culture to rediscover the truth of goodness and the goodness of truth—and thus recover that sense of awe and wonder at the mystery of being that is essential to any true humanism?

That is something for the Church to pray for as it sings its hymn to God's beauty, the *Sanctus*, every day.

VOLTAIRE CONFOUNDED
The Church in Defense of Reason

Jagiellonian University, Kraków, Poland, November 7, 2013

During the Liturgy of the Word in the Byzantine Rite, the deacon admonishes the congregation with the chants "Wisdom! Let us be attentive ..." and "Wisdom! Let us stand aright ..." The first chant reminds us that wisdom, one of the seven gifts of the Holy Spirit, is essential if we are to discern the full truth of things in the world created by the Trinitarian God. The second chant suggests that wisdom, drawing our attention to the full truth of things, empowers us to lead upright lives—lives in accord with the moral laws that, as John Paul II said at Sinai on February 26, 2000, were "written on the human heart as the universal moral law" before they were "written in stone."[1]

The *Catechism of the Catholic Church* defines wisdom as "a spiritual gift which enables one to know the purpose and plan of God."[2] Wisdom, in other words, sheds light on what can seem opaque and dark, random and meaningless. Every period of history needs wise men and women. Perhaps this postmodern age has particular need of wise counselors, for throughout Western high culture, there is a disturbing tendency to deny that human beings can grasp the truth of anything with a measure of certainty. There is nothing new in this, of course; Pontius Pilate imagined that his question, "What is truth?" (Jn 18:38), put an end to the conversation. But so do many of our contemporaries.

At her 2007 inauguration as the twenty-eighth president of Harvard University, Dr. Drew Gilpin Faust noted that the Latin word *Veritas* on Harvard's coat of arms "was originally intended to invoke the absolutes of divine revelation, the unassailable verities of Puritan religion." But "we understand it quite differently now," she continued. For, according to Dr. Faust, in the twenty-first century there is only the aspiration to truth; truth is not a "possession," and there are certainly no "unassailable verities." Those engaged in higher learning and higher education in the twenty-first century, Dr. Faust concluded, "must commit ourselves to the uncomfortable position of doubt." And by "doubt," we may assume that Dr. Faust did not mean a healthy spirit of inquiry, but rather a stance of systematic skepticism toward the human capacity to know anything as, finally, true, save for some judgments of an a priori character (such as that one plus one will always equal two in the base-ten system). It is only from this stance of systematic skepticism, Dr. Faust and others would argue, that twenty-first-century men and women can live (as she put it in her inaugural address) with "the humility of always believing there is more to know, more to teach, more to understand."[3]

It was appropriate that Dr. Faust took as her example of a lost, unrecoverable, and not-to-be-lamented past what she termed the "absolutes of divine revelation." For in the long view of the history of ideas, Western high culture's Enlightenment skepticism about the possibility of speaking and thinking intelligibly about "divine revelation" was one of the turning points that eventually led us to today's crisis of the postmodern mind, in which there may be, at best, "your truth" and "my truth," but there is nothing recognizable as *the* truth: truth, plain and simple. This radical epistemological skepticism informs two other characteristics of postmodern high culture: metaphysical nihilism and moral relativism. And that unhappy cocktail—nihilism plus skepticism plus relativism—is not simply a debilitating intoxicant for intellectuals; it is making it very difficult to sustain the institutions of democracy.

For as John Paul II presciently taught in the 1991 encyclical, *Centesimus Annus*, there are real dangers encoded in the suggestion that "agnosticism and sceptical relativism are the philosophy and the basic attitude which correspond to democratic forms of political life." Why? Because "if there is no ultimate truth to guide and direct political activity, then ideas and convictions can be easily manipulated for reason of power." Thus, John Paul concluded, the history of the twentieth century had shown how "a democracy without values easily turns into open or thinly disguised totalitarianism."[4] Benedict XVI cited the same hard, but also essential, historical lesson in his warnings against the encroachments of a "dictatorship of relativism," in which coercive state power is used to impose a relativistic morality (itself grounded in metaphysical nihilism and epistemological skepticism) on all of society.[5] The validity of those warnings has been borne out time and again in recent years, in the debate over the life issues and the nature of marriage.

At the beginning of the continental Enlightenment, Voltaire urged his countrymen, "*Écrasez l'infâme!*" ("Crush the infamy!"), by which he meant the power of royalty and an established Church, drawing their authority from "divine right," to control societies in which ordinary people lived in servitude and poverty. Only when the illusion of divine revelation had been dispelled, Voltaire believed, would the *ancien régime* fall and the power of reason be unleashed—and from the free exercise of reason would come the power "to begin the world anew," as Thomas Paine, a later Enlightenment thinker and activist, famously put it. It was, in some respects, a noble aspiration, but the final result of this cultural revolution was not the utopia imagined by Voltaire and Paine; it was the birth of the greatest tyrannies in human history—the tyrannies that lived out what John Paul II's friend Father Henri de Lubac, S.J., called "the drama of atheistic humanism." Or, as Father de Lubac put it in his book by that title, "It is not true, as is sometimes said, that man cannot organize the world without God. What is true is that, without God, he can only organize it against man."[6]

John Paul II understood this intellectual history as well as any great figure of our time. He knew that, untethered to revelation and the biblical idea of man as the *imago Dei*, reason would be self-cannibalizing: Reason would destroy itself or, to put it more precisely, reason would deconstruct itself to the point where it would celebrate systematic skepticism and doubt. Unlike Harvard's president, John Paul II knew that faith in the God of the Bible and acceptance of the biblical vision of man as the *imago Dei* builds up within us what Dr. Drew Faust rightly commended as "the humility of always believing that there is more to know, more to teach, more to understand." Radical skepticism does not build that humility within us; rather, it builds what the French political philosopher Pierre Manent called the "self-adoration" and "fateful hubris" that led to the mass slaughters and enslavements of the twentieth century.[7]

Refusing to be cowed by those intellectuals who continued to insist, with Voltaire, that reason and revelation had nothing to do with each other, that rational inquiry and faith in the God of the Bible could not coexist, and that the God of the Bible had to be buried so that humanity could be mature and free, John Paul II, in the 1998 encyclical *Fides et Ratio*, repositioned the Catholic Church as the world's premier institutional defender of the potential and prerogatives of reason.[8]

In that encyclical, John Paul challenged philosophy's "false modesty,"[9] a self-limiting skepticism that had precluded philosophy asking the great questions, Why is there something rather than nothing? What is good and what is evil? What is happiness and what is delusion? What awaits me after this life? This false modesty had not only reduced philosophy to a kind of mathematics; it had opened the path to a culture too often dominated by an instrumental or utilitarian view of human beings, to a false faith in technology as the sovereign cure for all human ills, and to the triumph in politics of Nietzsche's will-to-power. It was time, John Paul suggested, for humanity to recover its faith in reason and for philosophy to recover that sense of awe and wonder that directs it to transcendent truth. Human beings can know what is true, what is good, and what is beautiful, John Paul II taught, even if we can never know the true, the good, and the beautiful completely.

In a powerful image at the very beginning of the encyclical, John Paul II employed an evocative image to sum up the case he was about to make: "Faith and reason," he wrote, "are like two wings on which the human spirit rises to the contemplation of truth."[10] Trying to fly on one wing had led to human catastrophe throughout the twentieth century. It was time to fly with two wings again.

In rereading the Book of Wisdom recently, I was struck by how its ninth chapter, presented as a prayer of King Solomon, provides a poetic framework for grasping key themes of the Catholic Church's twenty-first-century defense of reason, which is largely John Paul II's defense of reason. Permit me, then, to quote Wisdom 9:1–6, 9–11, while providing a contemporary commentary on the implications of the biblical text, drawn from the teaching of *Fides et Ratio*:

> O God of my fathers and Lord of mercy,
> who have made all things by your word,
> and by your wisdom have formed man,
> to have dominion over the creatures you have made,
> and rule the world in holiness and righteousness,
> and pronounce judgment in uprightness of soul. (Wis 9:1–3)

The intelligibility and coherence of creation are the result of creation "through" the Word, the Logos of God, who imprints on creation the divine intelligibility—the self-knowledge of the Trinitarian godhead—thus making creation itself intelligible to the mind of that creature, man, who bears the imprint of the Logos in his reason. Thus man does not simply apply his own rational organizing categories to creation; by the use of his reason, man discovers the rationality and the truths that God has encoded in the creation "in the beginning" (Gen 1:1), through the Word who was with God "in the beginning" (Jn 1:1) and by whom all things came into being and are sustained.[11]

> Give me the wisdom that sits by your throne,
> and do not reject me from among your servants.
> For I am your slave and the son of your maidservant,
> a man who is weak and short-lived,
> with little understanding of judgment and laws. (Wis 9:4–5)

Revelation helps reason, for reason without revelation—Athens without Jerusalem—cannot maintain a firm conviction of its own capacity to grasp things truly. That is the lesson of the decline of Enlightenment rationalism into postmodern epistemological skepticism, a decline mediated through the positivism of Auguste Comte (empirical science is humanity's only reliable tutor), the subjectivism of Ludwig Feuerbach ("God" is the mythical projection of human aspirations), the materialism of Karl Marx (the spiritual world is an illusion), and the radical voluntarism of Nietzsche (exercising the will-to-power is the index of human greatness). By the same token, reason purifies religious experience and prevents its degradation into superstition. As John Paul II put it in *Fides et Ratio*, citing Saint Augustine, believing "is nothing other than to think with assent.... Believers are also thinkers: in believing, they think, and in thinking, they believe.... If faith does not think it is nothing."[12]

> For even if one is perfect among the sons of men,
> yet without the wisdom that comes from you he will be regarded
> as nothing. (Wis 9:6)

Reason by itself falters, stumbles, and eventually falls. And the results are not to be found only within the walls of the academy. The results are to be found throughout society, in that "anthropological crisis," that diminishment of faith in man and his innate dignity and value, that John Paul II put at the center of the crisis of late modernity.[13]

> With you is wisdom, who knows your works
> and was present when you made the world,
> and who understands what is pleasing in your sight
> and what is right according to your commandments. (Wis 9:9)

Wisdom leads to happiness, beatitude, which is the goal of the moral life. Wisdom reminds us that freedom is not a matter of doing whatever we like, which is a very inhuman (and inhumane) form of freedom. Wisdom helps us understand that freedom is always tied to truth and ordered to goodness, so that the truly free man freely chooses what is good and does so as a matter of moral habit. Thus, wisdom increases intelligence, helping reason to grasp the deeper moral truths that can seem beyond reason's grasp: the truths of the Beatitudes, as expressed in Matthew 5:3–11.[14]

> Send her forth from the holy heavens,
> and from the throne of your glory send her,
> that she may be with me and toil,
> and that I may learn what is pleasing to you. (Wis 9:10)

Wisdom is a spiritual gift that develops in us, a gift that is nourished and nurtured by both reason and revelation. Faith in the God of the Bible enhances faith in the capacities of reason to reach the truth, even as reason purifies faith from any taint of superstition or irrationality.[15]

> For she knows and understands all things,
> and she will guide me wisely in my actions
> and guard me with her glory. (Wis 9:11)

Both reason and revelation guide us to an understanding of the moral law that is written into nature and into us, and that provides a "grammar" by which the world can turn discord into an orderly conversation about the common good (as John Paul II put it at the United Nations in 1995).[16] Thus public life in its social, political, cultural, and economic dimensions is enhanced by reference to both reason and revelation, the two wings on which the human spirit ascends to the truth.[17]

As we approach the midpoint of the second decade of the first century of the third millennium, what John Paul II described as the Church's "*diakonia* of the truth," the evangelical service of truth, will be lived out according to the rule laid down in the 1990 encyclical *Redemptoris Missio*: "The Church proposes; she imposes nothing."[18] And what shall the Church propose to the postmodern world, as humanity wrestles with the questions of truth and meaning?

The Church will remind humanity that the quest for truth and meaning is built into the human heart, and that the answers given to the questions of truth and meaning decide "the direction which people seek to give to their lives."[19]

The Church will remind humanity that wonder, not technique, is the beginning of knowledge and wisdom in their most ample dimensions.[20]

The Church will call men and women out of what the late Polish philosopher Wojciech Chudy called the "trap of reflection," recognizing with John Paul II that "reason, in its one-sided concern to investigate human subjectivity, seems to have forgotten that men and women are always called to direct their steps towards a truth that transcends them."[21] The Church will also recognize, and remind humanity that, as John Paul II put it, detached from transcendent truth, "individuals are at the mercy of caprice, and their state as persons ends up being judged by pragmatic criteria based essentially upon experimental data, in the mistaken belief that technology must dominate all."[22]

The Church will recover, and make part of its evangelical mission, the ancient maxim *Credo ut intelligam*. Faith respects reason's autonomy, but faith also reminds reason that reason cannot "bracket" revelation, drive theology and its reflection on revelation to the margins of academic life, or declare revelation irrelevant to the human quest for meaning and understanding.[23]

The Church will recover, and make part of its evangelical mission, the related, ancient maxim, *Intelligo ut credam*, reminding the world that true knowledge and wisdom lead to that gift of self which is fundamental to living nobly. Thus, with John Paul II, the Church will propose that "human perfection ... consists not simply in acquiring an abstract knowledge of the truth, but in a dynamic relationship of faithful self-giving with others. It is in this faithful self-giving that a person finds a fullness of certainty and security."[24]

In its *diakonia* of the truth, the Church of the twenty-first century will propose Christ the Lord as the answer to the anthropological crisis of late modernity and postmodernity, recognizing with the Second Vatican Council and John Paul II that it is "only in the mystery of the Incarnate Word" that the "mystery of man" is fully illuminated: "Christ the Lord ... the new Adam, in the very revelation of the mystery of the Father and of his love, fully reveals man to himself and brings to light his most high calling."[25] The Church will make this proposal in fidelity to the Great Commission of Matthew 28:18–20, from which the Church takes its identity as a communion of disciples in mission, and to meet the challenge of a world grown cynical in the "disenchantment" described by Max Weber—a disenchantment that has led to a crisis of meaning which can only be addressed by a recovery of the sapiential spirit in learning and teaching and a recovery of the metaphysical sensibility that was, until the continental Enlightenment, a central part of Western civilization.[26]

And in all of this the Church will, with Saint Bonaventure, invite humanity to recognize the humanly debilitating and intellectually disabling character of "reading without repentance, knowledge without devotion, research without the impulse of wonder, prudence without the ability to surrender to joy, action divorced from religion, learning sundered from love, intelligence without humility, study unsustained by divine grace, thought without the wisdom inspired by God."[27]

VERITATIS SPLENDOR
A Gift to the Church and the World

Pontifical University of John Paul II, Kraków, Poland, October 17, 2018

Thank you for inviting me to share with you this celebration of the fortieth anniversary of Karol Wojtyła's election as Pope John Paul II—an event of extraordinary consequence for both the Church and the world. Your focus on *Veritatis Splendor* reflects that dual importance of John Paul II as a reformer in the Church and as a man with many important things to say about the state of the world and its future. I would like to discuss this remarkable encyclical in light of those two dimensions of the pontificate: the ecclesial dimension and the public dimension. Let us begin with the ecclesial, or Catholic, dimension of the encyclical.

Why was *Veritatis Splendor* necessary? Why did John Paul II feel it obligatory to write an encyclical on the reform of moral theology in the Church?

We must go back to the period immediately after the Second Vatican Council to get the answer to that question. In that period—indeed, while the Council was underway—a new way of doing moral theology, often called "proportionalism," was being developed, largely in the German-speaking Catholic world. According to this theory, the morality of an act should be judged by a calculus of intention and consequence, plus a moral measure of the act itself. And embedded in this theory of proportionalism was the claim that there are no intrinsically evil acts: things that are simply wrong in themselves; what an older moral theology called acts that are *malum in se*.

This proportionalist theory was part of the Church's great, post–Vatican II debate over the appropriate means of regulating fertility. Pope Paul VI, as you will remember, established a commission to look into questions of family life, birth, natality, etc., and a great argument ensued within that commission. Cardinal Karol Wojtyła set up a Cracovian commission to look at these problems. And that commission came to the conclusion that, while the traditional teaching of the Church on the appropriate means of regulating fertility should be reasserted in the encyclical, better, more accessible arguments in favor of that teaching ought to be advanced.

In any event, during this intense debate in what became known as "the birth control commission," Paul VI came to understand that what was really at stake here was the nature of Catholic moral theology. Those who were pressing for a change in the Church's teaching on the appropriate means of regulating fertility were not just arguing for that change. They were attempting to enshrine the proportionalist method of moral reasoning as the official moral theology of the Catholic Church. And Paul VI understood—as Karol Wojtyła understood—that that would be a terrible mistake.

It would be a terrible mistake because it would empty the moral life of all of its drama. If there are no things that are simply wrong in themselves, things that are so humanly degrading that they fundamentally deny the dignity of the human person—if it is all just a matter of balancing intentions and consequences and specific acts—then the moral life loses its drama. And as happened in liberal Protestantism throughout Europe and North America during the second half of the twentieth century, all moral boundaries eventually dissolve.

The proportionalists lost the battle at the time of the writing of *Humanae Vitae*, but they were determined to continue the war. And it was partially in response to that grim determination John Paul II decided to write *Veritatis Splendor*. There, he tried to restore ballast to Catholic moral theology, not least by asserting the reality of intrinsically evil acts—some things that are just wrong by their very nature, and that no combination of intentions and consequences can make right. Think of sexual assault, think of the torture of children, think of the willful homicide of an innocent person. These things are simply (as the old language would have it) *malum in se*. And to deny that is to empty the moral life of all ballast.

But John Paul II was not simply making philosophical arguments in *Veritatis Splendor*; he wanted to re-center Catholic moral theology and the Catholic moral life on the Beatitudes.

There's a great misunderstanding in much of the world, even today, that Catholic moral teaching is essentially a laundry list of "dos" and "don'ts": You can't do this, you can't do that, you should do this, you should do that. As John Paul II wrote in *Veritatis Splendor*, that is not the nature of the moral life. The Beatitudes are the Magna Carta of all Christian morality. Those eight statements of the Lord in the Sermon on the Mount about human flourishing, human happiness, or what in theological language we would call "beatitude" are the framework in which Christians live the moral life. Christians, through the grace of God, seek beatitude. And in seeking beatitude, they are also seeking genuine human flourishing. So, the Beatitudes, not rules, are at the center of the moral life in the teaching of *Veritatis Splendor*.

That does not mean there aren't rules. But in *Veritatis Splendor* and in the thinking of John Paul II, "the rules" are repositioned. Rather than simply being a list of "dos" and "don'ts"—and especially "don'ts"—moral rules become understood as guardrails to guide us on the journey to beatitude. We have moral laws in the Church—we believe that God built moral laws into creation—precisely to guide us on the path to beatitude and to genuine human flourishing. That is what John Paul II tried to do in terms of redirecting moral theology in the Church. He not only taught that the proportionalist method would lead to moral wreckage; he tried to re-center the whole discussion around the question, What are we striving for? What does the grace of God call us to? It calls us to beatitude. It calls us, ultimately, to a life within the communion of the Most Holy Trinity in the Kingdom of God. That is the ecclesial dimension of *Veritatis Splendor*, if you will.

As for its public dimension, *Veritatis Splendor* was written at a time when moral language and moral concepts were becoming deeply confused throughout the Western world. Someone's fundamental human right was regarded by others as something intrinsically wrong. There was great confusion over the very idea of freedom. Is freedom merely willfulness? Or does freedom have something to do with truth and goodness?

Remember that in 1993, when *Veritatis Splendor* was issued, we were only four years away from the fall of the Berlin Wall. New democracies were shaping their public cultures. John Paul II thought it important for the Church to help shape those public moral cultures in ways that they could in turn influence free democratic politics and free economics in a postcommunist world.

I think the Pope also had another concern here. John Paul II was deeply marked by the history of the twentieth century, and he knew that its bloody history taught us a very valuable lesson. And that lesson is that if morality is simply sentiment—if the moral life is not rooted in truths built into the world and into us, truths that we can know by reason—then chaos ensues. Freedom detached from truths easily degrades into license. And a society in which license prevails, a society in which freedom is detached from truth, in which freedom is not ordered to goodness, is a society heading for deep trouble. Why is that?

If freedom is simply license, if freedom is simply willfulness, then society quickly degrades into a contest of everyone's will-to-power set against everyone else's. I've often suggested to audiences in North America and in Europe that they think about this in terms of the collapse of the idea of truth. If there is only "your truth" and "my truth" and neither one of us recognizes some reality called "the truth," then what happens when your truth and my truth collide, and neither one of us recognizes something called "the truth" by which we can adjudicate and settle our differences?

What happens, as Friedrich Nietzsche knew, is that you will impose your power on me or I will impose my power on you. If there is no truth-grounded moral horizon for social life, then society really does decompose into a contest over the will-to-power. That's a kind of Nietzschean nightmare. And because human beings cannot tolerate chaos—the chaos that would ensue from an endless contest of my will-to-power versus yours—the result of that collapse of morality into sentiment is a chaos that eventually leads to tyranny. People will reach for chains if chains are perceived to be the only alternative to chaos.

Veritatis Splendor tried to address that set of problems by restoring a richer, nobler understanding of freedom to the public life of the West. Here, John Paul II drew on the thinking of a Belgian Dominican, moral theologian Father Servais Pinckaers, who in his extraordinarily important book, *The Sources of Christian Ethics*, analyzed the difference between what he called the "freedom of indifference" and what he called "freedom for excellence."[1]

Pinckaers illustrated this difference by asking us to think about two very common human situations. First, learning to play a musical instrument. When I was a boy learning to play the piano, I was given a book called *Scales, Chords, and Arpeggios*. It was an awful book—many of you may have known it in your own childhood. It was awful because it forced you to do exercises that trained your fingers to play the piano properly. That seemed terribly restrictive at the time. It seemed like a burden. And yet if you think about it, it is precisely those exercises that allow one to play the music one wishes to play. It is precisely those exercises that allow one to create new music, because a disciplined understanding of how to play the piano correctly has been learned, has become a habit—and we know that one Latin word for "virtue" is *habitus*. We have learned the virtue of learning to play the piano properly.

Contrast that to a three-year-old child simply banging on the piano. You can say that is playing the piano, but it's not a human way of making music; it's a childish, infantile way of making music. It's sheer noise. Pinckaers, and John Paul II, would say that it's the freedom of indifference at work: a freedom without the disciplines that allow us to lead a truly human life commensurate with our human dignity.

Pinckaers offered a second example, which I think made a lot of sense to John Paul II, in illustrating this difference between the freedom of indifference and freedom for excellence. Think about learning a new language. Everyone knows that the best way to learn a new language is to speak it, haltingly at first, in conversation with others. Eventually, though, one has to learn vocabulary and grammar. Grammar and vocabulary are rules. They're rules that allow us to speak a language properly. They're rules that allow us to speak that language so that we can actually communicate with others, share ideas, and learn. That's another example of the difference between the freedom of indifference and freedom for excellence.

The freedom of indifference is my beautiful one-and-a-half-year-old granddaughter, Lucy, babbling. Eventually, though, Lucy is going to have to learn vocabulary and grammar so that she can speak English properly. And that will allow her to live out her human dignity in a much more satisfying way, both for herself and for others.

John Paul II understood that grasping this difference between the freedom of indifference, which is an infantile freedom, and freedom for excellence, which is a mature freedom, is essential for democracy. Democracy is not a machine that can run by itself. It takes a certain critical mass of people living certain virtues to make the machinery of democracy work, so that the net result of democratic politics is social solidarity, the advance of the common good, and the human flourishing of individuals. Getting clear on this distinction between the freedom of indifference and the freedom for excellence, which was one of the key teachings of *Veritatis Splendor*, is thus essential for the future of democracies.

There was another point that John Paul II made in *Veritatis Splendor* that deserves reflection by people concerned about the democratic future throughout the Western world. The Pope posed an interesting question about equality. The equality of human beings—the moral equality and the legal equality of human beings—is a bedrock principle of democracy, he noted. Yet how can we assert that equality in a world in which we are constantly encountering human inequality? Some people are more intelligent than other people. Some people are more beautiful than other people. Some people are more athletically gifted than other people. Some people are more musically gifted or linguistically gifted than other people. Some people are great at making money, some people have great entrepreneurial skills, other people can barely balance a checkbook.

How do we assert human equality in a world where inequality presents itself to us every day? The Pope made an interesting suggestion in *Veritatis Splendor*. He said the most secure ground on which to assert the fundamental equality of all people, so crucial to democracy, is to recognize the responsibility of every human being before the moral law: before the truths of the moral law that we can know by reason. I think that is a fascinating idea: to ground democratic equality on equal moral responsibility before the truths of the natural moral law we can know by reason. I hope that someday political theorists and political philosophers will take up that proposal and develop it further.

So, as you ponder this important encyclical on the fortieth anniversary of John Paul II's election, let me urge you to consider both its importance in the life of the Church, which is being challenged by many today, and its importance in public life. *Veritatis Splendor* is not an encyclical for the Church alone; it is very much part of the

Church's proposal to society at large. And throughout the Western world today we are badly in need of that Catholic proposal, which distinguishes the freedom of indifference from freedom for excellence, and which understands that freedom must be tied to truth, and ordered to goodness, if freedom is not to self-destruct.

JOHN PAUL II, THE PRIORITY OF CULTURE, AND THE CONTEMPORARY CULTURE WARS

Pontifical University of St. Thomas Aquinas, Rome, Italy, November 29, 2023

While these lectures during the 2023–2024 academic year, co-sponsored by the institute *Teologia Polityczna* and the Angelicum, take as their primary reference point John Paul II's 1999 *Letter to Artists*, I am going to take a somewhat different tack, addressing this year's theme of John Paul II and culture through the prism of John Paul's thinking on public life in the free and virtuous society of the twenty-first century. And I shall do so in part through a different textual reference point, the Polish pope's 1991 encyclical, *Centesimus Annus*.

In that epic encyclical, John Paul taught that the free and virtuous society of the post–Cold War future would have three interlocking components: a democratic polity, a free economy, and a vibrant public moral culture.

By democratic polity, John Paul meant a political community in which fundamental rights are constitutionally defined and legally protected; in which the legislative, executive, and judicial powers of government are distinct and mutually limiting rather than unitary and omnicompetent; in which those who govern do so according to the rule of law; and in which the natural and voluntary associations that make up civil society are, in their proper spheres of responsibility, protected in law from the encroachments of the state.

By free economy, the Pope meant a legally regulated, market-centered economic system, rather than a state-centered and state-dominated economy.

Yet it was the third sector of the free and virtuous society—the public moral culture—that John Paul believed to be the key to the proper functioning of the democratic polity and the free economy, and thus of the entire edifice of the free society. Political and economic freedom, he knew, let loose tremendous human energies. Disciplining and directing those energies so that they lead to genuine human flourishing and social solidarity is, he taught, the task of the public moral culture. Its health was thus crucial to the well-being of free politics and free economics. Absent a vibrant, truth-based public moral culture, rooted in a true understanding of the human person and human community, free politics and free economics could, and likely would, self-destruct.

The sad experience of the Weimar Republic, never far from John Paul II's imagination when it came to an analysis of twentieth-century politics, was a powerful example of this. Interwar Germany had a well-designed political system, of the sort noted above; yet despite German achievements in the hard sciences and technology, the Weimar years were also marked by a high culture of rather extraordinary decadence—think of the musical *Cabaret* (which actually toned things down considerably). Thus, when the pressures of historic resentments and the economic follies of the Treaty of Versailles combined with the world financial collapse of the Great Depression, the Weimar Republic lacked the solid moral-cultural foundation on which to resist the siren song of totalitarianism as the answer to the resulting political gridlock, lethal inflation, and social dissolution. Weimar democracy then voted into power the National Socialist or Nazi regime that immediately used the legal tools of the Weimar constitution to dismantle German democracy and install a dictatorship run by the *Führerprinzip*. The result was a second world cataclysm that Karol Wojtyła knew firsthand, through his experience of the Nazi occupation of Poland from September 1939 through the spring of 1945.

Put another way, John Paul II in *Centesimus Annus* taught that democracy and the market economy are not machines that can run by themselves, if only the mechanisms of politics and the economy are properly designed and built. Democracy and the free economy, he understood, are ongoing experiments, and their success can never be taken for granted. That success requires a critical mass of virtuous people so that the machinery of freedom works properly in the political and economic spheres. In the tripartite free society, it is the responsibility and task of the public moral culture to form that critical mass of citizens. And it is the Church's task to shape that culture formation according to the moral truths inscribed in us and in nature, forming virtuous citizens who live the cardinal virtues of prudence, justice, courage, and moderation in their personal and public lives.

John Paul II came to understand the priority of culture in human affairs from his philosophical work and his theological reflection on the Christian experience of the Church as itself a culture. I would like to suggest here that the Pope's thinking and teaching on culture and its power also reflected his Polish heritage and experience.

Poland-the-state disappeared from the map of Europe in 1795 at the time of the Third Polish Partition, when Russia, Austria, and Prussia completed the vivisection of an eight-hundred-year-old state, which had begun with the partition of 1772 and had continued in the partition of 1793. Yet Poland-the-nation survived. Indeed, Poland-the-nation survived with such vigor that the Polish nation could give birth to a new Polish state in the aftermath of World War I. Later, in the years following the partition of September 1939, when Nazi Germany and the Soviet Union "cancelled" Poland and the Polish state disappeared from the map of Europe from late 1939 until mid-1945, the Polish nation survived—and with sufficient strength that, after another four and a half decades of struggle, the Polish nation, in the Revolution of 1989, gave birth to a truly Polish state, which replaced the bogus Polish People's Republic created in 1945 by the tanks and bayonets of the Red Army. How did this happen?

It happened in 1918 because, after the final partition of 1795, the Polish nation survived through its language, its literature, and its Catholic faith, as the Church became a kind of safe-deposit box of Polish identity. In a word, Poland-the-nation survived because of the vitality of Polish *culture*. The same dynamic was at work during World War II, and during the forty-five years when Polish communists allied with the Soviet hegemon usurped the liberties of postwar Poland. It was authentic Polish culture—and particularly Polish Catholicism—that successfully resisted communism's attempt to create New Soviet Man in Poland by, among other things, rewriting Polish history and eradicating traditional Polish culture. (This resistance, it might be noted, led to one of the only jokes ever attributed to Stalin, who said that making Poland communist was like "fitting a saddle to a cow.")

Knowing all this and knowing from his Christian faith and his philosophical reflection that the power of the truth, courageously articulated, can be a liberating force in human affairs, John Paul II saw in that tenacious Polish culture the key to a future of authentic freedom for his people. And it was that tenacious culture to which John Paul appealed, and which he revitalized, during his epic first papal pilgrimage to his homeland, June 2–10, 1979—nine days, we can now see, on which the history of the twentieth century pivoted in a more humane direction.

What did John Paul II do during the Nine Days? He gave back to his people the truth about themselves as a nation formed by a distinctive culture—and did so without a single reference to either politics or economics. You are not, he said in many variations on one great theme, who *they* (the communist authorities) say you are. Let me remind you who you really are. Own that, and you will find tools of resistance that communist totalitarianism will not be able to match. It is true that you do not have power, as the world understands power in material terms. But you have a spiritual and cultural power that, unleashed, will eventually prove invincible.

Which is what happened over the next decade, as a revolution of conscience swept through east central Europe and made the nonviolent Revolution of 1989 possible. A revolution of the spirit brought down the empire that had monopolized material power since 1945. That was the gist of John Paul II's analysis of "The Year 1989" in chapter 3 of *Centesimus Annus*. And while some are still unwilling to recognize the power of a culturally based resistance informed by religious conviction to defeat a foe that held all the levers of worldly power, America's premier historian of the Cold War, John Lewis Gaddis of Yale University, got it exactly right when he wrote that the beginning of the end of European communism came on June 2, 1979, when John Paul II got off the plane at the Warsaw airport, kissed the ground of his homeland, and then called the Holy Spirit to once again renew the face of the earth—"of this land!"

The deficiencies of Weimar Germany's public moral culture were a major factor in the collapse of the free society in a Germany that became a totalitarian state. The power of Polish culture was a crucial factor in the auto-liberation of Poland in the Revolution of 1989. Culture—what a people believes, worships, and cherishes—is the driver of history over the long haul. Believing in false deities, worshipping that which is not worthy of worship, and cherishing that which is not truly noble leads to forms of cultural decadence that can promote neither human flourishing nor social solidarity. Culture is the driver of history over the long haul—and a culture that draws sustenance from authentic belief and worship will promote noble desires that can sustain the institutions of political and economic freedom or help restore them when they have been lost.

In the thinking of John Paul II, then, the question of culture and history cuts both ways: Cultural decadence leads to immiseration of various forms; cultural vitality rooted in the truth about the human person can lead to liberation. Which brings us to the question of what have been termed today's "culture wars."

The very term "culture wars" alarms some Catholics, who do not wish to be derided by the progressive public culture of the West as "culture warriors"—and who apply that epithet, "culture warrior," to those fellow Catholics who judge that something is seriously awry in the West today. "Culture warrior" has thus become a term of shunning, even disparagement, in certain Catholic circles. But this is not right. And if the mistake in not recognizing that there are indeed "culture wars" that must be fought—which means that there must be courageous "culture warriors" to fight—is repeated often enough, the Church will be weakened in its capacity to renovate Western culture so that it can sustain the free and virtuous society of the twenty-first century.

The term "culture war" was coined to describe what happened between 1871 and 1887, the years in which German Chancellor Otto von Bismarck tried by various strong-arm tactics, including the imprisonment of bishops, to bring the Catholic Church under the control of the newly established German Reich. The contemporary culture war is being fought across a much broader terrain. And it involves far more than the relationship of the Church to state power, although it also involves that.

The contemporary culture war, reduced to essentials, is a contest for the moral and cultural future of the West. It is a contest between those who believe, on the one hand, that there are truths built into us and into the world that we can know by reason and revelation—truths that illuminate the path to human flourishing and social solidarity—and those, on the other hand, who believe that there is no such thing as "human nature"; who believe that humanity is infinitely plastic and malleable, and that the only limits to that malleability are technological; and who, while tacitly accepting Kant's alleged destruction of classical metaphysics, reject Kant's dictum that "out of the crooked timber of humanity, no straight thing was ever made." For, they assert, human willfulness married to technological capacity can bring about a worldly utopia, if only those of a classical and biblical cast of mind, who insist that there are deep truths built into the world and into us that we ignore at our personal and civilizational peril, would get out of the way.

And if they—meaning us—will not get out of the way by our own volition, then we must be gotten out of the way. This is an important point to grasp. It is not understood by those Catholics who disparage and dismiss other Catholics as "culture warriors." In doing so, they deny the fundamental fact shaping the contemporary culture war in the West: *The culture war was declared on us*. We did not declare it. Those of a classical and biblical cast of mind—those who believe in "built-in" moral truths—were quite willing to debate and dialogue with those who denied the reality of those truths, and who declared, in a Nietzschean fashion, that human willfulness was the full meaning of human liberation and maturation. But the invitation to dialogue was rejected and the war was declared.

And it is folly to think that we can decline to fight it by retreating into the quasi-Benedictine enclaves of Mr. Rod Dreher's fertile imagination.[1] For progressive culture warriors are implicit, and in some respects explicit, totalitarians, who are determined to enforce their power everywhere.

When the Second Vatican Council met sixty years ago, it was literally unimaginable to many of the Council Fathers that, within two generations, abortion would be legally permitted throughout the Western world as a means of ex post facto (and quite literal) "birth control"—just as it was unimaginable that a *Washington Post* headline would deride as "forced-birth zealots" those who defend the right to life of the unborn and want to offer women in crisis something better than a technological "fix" to their "problem."[2] It was unimaginable that the Hippocratic Oath would be consigned to the ash heap of history as doctors, with cultural approbation and legal sanction, willingly participate in abortion and in the macabre practice euphemistically known as "physician-assisted suicide." The Council Fathers may have been concerned about family stability and rising divorce rates in the West; but they could not imagine a situation in which "marriage" would be redefined to include Adam and Steve as well as

Adam and Eve. And anyone who, in those days, suggested that "gender" was a "cultural construct," such that by technologically implemented acts of willfulness a man could declare himself a woman and be legally recognized as such, chromosomes notwithstanding, would have been thought bizarre, if not insane.

Yet that which was so recently unimaginable is now prominently on display.

The "trans" movement is perhaps the clearest indicator of the character of the contemporary culture war. There is no clinical evidence that the euphemistically described procedure known as "sex-reassignment surgery" produces positive mental health outcomes over time. None. On the contrary, there is abundant evidence that those who have "transitioned," even in less dramatic ways than by undergoing surgical "sex reassignment," are more prone to mental health disorders and suicide than others. Yet the legal capacity to "transition" oneself is now regarded in progressive circles as a basic human right. And this past November 20, the United States Department of State issued a statement on the Transgender Day of Remembrance that recommitted American diplomacy to "ensuring acceptance and support for transgender, non-binary, and gender non-conforming persons."[3]

The contemporary culture war is, in essence, a war over the meaning of the human person. And while the specific characteristics of today's battles may have been unimaginable sixty years ago, the fundamental character of the conflict was anticipated by one Council Father, Karol Wojtyła of Kraków, who, shortly after the Council, wrote about his current intellectual project in a letter to his friend, the French Jesuit Henri de Lubac:

> I devote my very rare free moments to a work that is close to my heart and devoted to the metaphysical sense and mystery of the PERSON. It seems to me that the debate today is being played out on that level. The evil of our times consists in the first place in a kind of degradation, indeed in a pulverization, of the fundamental uniqueness of each human person. This evil is even much more of the metaphysical order than of the moral order. To this disintegration planned at times by atheistic ideologies, we must oppose, rather than sterile polemics, a kind of "recapitulation" of the inviolable mystery of the person.[4]

How prescient was that? And while one "atheistic ideology" determined to remake the human condition may have been overcome by the Revolution of 1989, others have come to the fore. For we are living in a moment where it has become ever clearer that the most successful Marxist theoretician of the twentieth century was not Lenin or Trotsky; it was the Italian Marxist theoretician Antonio Gramsci, who argued that conquering the means of *cultural* production was the key to the ultramundane Marxist utopia of the future. And Gramsci has been vindicated, perhaps beyond even his imagining. For the contemporary culture war in the West is the result of the conquest of the means of cultural production—the universities; the worlds of art, music, and theater; various religious institutions; and the great foundations that support the means of cultural production—by a self-described "progressive" ideology. That ideology denies that there is anything properly describable as "human nature." It thinks of the human person as, essentially, a bundle of morally commensurable desires, the satisfaction of which is the meaning of "human rights." And it is determined to use the instruments of state power—and, here in Europe, transnational power—to impose that ultramundane ideology on all of society.

Aldous Huxley, while strikingly insightful about future scientific developments, was not a very distinguished novelist; George Orwell was the more gifted writer of dystopian fiction. Be that as it may, if you marry the stunted and manufactured humanity described in Huxley's *Brave New World* with the totalitarian brutality on display in Orwell's *1984*, you get something alarmingly similar to what those who declared the culture war imagine the desirable human future to be: a future that is unashamedly secular and hedonistic. And that must be fought.

How is the Church to address this civilizational crisis, this culture war, in light of the thought and teaching of Pope Saint John Paul II? And with what instruments should dynamically orthodox Catholicism engage the war that has been declared on the biblical and Christian concept of the human person?

It will be helpful in considering those questions to understand what *New York Times* columnist Ross Douthat and Cambridge historian Richard Rex both have proposed: that we are living through the third great crisis of the Catholic Church in the two millennia of Christian history.

The first such crisis was the Arian crisis of the fourth century. As Professor Rex wrote in 2018 in a review of Douthat's book *To Change the Church: Pope Francis and the Future of Catholicism*, the Arian crisis "gripped the Church from the Council of Nicaea to the Council of Chalcedon and beyond. This was an agonized and church-rending argument over the question, 'What is God'? The second crisis was that of the Reformation ... [which] was an agonized and church-rending argument over the question, 'What is the Church'? Our crisis, at least as great as those, is all about a question that once would have been expressed as 'What is man'? The fact that this wording is now itself seen as problematic is a symptom of the very condition it seeks to diagnose. What is it, in other words, to be human?"[5]

In the October 2023 issue of *First Things*, Professor Rex sharpened this analysis further, and in these terms:

> Christianity itself is beset by the third existential crisis in its history, a contemporary crisis over the nature of humanity itself, a crisis manifest on the same global scale as the Church herself. More than ever, the question for our times is "What is man"? For Christians, it's a crisis over the concept of creation, over Genesis itself. Is man created in God's image? Or are we our own creators? The hypersubjectivism of postmodern culture makes each man or woman, in principle, the unmoved mover of his or her own existence. "You can be anything you want" is the mantra pushed endlessly by the panoply of consumer capitalism, which preaches the gospel of, in Brad Gregory's lapidary phrase, "the goods life." And the goods life finds theoretical expression in the identity politics peddled by academic postmodernism, which fancies itself critical of consumer capitalism but is perhaps better understood as consumer capitalism's established church. How readily, after all, global corporations have imbibed woke values. The ethics of "autonomy" is pretty much the spiritual equivalent of the supermarket. The reification and idolization of identity are a perfect fit for the theory and practice of marketing in the goods life: It's all about self-image.[6]

In a recent speech accepting the Herzl Prize of the Tikvah Fund, the great bioethicist Leon Kass took this a step farther and dug deeper when he described the civilizational crisis and culture war in which we find ourselves as a war against idolatry. He spoke of the special obligations of Jews, but his call to resistance against the culture warriors who seek to "cancel" the biblical concept of the human person speaks to Christians as well as those John Paul II described as our Jewish "elder brothers":

> We are summoned to bear witness against idolatry—that universal temptation to fill the God-shaped hole in the heart with things that can never satisfy and that always lead astray. Long ago, idolatry was once the worship of the sun, the moon, and the earth—and the golden calf.... In modern times, it has come in the diabolical form of ideology: national socialism, communism, Maoism, and radical Islam, deadly false gods to which millions of innocent lives have been sacrificed.... Idolatry also includes worship of the market, of art and culture, and of human choice and human fiat as the sole source of value. Against all these false gods, the Jewish people bear witness to presence of a higher power and source of goodness.[7]

As must Catholics, who acknowledge in the Roman Canon "Abraham, our father in faith."

The contemporary culture war inevitably involves the Catholic Church, for if the Church is faithful to its Lord, it will defend and promote the truth about the spiritual and moral dignity of those the Lord died and rose to save. And the Church must fight this culture war as a culture-reforming counterculture, with the distinctive weapons of evangelical clarity and pastoral charity. Thinking about this is enriched by an encounter with the patristics scholar Robert Louis Wilken, who grew up in Missouri Synod Lutheranism and entered into full communion with the Catholic Church in 1994. In the April 2004 issue of *First Things*, he penned a masterful essay, "The Church as Culture," which included an assertion that is of great importance to our topic, and fully aligned with the thought of John Paul II on culture and history: "The Church is a culture in its own right. Christ does not simply infiltrate a culture; Christ creates culture by forming another city, another sovereignty."

The divisions in Catholicism over the Catholic relation to the contemporary culture war, evident at last month's Synod and in the discussions preceding it, can be understood through the prism of Wilken's insight. There are Catholics who understand that the Church is a culture with a unique foundation in Christ, and who live that understanding. Then there are those who, while formally professing the Creed, do not quite grasp the full import of the fact that the Church is a unique, Christocentric culture, charged with converting to Christ the cultures in which it finds itself, from classical Greco-Roman to postmodern Western.

This division often expresses itself in the so-called hot-button issues:

- Does the Church, as a unique, Christocentric culture, have (and live) an understanding of marriage as the stable, fruitful, lifelong union of a man and a woman?
- Does the culture that is the Church teach a way of expressing human love in intimate relationships that are formed and bounded by both divine revelation and the deep truths inscribed in human nature?
- Should the culture that is the Church, in its interaction with society, give priority to the task of promoting a socially embedded and legally recognized reverence for the sanctity of human life at every stage of life and in every condition?
- Does the culture that is the Church believe itself capable of ennobling all human cultures, because the culture that is the Church is an expression of the Christ who is the unique and universal savior of humanity? And if so, does the Church act on that conviction in its evangelization and the ordering of its own life?

The last of these questions came into sharp focus when Archbishop Mark Coleridge of Brisbane, who served as president of the Australian bishops' conference from 2018 until 2022, proposed in a pre-Synod interview that indigenous (aboriginal) Australian men should be exempt from the Latin-Rite Catholic practice of ordaining only celibates to the priesthood, stating that there is "no way you're going to recruit a celibate clergy in those cultures."[8]

Really?

Are some cultures impervious to Christ's call to live celibacy for the sake of the Kingdom? Are some cultures impenetrable to the Gospel? One can imagine such claims being made in the past about any number of "indigenous" peoples: peoples of different races and ethnicities, people with different histories. But at the risk of stepping into the minefields of wokery, does not the assertion that indigenous

Australians are incapable of living celibacy verge on racism? Or to get down to the theological bottom line, isn't the claim that people in certain cultures cannot hear, much less accept, the more challenging demands of the Gospel perilously close on blasphemy? Is the power of the Holy Spirit so circumscribed?

Similar questions arise from the assertions of the LGBTQ+ insurgency within the Church that certain people are "made" a certain way and thus can only love a certain way. This would seem to contradict one of the basic Christian truths that form the Church as a unique culture: the truth that, as we all "fall short of the glory of God" (Rom 3:23), we are all "justified" (3:24)—that is, made whole—by the grace of God poured out through Christ crucified. Which is to say that, whatever our desires and whatever our confusions, everyone is called to an ongoing, deepening conversion, sanctification, and, ultimately, glorification *that is available to all*: if we allow ourselves to be welcomed by Christ on *his* terms, not our own.

The culture that is the Church has converted and transformed cultures that may originally have seemed impervious to the Gospel for two millennia. The Church of the twenty-first century must reckon with that truth, or it will end up tacitly denying the Lord, who said, "I, when I am lifted up from the earth, will draw all men to myself" (Jn 12:32). Not some. All.

The threats to civilization today—the threats to the human future today—seem almost innumerable. If there is a common thread running through them, it is their denial of the inalienable dignity and infinite value of every human life from conception until natural death. That is what the "culture of death," identified as such by John Paul II in the 1995 encyclical *Evangelium Vitae*,[9] denies about the unborn, the vulnerable elderly, and the severely disabled. That is what Hamas and its imbecile supporters in elite Western universities deny about Jews. That is what Vladimir Putin denies about Ukrainians. That is what Xi Jinping denies by persecuting Christians and committing genocide against Uyghurs. The list goes on and on.

In the face of these assaults on the *humanum* and the vast suffering they cause, the Church-as-culture has no option but to be a counterculture: to be a culture-reforming counterculture that offers humanity a nobler view of itself through the Gospel, in the acceptance of which (as we are taught in *Gaudium et Spes*, no. 22) we learn the truth about ourselves as well as the truth about God.

That means being culture warriors who wield the sword of the Spirit and call all to conversion in Christ—not only, and perhaps not primarily, by argument, but by displaying a nobler, more humane way of life. Failure to engage the contemporary culture war is not just imprudent or cowardly. It is a dereliction of duty. For only by returning to the truths disclosed by both reason and revelation can we avoid self-destruction and survive, even flourish, as a civilization. That rescue mission is one the Church has undertaken in the past; that is what the Church must do today and in the future.

In that very Catholic sense, "culture warrior" is a title to be welcomed, indeed embraced. And we find the ideal of the Catholic culture warrior in the apostle of culture, Pope Saint John Paul II.

Men of Genius

JOHN PAUL II, DOCTOR OF THE CHURCH?

Academy of Music, Kraków, Poland, November 6, 2013

Over almost two millennia of Christian history, thirty-five men and women have been honored with the title *Doctor Ecclesiae*, "Doctor of the Church." This singular honor typically comes centuries after the honoree's death.

The four great Latin Doctors, recognized as such in 1298, were Saint Ambrose (+397), Saint Jerome (+420), Saint Augustine (+430), and Saint Gregory the Great (+604), while the four great Eastern Doctors, designated as such by Pope St. Pius V in 1568, were Saint Athanasius (+373), Saint Basil the Great (+379), Saint Gregory Nazianzen (+389), and Saint John Chrysostom (+407). Saint Thomas Aquinas and Saint Bonaventure, who both died in 1274, were recognized as Doctors in 1568 and 1588, respectively. Pope St. Leo the Great waited almost thirteen hundred years to be declared *Doctor Ecclesiae*. And Saint Cyril of Jerusalem's designation as a Doctor came two years short of a millennium and a half after his death. The Church, it seems, has been very careful in measuring, over time, the enduring contribution of great men and women to the Church's self-understanding and teaching.

Still, it may not be too early to suggest the possibility that the Church will one day recognize the enduring value of John Paul II's magisterium with the title *Doctor Ecclesiae*, such that the Polish pontiff will be known as Pope Saint John Paul II, Doctor of the Church. Were that to happen, that recognition would likely involve five aspects of John Paul II's accomplishment.

1. **The magisterium of John Paul II provided authoritative keys to the proper interpretation of the Second Vatican Council.** The Second Vatican Council did not provide authoritative keys to its interpretation, as the previous twenty ecumenical councils had done by defining dogma, condemning heresies (and heretics), legislating canons

for the Church's legal system, writing creeds, and/or commissioning catechisms. Vatican II produced sixteen documents of varying magisterial weight. But the Council did not provide the authoritative keys that would allow the Church to receive and appropriate that body of teaching as a coherent whole.

The magisterium of John Paul II provided those authoritative keys, through the Pope's apostolic constitutions, encyclicals, post-synodal apostolic exhortations, and apostolic letters, as well as through the Latin and Oriental codes of canon law, and the *Catechism of the Catholic Church*. That authoritative interpretation was also advanced by the 1985 Extraordinary Assembly of the Synod of Bishops, which John Paul II summoned to assess the reception of the Council, twenty years after its completion, and which suggested the idea of the Church as a *communio* (communion) of disciples in mission as the thread which could bind the various "pieces" of Vatican II into a single, unified, and beautiful Catholic tapestry.

This process of providing an authoritative interpretation of the "Council without keys" put a period (or at least a semicolon) on a period of confusion in the history of the Church, while concurrently setting in place a grand strategy for the Church of the third millennium, of which more will be said below.

2. **The magisterium of John Paul II addressed the critical problem of presenting the full symphony of Catholic truth in categories that could be grasped by the modern mind.** At the time of John Paul II's election in 1978, Catholic theology, and especially Catholic moral theology, was in crisis. The neo-scholastic consensus that had long shaped Catholic intellectual life had shattered, and it seemed that both Catholic doctrine and Catholic moral teaching were condemned to suffer from that incoherence that was a prominent characteristic of late modern and postmodern Western thought. By skillfully deploying modern philosophical and theological tools on a firm foundation of classic Aristotelian-Thomistic convictions about the human capacity to grasp the truth of things, John Paul II's magisterium provided a model for Catholic theology that practiced the ecumenism of time (i.e., preserving the wisdom of the tradition) while demonstrating that the ancient truths of the tradition could be understood and proclaimed in categories familiar to post-Enlightenment minds.

This accomplishment was embodied in the 1993 encyclical, *Veritatis Splendor* (The Splendor of Truth). There, a phenomenological analysis of the moral life and a thoroughly contemporary approach to pastoral ministry surround a classic Aristotelian-Thomistic analysis of some urgent questions in late twentieth-century moral theology (e.g., the possibility of exceptionless moral norms), all in the service of exploring a contemporary recovery of the virtue ethics of Aristotle and Saint Thomas.

3. John Paul II's philosophical acumen and his broad pastoral experience gave him keen insight into the rise, in the late twentieth century, of a new Gnosticism that treated everything in the human condition as plastic, malleable, and subject to change by human willfulness. Such a Gnosticism, John Paul understood, was the most culturally, socially, and personally destructive expression of the central crisis of late modernity that he had identified in his submission to the Ante-Preparatory Commission of the Second Vatican Council: the crisis of Western humanism.

John Paul's Theology of the Body, which he laid out in an epic series of general audience addresses between 1979 and 1984, and other aspects of his Christian anthropology, including his writings on the meaning of suffering and his "papal feminism," may well come to be regarded as an especially effective Catholic response to what Cardinal Karol Wojtyła described, in a 1969 letter to French theologian Henri de Lubac, S.J., as the principal "evil of our times ... a kind of degradation, indeed ... a pulverization, of the fundamental uniqueness of each human person."[1]

4. John Paul II's social doctrine deepened and extended the primary themes of Catholic social teaching as they had been identified by Popes Leo XIII and Pius XI. And in the course of that development, John Paul cemented a fourth basic principle, the principle of solidarity, into the foundations of the social doctrine, in addition to Leo's principles of personalism and the common good (set out in the 1891 encyclical *Rerum Novarum*) and Pius' principle of subsidiarity (identified in the 1931 encyclical, *Quadragessimo Anno*).

In the 1991 encyclical *Centesimus Annus*, John Paul offered the post–Cold War world a compelling vision of the tripartite free and virtuous society, in which a democratic political community, a free economy, and a vibrant public moral culture work together in such a way that human freedom is tethered to moral truth and ordered to goodness and human flourishing. This was not only a significant contribution to late twentieth-century democratic theory; it was also a challenge to the regnant materialism and functionalism of both political and economic thinking in the West. By insisting that it took a certain kind of people, possessed of certain virtue, to make the free institutions of democracy and the market work properly, John Paul II recovered public moral culture as a crucial factor in the structure of freedom lived nobly. Democracy and the market, he taught, were not machines that can run by themselves. The machinery of freedom must be tended by virtuous citizens, entrepreneurs, and consumers, if the machinery is to function properly and avoid breakdown.

This was a bold recovery of lost aspects of classic western political thought, an important proposal for the future—and an analysis thoroughly vindicated by events in the last decade of the twentieth century and the first decades of the twenty-first.

5. **In calling the Church to celebrate the Great Jubilee of 2000, John Paul II reminded both the Church and the world that the Christian proposal is not a myth, but a set of truth claims rooted in history, in time and space.** In concluding the Great Jubilee with the apostolic letter *Novo Millennio Ineunte* (Entering the New Millennium), John Paul II issued a bold call to the entire Church to "put out into the deep" (Lk 5:4)[2] of the New Evangelization in a postmodern world increasingly skeptical of the truth of anything.

Thus, John Paul II led the Church into a new moment of its history, the era of Evangelical Catholicism: As the early Church was succeeded by the Church of the Fathers, and the patristic Church was succeeded by medieval Christendom, which in turn was succeeded by Counter-Reformation Catholicism, so the latter is now being succeeded by Evangelical Catholicism. It is the same Church because that Church confesses the same Lord, professes the same faith, and offers the same baptism; but the mode of being Catholic, and certain institutional forms in the Church, change over time to meet the demands of the Great Commission (Mt 28:19). And it was the genius of John Paul II to give structure and content to the insight of John XXIII in summoning the Second Vatican Council—that is, to call the Church into the experience of a "New Pentecost," that would in turn propel the Church into the era of the

New Evangelization. Thus if the Church should declare Pope Saint John Paul II a *Doctor Ecclesiae*, at some moment in the future that we cannot know now, it will be because these, and perhaps other, facets of John Paul's magisterium have been judged to be enduring contributions to the entire Catholic Church's self-understanding, witness, and teaching.

BENEDICT XVI
Voice in the Secular Wilderness

London, England, September 2010

On May 13, 2004, a septuagenarian German intellectual gave a lecture in the Capitol Room of the Italian Senate. Ironies—or at least paradoxes—abounded.

The lecturer was a Catholic priest and bishop; the modern Italian state was born in a decades-long spasm of anti-clericalism. The lecturer, Cardinal Joseph Ratzinger, was known throughout the world as the living embodiment of Catholic orthodoxy; the man who had invited him to speak, Senate president Marcello Pera, was a nonbeliever and a philosopher of science in the school of Karl Popper. Cardinal Ratzinger chose as his topic "The Spiritual Roots of Europe: Yesterday, Today, and Tomorrow"; as he spoke, Europe was nearing the end of a fierce, year-long debate over whether biblical religion had had anything to do with what was noble in Europe's past, or whether biblical religion might have something important to say about Europe's present or future.

As Joseph Ratzinger, the man who became Pope Benedict XVI, comes to Great Britain on a state visit that will include the beatification of John Henry Newman, his lecture in the Italian Senate some six years ago is well worth revisiting—not least as a reminder that seemingly endless stories of clerical sexual abuse and the mismanagement of these sins and crimes by Catholic bishops are not the only story to be told about the Catholic Church at the end of the first decade of the twenty-first century. Important as the airing of the abuse story has been in compelling the Church to address grave problems that had long been buried beneath the carapace of a self-protective clerical culture, the press' obsession with clerical sexual malfeasance has also been a distraction—doubtless welcome in some quarters—from grappling with important arguments the present pope and his predecessor have made about the ideas shaping democratic societies today: arguments that invite serious men and women to think seriously about the democratic future. And if the sanguinary twentieth century ought to have taught the West anything, it was the truth of Keynes' famous observation that "ideas ... both when they are right and when they are wrong, are more powerful than is commonly understood. Indeed, the world is ruled by little else."[1]

The man who comes to Britain as the 264th successor of Saint Peter is many things, and Britons who rely on media imagery to form their impressions of public personalities will find some of those things surprising. Those who expect to meet "God's Rottweiler" (as his theological enemies caricatured Joseph Ratzinger decades ago) will find instead a shy, soft-spoken man of exquisite manners. Those determined to portray Pope Benedict as the central figure in a global criminal conspiracy of child rapers and their abettors will, it may be hoped, discover the man who did more than anyone else in the Roman Curia to compel the Church to face what he once called the "filth" marring the priesthood. Those looking for a hidebound clerical enforcer will meet instead a man of deep faith, a gentle pastor who has met with, wept with, and apologized to the abused victims of his brother priests and brother bishops.

Joseph Ratzinger is also a man of ideas: a world-class European intellectual with an intriguing analysis of contemporary's Europe's present circumstances and bold proposals to make about Europe's future. During the Pope's visit to Britain, those who ignore those proposals because of their fixation on scandal are depriving themselves of an opportunity to think seriously about the moral and cultural condition of the West—and indulging that intellectual anorexia at a moment when the West's future seems anything but secure demographically, economically, fiscally, strategically, or morally.

Like other notable German intellectuals of his generation (Ratzinger was born in 1927 and was reluctantly conscripted into the Wehrmacht during World War II), Benedict XVI's thinking about the West and democracy unfolds under the long shadow of the Weimar Republic: a meticulously constructed democratic edifice that rested on insecure moral and cultural foundations. The architects of Weimar, including the great social scientist Max Weber, imagined that they were building a rational structure of governance; Weimar's political institutions and their relationship to one another would be the products of reason, not tradition—and certainly not revelation. Yet as Joseph Ratzinger put it to the Italian Senate in 2004, "reason is inherently fragile," and political systems that imagine themselves to have solved the problem of democratic legitimacy by relying on reason alone "become easy targets for dictatorships."[2] That, in his view, is what happened in the Germany of his youth: "The collapse of Prussian State Christianity" in the aftermath of World War I "left a vacuum" that Weber and his fellow architects of Weimar imagined could be filled by rationality, but which in fact "would later provide fertile soil for a dictatorship."

After that dictatorship was defeated at an immense cost in human suffering (and with half of Europe consigned to the suzerainty of another dictatorship), efforts were made to reconstruct Europe on the basis of what the founding fathers of today's European Union—Robert Schumann, Alcide de Gasperi, Konrad Adenauer—believed to be a moral consensus derived from biblical religion. Their efforts, Ratzinger readily acknowledges, produced three generations of a Europe at peace and enjoying unprecedented prosperity. Yet, as he told the Italian Senate, the new Europe still suffers from an idea deficit, the implications of which were becoming ever more troubling as the twentieth century gave way to the twenty-first. For, as he put it in 2004, "the complex problems left behind by Marxism continue to exist today. The loss of man's primordial certainties about God, about himself, and about the universe—the loss of an awareness of intangible moral values—is still our problem ... and it can lead to the self-destruction of European consciousness."

The key to grasping Ratzinger's analysis is to see that he thinks of Europe's contemporary crisis of cultural morale as a matter of *self*-destruction. Or, as he put it in an earlier version of his address to the Italian Senate, it is impossible not to "notice a self-hatred in the Western world that is strange and can even be considered pathological." For as "the West is making a praiseworthy attempt to be completely open to foreign values ... it no longer loves itself; [indeed], it sees in its own history only what is blameworthy and destructive [and] is no longer capable of perceiving what is great and pure."

This, it seems to Benedict XVI, is little short of suicidal: for "in order to survive, Europe needs a new—and certainly a critical and humble—acceptance of itself—that is, if it *wants* to survive." But that will-to-survive (which is not for Ratzinger a will-to-dominate, but a commitment to share with others the truths the West has discovered about the dignity of the human person), will not attain critical mass in contemporary Europe for so long as Europe is "on a collision course with its own history."

And that, in turn, is why Ratzinger constantly asks the contemporary West to reconsider its hypersecularist reading of the past, in which black legends of Christian perversity dominate the historical landscape, and the dignity of man is only asserted with effective cultural and political force in the Enlightenment.

Thus, in his lecture to the Italian Senate, Ratzinger, echoing the opening sequence in Kenneth Clarke's series, *Civilization*, reminded his audience that Christian monasticism saved European culture when it was in grave danger of losing hold of its classical and biblical heritage. In remote places like Iona and Lindisfarne, the monks of Saint Benedict, he recalled, were the agents of a rebirth of culture, and did so precisely as "a force prior to and superior to political authority" (which, in the so-called Dark Ages, had largely disappeared from the scene). Moreover, Ratzinger proposed, it was Christianity itself that initially proposed and defended that "separation" of religious and political authority (or, in the vulgate, the "separation of Church and state") so prized by modern secularists: in the first instance, when the late fifth-century pope Gelasius I drew a crisp distinction between priestly and political authority; later, in the eleventh century, when Pope Gregory VII defended the liberty of the Church against the Holy Roman Emperor Henry IV's attempts to turn the Church into a department of the state by controlling the appointment of bishops. Absent Gelasius I and Gregory VII, Ratzinger suggested, the rich social pluralism of European life in the first centuries of the second millennium would have been much less likely to develop—and, to bring the point home in terms of Britain, there would have been no Magna Carta and all that flowed from there. It was the *Church*, in other words, that made the first arguments for the "separation of Church and state," not the *philosophes* of the continental Enlightenment.

Which, as Ratzinger surveys contemporary European high culture, brings us to yet another irony: the inability of the rationalism proclaimed by the Enlightenment to sustain Europe's confidence in reason. As the late John Paul II saw it, and as Benedict XVI sees it, "Europe" is a civilizational enterprise and not simply a zone of mutual economic advantage. That civilizational project rests on three legs, which might be labeled "Jerusalem," "Athens," and "Rome": biblical religion, which taught Europe that the human person, the child of a benevolent Creator, is endowed with inalienable dignity and value; Greek rationality, which taught Europe that there are truths embedded in the world and in us, truths we can grasp by reason; and Roman jurisprudence, which taught Europe that the rule of law is superior to the rule of brute force. If Jerusalem goes—as it has in much of post-Enlightenment European high culture—Athens gets wobbly: as is plain in the sandbox of postmodernism, where there may be your truth and my truth, but nothing properly describable as *the* truth. And if both Jerusalem and Athens go, then Rome—the rule of law—is in grave trouble, as is plain when coercive state power is used throughout Europe and within European states to enforce regimes of moral relativism and to punish the politically incorrect.

The collapse of faith in reason, the embrace of crank theories of racial superiority, and the emotive power of atavistic nationalism brought down the Weimar Republic and led to the brutal dictatorship of German National Socialism. The collapse of faith in reason today—the insouciance about truth displayed in postmodernism—will also have its consequences, in Ratzinger's view. Some are already evident, as in the soul-withering nihilism that is one cultural root of Europe's demographic suicide. Others lurk menacingly on the near-term political horizon, in the threat of what Ratzinger famously called, the day before his election as pope, the prospect of a "dictatorship of relativism." For, as he put it to Italy's senators, "In recent years I find myself noting how the more relativism becomes the generally accepted way of thinking, the more it tends toward intolerance, thereby becoming a new dogmatism." Thus relativism becomes a "kind of new 'denomination'" that seeks to "subordinate" every other form of conviction "to the super-dogma of relativism."

These are not, to be sure, popular claims to make, on either side of the English Channel (or either side of the Atlantic, for that matter). But that they are claims deserving close attention and not clownish dismissal (*pace* the New Atheists), only the truly rigid dogmatists of the secularist superdenomination will deny.

Those who wish to explore how Pope Benedict's analysis of the current civilizational crisis of the West is engaged by a serious mind can do so by reading the lectures given by Ratzinger and the German philosopher Jürgen Habermas at a joint appearance in Munich three months before Ratzinger's address to the Italian Senate.[3] Many expected an intellectual donnybrook at the Catholic Academy of Bavaria on January 19, 2004: in one corner, the preeminent European secularist philosopher of "democratically enlightened common sense," himself deeply influenced by the neo-Marxism of the Frankfurt School; in the other, the Prefect of the Vatican's Congregation for the Doctrine of the Faith, inevitably described by most reporters as "the successor to the Inquisition." The question Habermas and Ratzinger were to examine was also contentious, especially in the context of a Europe then furiously debating whether Christianity ought to be mentioned when the draft European constitutional treaty described the sources of twenty-first-century Europe's commitments to civility, tolerance, human rights, democracy, and the rule of law. The issue put to Habermas and Ratzinger in the language of political theory—the question of the "pre-political moral foundations of a free state"—was in fact the very same question being argued passionately throughout Europe: Do twenty-first-century democracies, in which political and spiritual authority is separate and the public sphere is "secular," depend for their legitimacy on moral presuppositions the secular state itself can't provide or guarantee?

Habermas, who had previously coauthored an op-ed article with the French postmodernist Jacques Derrida, arguing that the new Europe must be "neutral between worldviews," was expected by many to uphold the standard of the European naked public square: a public space constitutionally shorn, not only of religious conviction, but of religious informed moral argument.[4] Ratzinger, the guardian of Catholic orthodoxy, would, it was assumed, denounce the false claims of secularism and warn sternly that an apostate Europe would be an offense against God and man. Both men gravely disappointed the conventional expectations.

For his part, Habermas lamented "the transformation of the citizens of prosperous and peaceful liberal societies into isolated monads acting on the basis of their own self-interest, persons who use their subjective rights only as weapons against each other." He also expressed concern over what he termed (in language demonstrating that German philosophers continue to speak a *gespracht* uniquely their own) "the ethical abstinence of post-metaphysical thinking, to which every universally obligatory concept of a good and exemplary life is foreign." The European future he imagined was one in which "secularized citizens" do not, "in their role as citizens of the state," deny "in principle that religious images of the world have the potential to express truth"—including the truths about the human person that are the moral-cultural foundations of democratic self-governance. Religious fellowships, Habermas conceded, had "preserved intact something which has elsewhere been lost." Might that "something" be the will to live in solidarity with others, coupled with the capacity to give a reasoned account of one's democratic commitments?

For his part, Joseph Ratzinger acknowledged "pathologies in religion that are extremely dangerous and that make it necessary to see the divine light of reason as a 'controlling organ'" in public life. As the first millennium Fathers of the Church had taught, "religion must continually allow itself to be purified and structured by reason." At the same time, there were "pathologies of reason" that had led to a loss of faith in reason. Thus, the prime cultural imperative of the moment was to recognize the "necessary relatedness between reason and faith and between reason and religion, which are called to purify and help one another," and which must "acknowledge this mutual need."

In brief, the Munich debate between Jürgen Habermas and Joseph Ratzinger was a serious exploration of the cracks in the foundations of the Western democratic project, conducted by two men determined to avoid what Edward Skidelsky once labeled the "Punch and Judy Show" character of so many debates between "science and religion." It seems that Richard Dawkins was not paying much attention to what transpired in Munich in January 2004. But perhaps others, less dogmatic in their antidogmatism, will pay attention when Pope Benedict XVI explores some of these same themes in his Westminster Hall address.

His 2004 debate with Habermas and lecture to the Italian Senate three months later give us, in capsule form, Ratzinger's analysis of Europe's cultural condition today. But what role does he envision for the Catholic Church in helping repair the damage that nihilism, skepticism, and relativism have done to what he called, in the Italian Senate, "that which holds the world together"?

Pope Benedict has sometimes been accused of being a nostalgic for the intact (Catholic) culture of his Bavarian youth, which was first destroyed by the Third Reich and then supplanted by a new Germany that eventually turned its back on both its Catholic and Lutheran roots. There is something to this, but Ratzinger is far too intelligent a man and far too sophisticated an analyst of the tides of history to imagine that any kind of rollback to a premodern (or pre-postmodern) past is possible. Rather, his first obligation, as he understands it, is to make Europe look closely at itself, in the unsparing but nonscolding way he did in the Italian Senate in early 2004:

> At the hour of its greatest success, Europe seems hollow, as if it were internally paralyzed by a failure of its circulatory system that is endangering its life, subjecting it to transplants that erase its identity. At the same time as its sustaining spiritual forces have collapsed, a growing decline in its ethnicity is also taking place.
>
> Europe is infected by a strange lack of desire for the future. Children, our future, are perceived as a threat to the present, as if they were taking something away from our lives. Children are seen as a liability rather than as a source of hope. There is a clear comparison between today's situation and the decline of the Roman Empire. In its final days, Rome still functioned as a great historical framework, but in practice it was already subsisting on models that were destined to fail. Its vital energy had been depleted.

Having held the mirror of reality up to faces that may have been reluctant to gaze into it, for fear of what they could find there, the man who became Benedict XVI then urged his audience of Italian political leaders to reject Spenglerian gloom and to refuse to concede that the West was "rushing heedlessly toward its demise." Rather, he proposed that men and women of conscience adopt a vision of possibility drawn from Arnold Toynbee, in which "the energy of creative minorities and exceptional individuals" can lead to a revitalization of culture that will allow "the inner identity of Europe to survive throughout its metamorphoses in history."

The Catholic Church, Benedict XVI believes, can be one of those "creative minorities" in twenty-first-century Europe, and indeed throughout the West. To be that, the Church must regain a clear sense of its own identity, primarily through a resacralization of its worship; it must recover a firm grasp on the truths it proposes, putting behind it the "liberalism" in religion that John Henry Newman deplored; it must raise up a generation of bishops and priests who are persuasive evangelists and witnesses, according to the model established by John Paul II; and it must demonstrate, not so much by argument as by sanctity and beauty, that it offers the men and women of today a path on which they can encounter "that which holds the world together."

And to do all of *that*, the Catholic Church must purge itself of its corruptions, a point on which Pope Benedict has been insistent for years, most recently in regard to the appalling defaults of Irish Catholicism. This will take some time, given the density of clerical culture and the fact that popes are not, *pace* media distortions, absolute monarchs who can effect massive institutional change at the flick of a finger; it will probably take more time than Anglophone cultures will like, given the still-languid, Italianate ways of the Vatican. No one should doubt, however, that Benedict XVI understands that, for the Church to become the "creative minority" of his imagination, it must be a credible minority that lives the truths it proclaims and deals decisively with those in its midst who betray the trust given them.

Benedict's vision of the Church in Europe's future has nothing to do with the rebuilding of a mythical *ancien régime*. He has shown himself sympathetic to the desire of some Catholics to worship according to the old ways, but he has no truck with the restorationist political fantasies that are at the root of the Lefebvrist movement. As he sees the Catholic future in Britain and elsewhere, the public task of the Church is to form alliances with those who understand that the democratic project requires a far more secure moral-cultural foundation than that offered by pragmatism or utilitarianism. And in the Pope's mind, those alliances ought to be built in a genuinely intercultural and pluralistic way, formed around the truths we can know to be true as a result of putting various religious and philosophical traditions into vigorous conversation.

That is the proposal of the man who will celebrate the beatification of John Henry Newman and challenge Britons to lift themselves out of the slough of secularist despond. If that proposal gets drowned out by a cacophony of media scandal-mongering (itself amplified by the usual Vatican communications incompetencies), and by the antics of the New Atheists (to which British and American editors seem curiously addicted), Joseph Ratzinger, Pope Benedict XVI, will not be the loser.

A word about the origin of this text is in order.

In mid-2010, planning for Pope Benedict XVI's pastoral visit to Great Britain that fall was in a shambles, to the point where the Catholic bishops of Britain asked the British government to take control of the situation. The government agreed and appointed the Catholic parliamentarian Chris Patten (Lord Patten of Barnes), former governor of Hong Kong and the chancellor of Oxford University, to bring order to the chaos. Part of that chaos involved the inability of the British hierarchy to respond effectively to the calumnies of Benedict XVI that were being regularly circulated in both the quality and tabloid press in the U.K., and that were as much a threat to the papal visit's success as the bishops' ineptitude in managing things. Daniel Johnson, editor of the monthly *Standpoint*, urged me to write a piece correcting the caricatures of the Pope, which could then be circulated widely in Whitehall and the media by Patten and the governmental event planners. This essay was my response to that request. And while it was not, strictly speaking, a lecture to an academic audience, it was certainly aimed in part at correcting the misapprehensions (and worse) of certain British intellectuals.

CARDINAL JEAN-MARIE LUSTIGER AND THE FUTURE OF THE WEST

Retrieving the Truths within Christian Ideas Gone Mad

Collèges des Bernardins, Paris, France, February 11, 2010

In June 2003, Pope John Paul II published the post-synodal apostolic exhortation *Ecclesia in Europa*, his last notable contribution to the Catholic Church's reflection on the culture of political modernity. Twelve years had passed since the pathbreaking encyclical *Centesimus Annus*, which had imaginatively and boldly inserted the universal Church into the debate over the shape of the post–Cold War world by insisting that both democratic political communities and free economies required a vibrant public moral culture, formed by the truths about man and society that can be known by reason, if democracy and the market were to result in genuine human flourishing and social solidarity. Viewed as an update of *Centesimus Annus*, *Ecclesia in Europa* can be read as a papal report card on how well, or how poorly, a newly united Europe was living its first period of uncontested peace and freedom since 1914.

The report card gave Europe mixed grades.

Amidst understandable satisfaction that freedom had triumphed over tyranny and that the artificial division of postwar Europe had ended, John Paul nonetheless was deeply concerned that the new Europe was suffering from spiritual malaise—from an "existential fragmentation"[1] that was evident in "grave uncertainties at the levels of culture, anthropology, ethics, and spirituality."[2] At what ought to have been a time of cultural renewal, Europeans seemed dubious about the worth of their civilizational accomplishment, guilt-ridden about the past, and confused about the relationship of the true, the good, and the beautiful to twenty-first-century life. Those characteristics of the European cast of mind displayed themselves in numerous ways, but the most striking was Europe's failure to create the future in the most elemental sense, by creating successor generations. And while Europe's demographic winter was undoubtedly the result of a complex of causes, something was clearly awry in the realm of the human spirit when an entire continent—wealthier, healthier, and more secure than ever before—was depopulating itself, not because of war, natural disaster, or plague, but by its own will. The Pope summed up his concerns by suggesting that the "most urgent matter Europe faces, in both East and West, is a growing need for hope, a hope that will enable us to give meaning to life and history and to continue on our way together."[3]

What was perhaps most striking about *Ecclesia in Europa*, however, was the biblical framework John Paul II chose for his analysis of twenty-first-century European public life: the Book of Revelation, originally addressed to the "seven churches" (1:4) of what we call Asia Minor. At the time of Saint John's visions, all these Churches were living, if struggling, Christian communities; in 2003, six were titular sees in the Vatican handbook, the *Annuario Pontificio*, and only one, Smyrna, was home to a bishop, although the name of his archdiocesan see had changed to Izmir. Such "framing" biblical reference points in a papal document are not accidental; they are intended to send a message. And if one part of John Paul II's message in *Ecclesia in Europa* was to lift up the New Jerusalem of Revelation 21:2 as a horizon of aspiration for our building the earthly City and a symbol of reassurance that God's purposes will ultimately be vindicated, then the parallel message was a warning: Twenty-first-century Europe was at risk of duplicating the unhappy fate of the classical world in which the "seven churches" of the Book of Revelation had taken root. There is nothing *given* about civilizational vitality and continuity, John Paul II seemed to be suggesting. The civilization of the West—the product of a fruitful encounter among Jerusalem, Athens, and Rome, biblical religion, Greek reason, and Roman law—was a gift to the present from the past. In order to be able to pass that gift to future generations of Europeans, however, the Europe of the twenty-first century had to take more secure possession of its moral-cultural heritage—not least by challenging certain secularist shibboleths and rediscovering how much of that heritage was the by-product of the leaven of the Gospel.

Cardinal Jean-Marie Lustiger, whose thinking about European civilization in its origins and in its contemporary struggles closely paralleled that of John Paul II, was keenly aware of how much what we call "the West"—Europe, and Europe transplanted into the Western hemisphere and other parts of the globe—owed to Christianity. Europe's unity as a common civilizational enterprise was not, in Lustiger's view, the "result of a political framework"; rather, the "basic [European] mold" was created by the meeting of "Judaeo-Christian tradition with Greek and Latin civilization."[4] Moreover, that "mold" had proven so liberating that it had had a universal impact. Thus in a 1984 interview in *La Croix*, Lustiger argued that Christianity had given Europe, and then, through Europe, the entire world, four of the cultural building blocks of modernity: science as the product of rational inquiry; the exploration of the planet and what Lustiger described as the drawing up of an "inventory of the human race"; the notion that the fundamental requisite of a just society was the rule of law "at the service of the common good of human beings and [of] their dignity as persons"; and the idea of "development," rooted in the biblical conviction that history can be a march toward greater justice in human affairs.[5]

Lustiger also anticipated another of John Paul II's concerns in *Ecclesia in Europa*: that if the "great values which amply inspired European culture" were "willfully separated from the Gospel," the result was likely to be "any number of aberrations."[6] In that same *La Croix* interview, given almost two decades before *Ecclesia in Europa*, Lustiger spoke of "the idols of the European nations as Christian ideas gone mad; they are reason taken to excess, the manipulation of communications, and the use of the state against the community."[7] Even so prescient an analyst as Jean-Marie Lustiger might not, however, have foreseen the ways in which a Christian idea gone mad—the idea of tolerance, lifted up by the Second Vatican Council's Declaration on Religious Freedom, *Dignitatis Humanae*—would, within a generation, lead to the "dictatorship of relativism" of which Cardinal Joseph Ratzinger warned at the Mass *Pro Eligendo Romano Pontifice* (Mass for the Election of the Roman Pontiff) on April 18, 2005.[8]

Both John Paul II and Jean-Marie Lustiger were acutely aware of the burden of guilt that shaped much of postwar European culture, and which continues to distort the continent's interior life today. In a 1981 address to the religious and political leadership of West

Germany and to the diplomatic corps in Bonn, Lustiger spoke of an "evil spirit which broods over Europe and its past ... the guilt which comes from achieving brilliant success at the cost of the very principles which have made such a success possible." Here, Lustiger had in mind "the proclamation of freedom [which] became the will to dominate ... the pursuit of equality [which] produced slavery," and "the affirmation of brotherhood [which] became the origin of bloody struggles and of hopeless divisions." Now, Lustiger said, "as if exhausted by violence, Europe is hardly capable of transmitting life to new generations; poor, wounded Europe is causing the springs of life to run dry. The fruitfulness of love is under attack and the fruits of love are being aborted."[9] Twenty-two years later, in *Ecclesia in Europa*, John Paul II wrote poignantly of the soul-withering effects of a European guilt that could not be expiated, because the notion of "sin" had been displaced: "One of the roots of the hopelessness that assails many people today is found in their inability to see themselves as sinners and to allow themselves to be forgiven, an inability often resulting from the isolation of those who, by living as if God did not exist, have no one from whom they can seek forgiveness."[10]

The displacement of the God of the Bible in the name of human liberation, a phenomenon brilliantly analyzed by Henri de Lubac as the "drama of atheistic humanism," has thus had precisely the opposite effects than those promised by the thinkers whose work shaped twenty-first-century Europe's post-Christian culture.[11] Rather than liberation from the alleged burdens of God-consciousness, there is an unexpiated and, in principle, unexpiable, burden of guilt. Rather than tolerance, there is, on the one hand, increasing nervousness about "difference," and, on the other, the imposition of moral relativism by coercive state power. Rather than international leadership, there is international impotence. Rather than civil responsibility, there is ever-expanding governmental bureaucracy. And at just the moment when Europeans can be reasonably confident that their children will not be cannon fodder, children are increasingly hard to find. Those who cannot see the connections between these phenomena and the aggressive secularism of European high culture are, at this stage of the game, willfully blind. If wise and experienced nonbelievers like Marcello Pera and Giuliano Ferrara can understand the linkages here, there is no excuse for Christians not to do the same.

Which brings us to a question famously posed by Lenin: "What, then is to be done?"

As I understand it, Cardinal Lustiger's pastoral strategy was one which began from the premise that the Church could no longer be (and in fact ought *not* be) a Church of power: either the power of the *ancien régime*, or the power to be found in an alliance with an ascendant European Left (as some proposed in the wake of the Second Vatican Council). Rather, the Church should reevangelize France, not through the mediation of politics, but through the conversion of culture. This magnificent Collège des Bernardins is one physical embodiment, in stone, glass, and wood—and, more importantly, in the exercise of the intellect and the enrichment of the human spirit that takes place within these walls—of that strategy, which is, again, closely analogous to the "culture-first" strategy by which John Paul II in *Centesimus Annus* proposed to save free societies from the madnesses of virtues gone awry. A similar concern for the conversion of culture was evident in Pope Benedict XVI's address here in September 2008, which concluded with the Holy Father's reminder that "what gave Europe's culture its foundation—the search for God and the readiness to listen to him—remains today the basis of any genuine culture."[12]

There is a tactical question that shapes the strategic analysis here, and that is the question of whether it is possible to engage with the culture of postmodernity seriously, given that culture's epistemological skepticism, moral relativism, and metaphysical nihilism. In his January 2004 debate with Jürgen Habermas on the moral-cultural foundations of the newly expanded European Union, Joseph Ratzinger demonstrated how it is possible to make at least some progress beyond the confusions engendered by postmodernism on the question of whether Europe can in fact be "neutral between worldviews," as Habermas and Jacques Derrida had earlier proposed. But bringing a man of Habermas' intelligence to concede the necessity of a more solid moral-cultural foundation for democracy than he had once imagined desirable is one thing; converting a culture stewed in the juices of nihilism is another.[13]

For that, as Rémi Brague has suggested, is Europe's—and the entire West's—real problem: nihilism. Thus, the twenty-first century, Brague has proposed, will be the century of "being-and-nothingness," as the twentieth century (dominated by the claims of totalitarian ideology) was the century of "good-and-evil," and the nineteenth century (shaped by the social question and the demise of traditional society) was the century of "true-and-false."[14]

If nihilism is indeed the core problem of Europe (and by extension, the entire West) today, that casts the strategy of converting culture in a new light—as does the new aggression in public life demonstrated by the European, Canadian, and American exponents of what the Orthodox Jewish legal scholar J. H. H. Weiler has called "Christophobia," itself another by-product of postmodern nihilism.[15] Thus permit me to make several suggestions for refining the "culture-first" strategy of Jean-Marie Lustiger and John Paul II.

First, intolerance in the name of "tolerance" must be named for what it is and publicly condemned. To deny religiously informed moral argument a place in the European public square is intolerant and antidemocratic. To identify the truths of biblical morality with bigotry and intolerance is a distortion of moral truth and an intolerant, uncivil act, which must be named as such. To imagine that any state, or the European Union, has the authority to redefine marriage, a human institution that antedates the state ontologically as well as historically, is to open the door to what John Paul II called, in *Centesimus Annus*, a "thinly disguised totalitarianism"[16]—and this, too, must be said, publicly. All of this will require European Christians—and especially European intellectuals and political leaders—to overcome what often seems to be a deeply engrained and internalized sense of marginalization within contemporary society.

Secondly, we must speak openly about the empirically demonstrable, deplorable effects of the sexual revolution on individuals and society, while calling our contemporaries to a new appreciation of the dignity and nobility of human love. In John Paul II's *Theology of the Body*, believers and unbelievers alike have a more compelling account of our human embodiedness as male and female, and the reciprocity and fruitfulness "built into" that embodiedness and differentiation, than theories of human sexuality that reduce sexual differentiation to a question of plumbing and human love to another sporting activity. Young people, deeply wounded by a culture of promiscuity that tells them simultaneously that they must be sexually active and that sex could kill them, are yearning for the truth about love, as the remarkable impact of the Theology of the Body on American university campuses and in marriage-preparation programs demonstrates. This weapon in the conversion of culture ought to be fully and unapologetically deployed, and if that requires making the public claim that the Catholic Church understands human sexuality better than the prophets of sexual liberation, then so be it.[17]

Third, the reduction of Christian history to the Crusades, the European wars of religion, Galileo's trial, and the Inquisition must be publicly challenged, for these "black legends" feed nihilism and put obstacles in the way of the conversion of culture—even as they reinforce the guilt that distorts twenty-first-century European culture. Contemporary scholarship has deepened our understanding of the Crusades as a legitimate, if often mismanaged and brutal, response to Islamic aggression, even as it has demonstrated that such horrors as the Thirty Years' War were far more about politics than about the fine points of the theology of justification.[18] As for the Inquisition, the Church has repented, publicly, of this and other unsavory alliances with state power; when will the European Left apologize for communism, which killed more men and women in a slow week than the Inquisition did in centuries?[19] As for science, absent Christianity and its convictions about a world imprinted with the divine reason through the Logos, it would almost certainly have not developed as it did in Europe (or anywhere else).[20] I raise these matters of historical record, not to score debating points, but to suggest that part of the challenge we face today is to recognize, with John Paul II and Cardinal Lustiger, that Europe (and indeed the entire West) is suffering from a false story about itself, and about the relationship of biblical religion to its formation and its history.

Fourth, the Catholic Church, while enriching its interior life through a deepened encounter with the sources of its faith in the Bible, the Fathers, and the sacraments (*ressourcement*), and while developing ever more winsome ways to make the Church's proposal to a post-Christian Europe (*aggiornamento*), must also join forces with men and women of conscience who may not be believers, in order to challenge publicly the ever-more-ominous dictatorship of relativism of which Cardinal Ratzinger warned.[21] The Church's engagement with European culture and politics, in other words, must be less diffident, less defensive, and more assertive—not in the sense of aggression, but of truth-telling "in and out of season" (2 Tim 4:2).

Finally, having offered you some unsolicited advice, let me suggest why all of this is important for the rest of the West, which is "Europe exported."

Because nineteenth-century American coal mines lacked proper ventilation, miners brought with them, deep down into the earth, a canary in a cage. When the canary began to wobble, it was a sign that the air was becoming toxic. If the canary toppled over and died, the air had become insufficient to support life and it was time to get out of the mine shaft.

Europe, which created "the West," is the West's canary-in-the-mine-shaft: the test of whether the ambient atmosphere of postmodernity, which is most advanced here on the continent, is becoming too toxic to sustain human life and genuine culture. The acids of postmodern nihilism have eaten into the cultural foundations of all our societies; little that I have described here, in terms of the public effects of postmodern nihilism, could not be found in the United States; it can certainly be found in Canada. Yet the United States, for all its flaws and confusions, has not become a post-Christian society, and a place for religiously informed moral argument remains reasonably secure in the American public square. That, I am convinced, is because of the efforts of those who, while seeking to convert the culture, have not hesitated to confront the culture and to organize politically so that the instruments of law do not reinforce the temptations of nihilism. We have not always succeeded. But we are fighting.

I commend that more combative stance to you, who stand watch over the societies that gave birth to my own, in contesting for the causes we share. You will not find Americans lacking as allies in the twenty-first century, as you did not find us lacking as allies in the century just past.

LEAD, KINDLY LIGHT
John Henry Newman and Us

Pontifical University of St. Thomas Aquinas, Rome, Italy, October 12, 2019

In February 2003, the fathers of the Birmingham Oratory honored me with an invitation to deliver the *laudatio* at the "Musical Oratory" marking John Henry Newman's 202nd birthday. It was a marvelous evening of music and intellectual reflection, wine and fellowship; but what remains most firmly in my memory was the half hour I had spent earlier that day in Cardinal Newman's rooms, which had been left the way they were at his death.

I sat in his chair before the fireplace, fingered the small brandy glasses from which he warmed himself of a chill evening, held the Latin breviaries with which he had prayed even before entering into full communion with the Church of Rome.

On one wall, there was a yellowed but still readable map from the *Times* of London, on which Newman had followed the path up the Nile of General Kitchener's expedition to relieve the siege of Khartoum and rescue General Charles Gordon; and I remembered that Gordon, who was murdered by the forces of the Mahdi before Kitchener's troops arrived, had prepared for death by reading Newman's poem, "The Dream of Gerontius."

Inside the old upright wardrobe was the *galero*, the ceremonial red hat bestowed on Newman by Pope Leo XIII.

And pinned around the altar were brief notes in Newman's own hand, or sent to him by others, reminding him of those for whom he had promised to pray.

The next day, I was given leave to ramble through Newman's horseshoe-shaped, two-tiered library. And it's not easy to convey the emotion I felt when I lifted off the shelf a large folio volume of the

Opera Omnia of Pope Saint Gregory the Great and read on the flyleaf the inscription, "To my dear friend J.H. Newman, E. Pusey."

But it was while sitting in Newman's room in his chair that the thought occurred, Was his a life of change or a life continuity?

When Cardinal Newman died in 1890, Archibald Primrose, who as Lord Rosebery would become prime minister of Great Britain four years later, came to the Birmingham Oratory church to pay his respects. Rosebery was the last of the Liberal grandees, a man of whom Winston Churchill's secretary, John Colville, once wrote that he "... was likely to have read *Das Kapital*, but probably in a rare edition, specially bound in calf."[1] In any event, after contemplating Newman laid out before the altar of the Oratory church, Rosebery wrote in his diary: "This was the end of the young Calvinist, the Oxford don, the austere vicar of St. Mary's. It seemed as if a whole cycle of human thought and life was concentrated in that august repose. That was my overwhelming thought. Kindly light had led and guided Newman to this strange, brilliant end."[2]

But was there something really "strange" about Newman's destiny, and the life in which he fulfilled it? However dramatic the changes in his life seemed on the surface of history, was there not far more continuity than change, when Newman's life was read in its true, spiritual depth?

It was, after all, Newman who, in the "Meditations on Christian Doctrine," insisted that God "knows what he is about."

It was, after all, Newman who demanded of himself and held himself to this challenging commitment: "I shall be a preacher of truth."

So while there was certainly change over the long course of Newman's eventful and contentious life, there was also a genuine, deep-running continuity.

That was the continuity of the radically converted Christian, who, having passed through adolescent skepticism, committed himself wholly and entirely to Jesus Christ, the answer to the question that is every human life—and to the Church that is Christ's Mystical Body in the world.

And amidst that continuity of faith, there was a continuity of conviction: that the faith, in modernity, was under assault from a particularly dangerous enemy, dangerous because it appealed to modern humanity's fascination with itself and modern humanity's constant temptation to confuse tolerance with indifference to the truth of things.

That conviction was most memorably expressed in the famous "*Biglietto* Speech," which Newman delivered on May 12, 1879, on receipt of the official notification of his enrollment in the College of Cardinals. There, after some preliminary words of thanks to Pope Leo XIII, Newman had this to say about himself:

> In a long course of years I have made many mistakes; ... but what I trust that I may claim all through what I have written is this—an honest intention, an absence of private ends, a temper of obedience, a willingness to be corrected, a dread of error, a desire to serve Holy Church, and, through divine mercy, a fair measure of success. And, I rejoice to say, to one great mischief I have from the first opposed myself. For thirty, forty, fifty years I have resisted to the best of my powers the spirit of liberalism in religion. Never did Holy Church need champions against it more than now....
>
> Liberalism in religion is the doctrine that there is no positive truth in religion, but that one creed is as good as another.... It is inconsistent with any recognition of any religion, as true. It teaches that all are to be tolerated for all are matters of opinion. Revealed religion is not a truth, but a sentiment and a taste; not an objective fact, not miraculous; and it is the right of each individual to make it say just what strikes his fancy.[3]

Throughout his life, Newman, the man of change and development amidst continuity, was guided by the promptings of his conscience, which he took to be the voice of God speaking to us through what he termed "the aboriginal Vicar of Christ."

Many of you will be aware of the impact that Newman's writings on conscience had on the young Joseph Ratzinger in the aftermath of the Second World War. Perhaps not so well known, however, is the impact that Newman's sermons on conscience had on the young Germans of the anti-Nazi White Rose movement, including the most famous member of that resistance organization, Sophie Scholl, who was beheaded for treason in 1943.

When Sophie Scholl's boyfriend, Fritz Hartnagel, was sent by the Wehrmacht to the Russian front in 1942, Sophie gave him two volumes of Newman's sermons. Fritz later wrote Sophie that "we know by whom we are created, and that we stand in a relationship of moral obligation to our creator. Conscience gives us the capacity to distinguish between good and evil"—words, British author Paul Shrimpton observed, that "were taken almost verbatim from a famous sermon of Newman's called 'The Testimony of Conscience.'"[4] On the witness stand before the odious Judge Roland Freisler in the notorious Nazi "People's Court" in Munich, twenty-one-year-old Sophie Scholl testified that it was her conscience, and her Christian conviction, that had led her to nonviolent resistance against Hitler and his gangsters. That Christian conscience was formed in part by a serious intellectual and spiritual encounter with the man we shall know from tomorrow as Saint John Henry Newman.

There is a lot of talk in the twenty-first-century Church about "conscience," and Newman is invoked by many prominent personalities in those debates. So, it might be useful for all concerned to ponder Newman's influence on these contemporary martyrs.

What did the members of the White Rose learn from Newman about conscience?

They learned that conscience could not be ignored or manipulated.

They learned that the voice of God speaking through our consciences sets before us what is life-giving and what is death-dealing.

They learned that conscience can be stern, but that in submitting to the truths it conveys, we are liberated in the deepest meaning of human freedom.

They learned that obedience to conscience can make us courageous, and that to strive to live an ideal with the help of grace is to live a truly noble life with an undivided heart.

These themes are of obvious significance for the Church today.

The continuity to be found in the life of the radically converted Christian disciple was also evident in Newman's work on the development of doctrine.

The marks of a true development of doctrine that Newman identified were, I suggest, themselves a development of the work of Saint Vincent of Lerins, which many of us read in the Divine Office yesterday. As you will remember, Vincent, anticipating Newman's *Essay on the Development of Christian Doctrine* by fourteen hundred years (and *Gaudet Mater Ecclesia*, John XXIII's opening address to the Second Vatican Council by fifteen hundred), insisted that the "development of religion in the Church of Christ ... must truly be a development of the faith, not [an] alteration of the faith. Development means that each thing expands to be itself, while alteration means that a thing is changed from one thing to another. The understanding, knowledge, and wisdom ... of the whole Church ought, then, to make great and vigorous progress with the passing of the ages and the centuries, but only along its own line of development, that is, with the same doctrine, the same meaning, and the same import."[5]

Development, not "paradigm shifts," was what characterized Newman's path in following the kindly light—as it was what characterized Newman's theological concept of how the Church's self-understanding deepens and expands over time. We see that theology vindicated in the Second Vatican Council's teaching on the nature of the Church, on divine revelation, on the office of bishop, and on religious freedom and the modern state.

The great continuity of Newman's life, as I have suggested several times here, was his radical discipleship. That discipleship, that deep conversion to Christ, informed a brilliant and subtle mind; it was a conversion so profound that Newman could say, and mean, that "ten thousand difficulties do not make one doubt";[6] and that discipleship was also at the core of Newman as a churchman.

"Churchmanship" is not a term in common use today. That is a shame, for the word suggests qualities of character that are always needed in the Mystical Body of Christ, but especially in times of cultural turmoil and consequent ecclesiastical turbulence. Newman's churchmanship was never better displayed than in his work before, during, and after the First Vatican Council.

As everyone here surely knows, Newman believed in the infallibility of the Bishop of Rome under certain well-defined circumstances. He also believed that a dogmatic definition of that infallibility at the end of the seventh decade of the nineteenth century was imprudent or, as the language of the day had it, inopportune. And he resisted, with his usual literary vigor, the attempts by some to give papal infallibility so broad a definition as to turn the pope into a kind of oracle on virtually every imaginable question of ecclesiastical and public life. Yet, when Vatican I adopted a carefully crafted definition of the nature and range of papal infallibility, Newman not only accepted it in his own mind but defended it in public against the deprecations of the former prime minister, William Ewart Gladstone, in his famous *Letter to the Duke of Norfolk*, in a defense of the integrity of Catholic faith that only Newman could have successfully made in the England of his time.

This was churchmanship of the highest caliber, and it is a quality of character from which every Catholic today can learn today.

Finally, there is a deep continuity to be found in Newman's life in his courage: another quality of mind, heart, and soul—another virtue—that is much needed in Catholicism today.

I will of course defer to great Newman biographers like Father Ian Ker on this point, but it does seem to me that Newman's displays of courage throughout his life—in his transition from youthful skepticism to evangelical belief, his transition from evangelicalism to the Newman of the *Tracts for the Times* and the Oxford Movement, his reception into full communion with the Catholic Church, his acceptance of the presidency of a nascent Catholic University in Ireland, his debate with Charles Kingsley, and his aforementioned work during and after Vatican I—did not come to him easily. His was a gentler spirit than the polemicists of his time, and one can easily imagine that he would have much preferred to be left to his scholarship and his life of prayer, rather than being constantly called into the lists of controversy.

But when those calls came, this consummate churchman answered it, spoke the truth (even when that meant speaking truth to power), and in doing so inspired others to do the same.

Newman's courage was another manifestation of his profound Christian faith. And in his courage, he lived out what he had espoused to others in that "Meditation on Christian Doctrine," when he wrote, and speaking of God, "Therefore, I shall trust Him.... If I am in perplexity, my perplexity may serve Him.... My ... perplexity ... may be [a] necessary [cause] of some great end, which is quite beyond us. He does nothing in vain.... He may make me feel desolate, make my spirits sink, hide the future from me—still, He knows what He is about."

We honor the memory of John Henry Newman, this newest of God's saints, by imitating that courage and the conviction that underwrote it.

MICHAEL NOVAK
An American Catholic Achievement

Ave Maria University, Ave Maria, Florida, September 20, 2013

In the fall of 1970, when I was a college sophomore, the first article assigned in my theology course on revelation and faith was entitled "What Is Theology's Standpoint?" The author argued that a "standpoint" was "a set of experiences, images, presuppositions, expectations, and operations (of inquiring and deciding)" by which human beings made sense of themselves and their relationship to the world. Late twentieth-century theology, he continued, should operate from an "open standpoint," engaging the human experience in full.

Reading that article was my first encounter with the mind and spirit of Michael Novak. Forty-three years later, it strikes me that the gist of the article's argument helps us to grasp the range of Michael Novak's achievement, as well as its distinctive location.

In those days, there was something of a fad for titling articles and books, "*Toward* a Theology of ..." this, that, or the other thing (a fad once parodied by my Toronto colleague, Margaret O'Rourke Boyle, in a nicely wrought nonsense essay entitled "Toward a Theology of Garbage," which was published in *Commonweal* in the days when that venerable journal displayed an occasional sense of humor). Indeed, the "toward" bug infected Michael Novak on one occasion, when he christened an extended essay "Toward a Theology of the Corporation." But that was, I am sure, a literary venial sin. For Michael's entire intellectual enterprise has never needed that faux rhetorical booster "toward." As he showed me in that 1968 *Theology Today* essay on theology's "standpoint," Catholic intellectual life, and especially Catholic theology, is *always* "toward": Catholic intellectual life, and Catholic theology, consciously engage the fullness of the human experience, which Catholic thinkers "read" through the prism of revelation and reason, casting the light of truth on human affairs so that men and women may come to know him who is the Truth, as well as the Way and the Life.

Over more than a half century of scholarship, journalism, and public service, Michael Novak trained his philosophical and theological skills on virtually every consequential aspect of the human condition. He did not follow a preset itinerary but deliberately charted previously unexplored territories and terrain. That choice—to break out of conventional patterns of thought and become one's own intellectual GPS—did not always make for an easy life.

Some did not appreciate having their disciplines and practices examined through lenses ground by theological reason; indeed, some of those whose turf Michael surveyed regard the very notion of "theological reason" as oxymoronic. Explorers make mistakes, and Michael would be the first to admit that what once seemed an interesting track eventually turned into a blind alley, or that the account he gave of this or that form of human activity was incomplete. In fact, one of the most impressive aspects of Michael Novak's intellectual personality was his openness to criticism and his willingness to say, when necessary, "You were right and I was wrong"—a confession that comes harder to intellectuals than to most. Like others who, in the standard political categories, made the pilgrimage from left to right, Michael Novak has been pilloried as a traitor to his class, when in truth he had the courage to face facts and hold fast to his deepest convictions about human dignity and human freedom, rather than adjust those convictions to the shifting fashions of political correctness. Like virtually everyone who enters the public arena with ideas that challenge the regnant wisdom, Michael Novak must have wished, from time to time, for a better class of enemies. But, unlike some of those enemies, he has maintained a commitment to charity, candor, and respect in controversy.

It was not easy being an intellectual trailblazer for a half century; perhaps it never is. Still, it is worth noting how nasty what passes for intellectual exchange often is, these days. Late in his life, which was built around debate and controversy, almost always conducted with robust good humor, G.K. Chesterton sighed that his friend Hilaire Belloc's controversies were always so "sundering." That had something to do with Belloc's demeanor, of course, but in our own time, controversy has become inexorably "sundering" because of the secular-messianic streak that has come to dominate late modern and postmodern intellectual life, especially at the sometimes-bloody crossroads where ideas meet public policy. Those who challenge the shibboleths of the politically correct academy are not merely mistaken; they are wicked, and they must be shunned. That this cast of mind has seriously eroded American public life has become all too clear—in, for example, recent judicial *dicta* that dismiss those who defend reality from postmodern Gnosticism as irrational bigots. Similar shunning dynamics, rooted in the same fideism that history's ratchet only works in one direction, have too often made intra-Catholic controversy a very unpleasant, not to say un-Christian, arena in recent decades.

But enough, already, about the difficulties that Michael Novak faced over a half century of Catholic intellectual trailblazing. What about his singular achievement? Others in this symposium have explored those accomplishments in detail, in specific areas of Michael's extraordinary range of interests. Perhaps what I can offer is an overview of Michael's achievement, and then suggest a thing or two about its distinctive location.

Novak and Economics

It is not within my competence to make judgments about Michael Novak's Catholic account of economic life; others are better equipped to judge what Michael got right, and what has been left incomplete, in his philosophical and theological analysis of markets, enterprise, the system of democratic capitalism, and the vocation of business. But however those judgments are rendered over time, it seems clear to me that Michael, with singular dedication and real effect in the evolution of Catholic social doctrine, introduced a new temper, a new tone quality, to Catholic thinking about economic life. That new temper, or tone quality, is perhaps best described as an empirical sensibility that never descends into empiricism.

Novak's account of economics begins, not with abstractions, but with keen observations of what *is*, which in turn lead to a disciplined reflection on how that *is* ought to be *understood*, such that light is cast on moral truths and responsibilities in the process. Or, as his friend the Italian philosopher Rocco Buttiglione put it, Michael's seminal thinking about economic life raised an important question that had not been much explored previously in Catholic social thought: Might there be "laws" in economic life that are analogous to the moral laws that can be discerned from a disciplined reflection on human moral action? Is there, in other words, a deep structure to economic life that helps explain why some economies "work," be those economies lodged in medieval Benedictine monasteries or modern business enterprises? And does that deep structure reflect certain truths about the human person and human relationships that we can discern by careful, empirically informed reasoning that is also attentive to the truths of revelation?

For all its insight between Leo XIII and John XXIII, Catholic social doctrine had a somewhat abstract quality about it. Principles were enunciated within what Russell Hittinger has called the social doctrine's "Leonine architecture," and applications to particular circumstances and issues were made; but there was a somewhat top-down quality to the enterprise. Thus the markedly empirical temper of *Centesimus Annus*, John Paul II's seminal 1991 encyclical on the free and virtuous society in its political, economic, and cultural dimensions, marked a real development in the evolving social doctrine of the Church. The Leonine architecture remained in place but was now filled out by a far more attentive reading of the realities of late modern political and economic life. That developing social doctrine "standpoint," to return to an earlier image, reflected the groundbreaking Catholic thinking on economics that had been done by Michael Novak. And if Catholic social doctrine continues to unfold along the trajectory of *Centesimus Annus*, it will continue to bear the imprint of Michael's thought.

The impact of Michael's writing on Catholicism and economic life was not felt in Rome alone, however. The *samizdat* translation of *The Spirit of Democratic Capitalism* that circulated in poorly printed and tattered editions during and after the martial law period in Poland helped shape the postcommunist future of that country by shaping the thinking of the leaders of the Solidarity movement—a contribution to free Poland that the Polish government acknowledged by awarding Michael the Commander's Cross with Star of the Polish Order of

Merit. In a different, but not unrelated, context, Novak's thinking on Catholicism and economics and his critique of the defective politics and economics of the sundry theologies of liberation helped turn the tide against a movement that threatened to reduce the Church in Latin America to a political agent advancing a totalitarian agenda; at the same time, Novak's creative extension of Catholic social doctrine helped Latin American Catholic scholars, clergy, and political leaders think beyond the authoritarianism and mercantilism that had too often characterized Catholic public cultures south of the Rio Grande.

Finally, in this field of endeavor, mention should be made of Michael's impact on an entire generation of younger Catholic thinkers about Catholicism and economic life, on Catholic officeholders in the United States (and non-Catholic officeholders, for that matter), on religious leaders of a variety of denominations, and on business leaders and entrepreneurs throughout the world. By demonstrating in his own work how empirical rigor about the realities of economic life in the late twentieth- and early twenty-first centuries could be married to core principles of Catholic social doctrine and to a profound Catholic philosophical and theological anthropology, Michael Novak helped open up countless conversations that were once unimaginable—and in doing so, he helped give Catholic truth new purchase in public life.

Novak on Civil Society and the American Founding

In *Centesimus Annus*, John Paul II described the free and virtuous society of the future as being composed of three interlocking parts—a democratic political community, a free economy, and a vibrant public moral culture—while stressing the crucial importance of the third sector, the cultural sector, in disciplining and tempering the energies unleashed by freedom so that those energies contribute to genuine human flourishing. That portrait of the free and virtuous society has been filled in over several decades by Michael Novak's reflections on the crucial importance of civil society to twenty-first-century democratic life, and on the importance of religious conviction to the formation of civil society in the thinking of the American founders.

Here, too, Novak was helping break new ground, for, seven decades into the twentieth century, political science tended toward a functionalist view of democracy in which the only relevant actors were the individual and the state and Christian religious conviction played a marginal role (at best) in the ongoing making of America. Novak's work on ethnicity was an important reclamation of the cultural richness of American society and the American body politic. And his various commentaries on Alexis de Tocqueville were reminders that (as Tocqueville and his fellow Frenchman, Jacques Maritain, both understood) the associational instinct—the building of those free associations that John Paul II described in *Centesimus Annus* as embodiments of the "'subjectivity' of society"[1]—was a crucial component in making the United States a home of freedom in a distinctive way, even as the withering of that associational instinct in other democracies presaged the deterioration of their political cultures.

As for the Founding, Novak's work, along with others', was a welcome challenge to the prevailing Whig historiography, in which religious conviction (of a decidedly Deist sort) was at best a minor factor in the making of America. The religious convictions of the Founders and Framers, Novak proposed, were far more complex than that, and any serious account of the cultural landscape of the Founding had to take that complexity into account. This was not only an important contribution to redressing a historiographic mistake; it was also, and perhaps even more importantly, a useful tool in combatting efforts to create in contemporary America what Richard John Neuhaus famously dubbed the "naked public square"[2]—a public arena shorn, not only of religious dogma, but of religiously grounded moral conviction.

Novak and Apologetics

In the immediate post–Vatican II years, the traditional theological subdiscipline of apologetics made many Catholic intellectuals uncomfortable. Apologetics seems to imply polemics, and polemics were not deemed congruent with the spirit of the post-conciliar Church, misconstrued as the Church of Nice. And so, just as the ambient Western culture turned toxic and Christophobic, Catholicism's apologetic muscles slackened, the truths of biblical faith (including those essential truths about the human person on which free societies rest) were too often left defenseless, and the wider culture too often assumed that what was not defended was, in fact, indefensible to modern and postmodern minds.

In this challenging situation, Michael Novak was one of the leaders in crafting a new Catholic apologetics, in books like *Confession of a Catholic* and the charming volume he wrote with his daughter Jana, *Tell Me Why*. *Confession of a Catholic* anticipated, and *Tell Me Why* embodied, what John Paul II meant in the 1990 encyclical, *Redemptoris Missio* (The Mission of the Redeemer), when he wrote that "the Church proposes; she imposes nothing."[3] Unlike older forms of apologetics that tended to bludgeon the reader into submission through hammer blow after hammer blow of airtight, unassailable logic, Novak's apologetic method was far more discursive—it was, to use an often ill-used word in its proper sense, dialogical. It invited the reader into a serious conversation about serious things, without ever getting lost in self-seriousness.

As scholar, teacher, and parent, Michael Novak brought to the task of explaining the truths the Church teaches an acute sense of the challenges that late modern and postmodern culture poses to Christian faith and Christian truth claims. Young people growing up in a culture that assaults Christian sensibilities, and that tacitly (or not so tacitly) mocks Christian convictions and Christian symbols, could not be convinced, he knew, by logic alone—any more than the Lord Jesus had drawn disciples to himself by logic alone. Clear convictions were not enough; patience, tact, and an ability to hear questions in such a way that the apologist can provide the appropriate answer—not just the correct answer—were all needed. Michael Novak had those skills, as his being voted most effective teacher at two major universities on several occasions demonstrated. Deploying those skills in order to make the Church's proposal credible to young people who had grown up in a post-Christian culture, Michael Novak was one of the pioneers of a new Catholic apologetics that sought to lead young minds and hearts into the adventure of belief: to ascend the mountain and fly with the dove, to use the images he adopted for the title of his invitation to religious studies; to experience the sacred and understand that that encounter enlarged, rather than diminished, human freedom.

Novak and Diplomacy

No account of the accomplishment of Michael Novak as an American Catholic intellectual would be complete without an acknowledgment of at least one aspect of his public service.

When President Ronald Reagan sent Novak to lead the U.S. delegation to the United Nations Human Rights Commission in 1981, American diplomacy was floundering. The Carter administration had adopted the language of "human rights," which had been introduced into the U.S. foreign policy debate by men like Henry M. Jackson and Daniel Patrick Moynihan in the mid-1970s; but Carter and his administration had then emptied the idea of "human rights" of any serious content, in part because of their conviction that America must transcend what the president called its "inordinate fear of communism."[4] Michael Novak helped fill that content vacuum with an understanding of human rights drawn in part from Catholic social doctrine and in part from the American experience, and used that understanding to pummel the Soviet Union, its allies, and its apologists in what we now know was the beginning of the last act of the Cold War.

There was no help to be had on this front from the Department of State, at least at the beginning. Novak and his able colleague, Richard Schifter, were on their own, in bureaucratic terms. But they were not on their own conceptually, because Michael Novak and others who had begun their public lives on the left had, in the course of their political journey, thought through the ideas that enabled them to become effective defenders of the rights of Solidarity, Charter 77, the Lithuanian Committee for the Defense of Believers' Rights, and the rest of that noble galaxy of east central European human rights activists who looked to the United States for support.

And in making the case for freedom, Novak and his colleagues at the U.N. Human Rights Commission demonstrated to one of the most thoroughly secularized sectors of the U.S. government—the

Foreign Service—and to the religiously tone-deaf foreign policy establishment that philosophy and theology had things to say to, and in, diplomacy. The revolution of conscience that eventually swept through east central Europe, sweeping European communism into the dustbin of history in the process, was inspired and led by John Paul II. But John Paul was not alone in that great work, and Michael Novak, diplomat, helped bring the Catholic human rights revolution to bear, with effect, in that most unlikely venue, the U.N. Human Rights Commission.

Novak on Sports

And then there is the world of sports, which for Michael Novak was very much a fit subject for philosophical and theological reflection.

I do have to confess to some queasiness here about the plenitude of Michael's orthodoxy. It was in the spring of 1985, if memory serves, that Michael and I first walked together into old Memorial Stadium in Baltimore for one of the first games of the new baseball season. Memorial Stadium was a brick horseshoe, and you accessed the seating bowl by walking up concrete ramps; one of those interior ramps afforded a brief glimpse of the great greensward of the outfield beneath the overhanging mezzanine section, and although Memorial Stadium is no more, that constricted view, with its promise of summer to come, remains one of my favorite visual memories. In any event, as we both inhaled the sweet scents of freshly mown grass rising from the infield, we heard the unmistakable *crack* of ash on horsehide as a batting-practice ball was propelled into the right-field bleachers. "Greatest sound in sports," I said. "Except for 'swish'," Michael replied.

That lapse into Naismithian heresy aside, Michael Novak's thinking and writing about sports helped us appreciate our games as something other than vehicles for marketing team accessories—an ever-present danger in today's professional and collegiate sports environment. Who but Michael Novak would, or could, or could get away with describing the National Football League as "the liturgy of the Bureaucratic State," as Michael did in *The Joy of Sports* (a fine book whose title was ruined by an editor's priggish sense of propriety; Michael wanted to call it *Balls*)? Who but Michael Novak could describe baseball as a signal of transcendence, what with the game's lack of clock time and the theoretically infinite extent of the foul lines? And who else but Michael Novak would see in baseball's distinctive combination of individualism ordered to team achievement (or, if you prefer, the pastime's unique embodiment of personal freedom and responsibility ordered to the common good) a unique metaphor for America—and a lesson for the world?

I have watched a lot of games in a lot of sports with a lot of people, but I never was with anyone who enjoyed sports more than Michael Novak—which in Michael's case is, I'm sure, not a psychological quirk but a matter of deep Catholic conviction about *homo ludens* and the relationship of our games to the Wedding Feast of the Lamb. From that ample theological standpoint whereby Novak surveyed the human scene, being a fan also meant being confirmed in one's convictions that the human story is, in the final analysis, a divine comedy, not a meaningless tragedy.

Novak as American Catholic

Michael Novak's life and thought was shaped by his love for his Slovak roots and, more generally, for the Slavic understanding of history (which, he once explained, is why great quarterbacks who pull the game out in the last minute are invariably from Slavic backgrounds in western Pennsylvania: "It's the fourth quarter, you're down by twenty; what's new?"). But while he is, in a sense, one of his own "unmeltable ethnics," Novak is also an American whose profound patriotism is informed by an equally profound love for Christ and his Body, the Church. That much is, I think, obvious to those who knew Michael. What may not be so obvious, or at least seems to me rather unremarked, is that the achievement of Michael Novak is a singularly American and singularly Catholic achievement.

It is really impossible to imagine a Michael Novak and his achievement anywhere else; it just couldn't happen in Europe or Latin America, much less among the new Churches of Asia and Africa. And it is just as impossible to imagine that accomplishment as anything other than a Catholic accomplishment; no Protestant thinker would bring

Michael's sacramental apprehension of reality to bear on the subjects he has addressed, just as no Jewish thinker would bring Michael's incarnational imagination to a reflection on politics, economics, or culture.

Catholic intellectual life has a distinctive texture in these United States. In the best of American Catholic thought, we find a combination of the empirical and the abstract, practical reason and theoretical reason, that we find, frankly, nowhere else in the world Church. Michael Novak exemplified that distinctively American expression of the famous Catholic "both-and" in a singular way for over half a century.

And then there is the breadth of Novak's mind. I do not know many other Catholic intellectuals in modern times who have been able to range so freely and with such command across such a broad intellectual landscape—an achievement that speaks to Michael's own talents, of course, but also to the freedom granted by that distinctively American invention, the freestanding scholarly research institute, or think tank.

And perhaps most strikingly of all, Michael Novak stretched the Catholic Church's self-understanding—and the wider culture's understanding of the Catholic Church—as a layman: a layman both faithful to the magisterium and committed to free inquiry of the sort that lay Catholics can best undertake. When the bishops of the United States undertook in the mid-1980s to write a national pastoral letter on economic life, Michael took the lead in organizing a "Lay Letter" on the economy. Some found this cheeky; others were openly hostile; Michael saw it as an opportunity to bring distinctive lay experiences and gifts to bear for the benefit of the shepherds in their exercise of the *munus docendi*. The "Lay Letter" was not an attempt to challenge the bishops' teaching office; it was an effort to strengthen that teaching office through a truly open and free conversation about Catholic truth and economic life. And that, too, could only happen in the United States.

Men and women of many different religious convictions and no religious convictions will be arguing about the works of Michael Novak for decades, perhaps even centuries, to come. But as that debate continues, something else should be remembered about the accomplishment of Michael Novak, at a very personal level.

Because of Michael's work, men and women in commerce, and entrepreneurs throughout the world, came to think of their distinct exercise of their God-given creativity as a vocation, not just a job; so, I believe, did some athletes. Because of Michael's work, countless students came to understand that religious experience is a field as worthy of study as algebra or zoology. Because of Michael's work, those who bear the burden of responsibility for the common good, at the highest levels of national government, were reminded of the importance of moral reason and moral commitment in the affairs of state. Because of Michael's work, Catholicism in America and elsewhere learned a new grammar and a new vocabulary for meeting the challenges of Christophobia and for making the Church's proposal in a winsome and compelling way. Because of Michael's work, Catholic social thought became much more capacious, and participation in the Catholic, ecumenical, and interreligious conversations over moral truth and public life (in its economic and political aspects) was broadened.

At the end of Chaim Potok's beautiful novel, *The Chosen*, Reb Saunders, the Hasidic sage who has conceded to his older son Danny's desire to become a healer in the world rather than a congregational rabbi, makes a kind of act of faith in his son's future—his son will be a *tzaddik*, a wise and compassionate man, a moral beacon, for the world. "And the world needs a *tzaddik*," the aged refugee from Russian pogroms testifies. Given the depth of Michael's ongoing conversation with Jewish thinkers, I don't think I am stretching the bounds of interreligious propriety to suggest in closing that the achievement of Michael Novak, this singularly American Catholic achievement, has been the achievement of a *tzaddik* for the world.

Navigating the New World Disorder

THE NATIONAL INTEREST AND THE NATIONAL PURPOSE

Moral Reasoning and U.S. Foreign Policy

Baylor University, Waco, Texas, March 23, 2010

Over the course of my life and the lifetimes of my parents, the debate over the national interest and the national purpose—or, more broadly, the debate over morality and foreign policy—has careened through almost a dozen cycles, resulting in numerous, and sometimes jarring, shifts in the U.S. government's approach to the world. The most recent of these changes has been particularly dramatic, resulting in an inversion of the locus of foreign policy "idealism" and foreign policy "realism" on the ideological map of American public life (to use the conventional secular terminology for the morality and foreign policy debate).

My mother was born in 1914 and my father in 1921: years that witnessed the emergence, the high-water mark, and then the collapse of Wilsonian idealism—an internationalism quite self-conscious in its moral assertiveness, in distinction from the Realpolitik internationalism of Theodore Roosevelt. The most memorable iteration of Wilsonian idealism came in the president's war message to Congress of April 2, 1917, when Wilson declared that America's aim in entering the conflagration then consuming Europe was to ensure that the world would be "made safe for democracy." That such noble sentiments could coexist with a curious political fastidiousness, bordering on prissiness, is evident in a less-remembered formulation of President Wilson's—*viz.*, that his interventions throughout the Caribbean and in Mexico were intended "to teach the South American republics to elect good men." Like Teddy Roosevelt's Realpolitik, Wilsonian idealism was thus shaped by notions of Anglo-Saxon cultural superiority that twenty-first-century progressives would likely find deeply embarrassing.

In the wake of the war to end all wars, Wilsonian idealism was displaced by the "normalcy" of Warren G. Harding and the rise of a strong isolationist current in American politics: a tide of public opinion so formidable that even as strong and crafty a president as Franklin Delano Roosevelt was compelled to tack carefully across it, even as he prepared the United States for its inevitable entry into World War II. American isolationism was another curious business, in that it found lodgments across the spectrum of political opinion. But whether it was the by-product of the progressivist politics of Burton K. Wheeler, the Anglophobia of Joseph P. Kennedy, the racial and eugenic speculations of Charles A. Lindbergh, or the traditional business-oriented conservatism of Robert A. Taft, isolationism was thought to be finished as a serious force in American public life by 5 p.m. Eastern Standard Time on December 7, 1941.

Over the next decade, the national consensus born at Pearl Harbor was strong enough to permit President Harry Truman, working with Secretaries of State George Marshall and Dean Acheson, and Republican leaders like Arthur Vandenberg and John Foster Dulles, to define and execute a vigilant internationalism across the full gamut of world affairs—an interventionist internationalism that continued through the Eisenhower, Kennedy, and Johnson administrations, albeit with different strategic and tactical accents, articulated in different registers of moral passion. That internationalist consensus, which was not without some elements of foreign policy idealism, took as its analytic starting point a realist reading of the mid-twentieth-century *Weltproblematik*: Totalitarianism, in its national socialist or communist form, was a mortal peril to free societies; resisting its aggressive encroachments required the United States to take the lead in the defense of the West after Europe had unmanned itself in the two mid-century world wars. Such leadership would take American power into lands about which Americans previously knew very little. But the expenditure of blood and treasure in remote parts of the world was deemed necessary for, as the inscription on the Korean War Veterans Memorial on the National Mall in Washington puts it, expressing a sentiment once broadly shared in these United States, "Freedom is not free."

Moreover, the creators of the postwar internationalist consensus thought it *vere dignum et iustum*, "truly right and just" as the Roman Missal says, that the United States take such a leading role in world politics, for, on balance and considering the alternatives, American power was a force for good in the world. The prudent exercise of American power was not only necessary; it was good, for it aimed at securing a morally worthy goal: peace through freedom. The rhetorical proclamation of this seemingly self-evident truth reached its apogee in President Kennedy's inaugural address of January 20, 1961, in words now carved into granite at Arlington National Cemetery:

> Let the word go forth, from this time and place, to friend and foe alike, that the torch has been passed to a new generation of Americans—born in this century, tempered by war, disciplined by a hard and bitter peace, proud of our ancient heritage—and unwilling to witness or permit the slow undoing of those human rights to which this Nation has always been committed, and to which we are committed today at home and around the world. Let every nation know, whether it wishes us well or ill, that we shall pay any price, bear any burden, meet any hardship, support any friend, oppose any foe, in order to assure the survival and the success of liberty.[1]

Within five years of President Kennedy's assassination, however, the postwar internationalist consensus shattered, and isolationism reemerged as a powerful force in American public life: not, now, an isolationism fearful of America becoming contaminated by the world, but the isolationism of the New Left, convinced that America was poison in and for the world. The new isolationism (which was far more moralistic than anything it found odious in the rhetoric of John Foster Dulles) quickly swept up the Democratic Party, such that, a mere eleven years after Kennedy's inaugural, the Democratic candidate for president of the United States was urging America to "come home"—and being cheered on in that neo-isolationism by the late president's younger brother and others who claimed JFK's political mantle.

Meanwhile, the Republican Party under Richard Nixon and Henry Kissinger had adopted a self-consciously realist approach to world politics, drawing on contemporary intellectual sources like Hans Morgenthau and Albert Wohlstetter, and European historical models such as the diplomacy of Metternich and Disraeli. In its pursuit of détente with what some realists judged to be an ascendant Soviet Union, the realism of the Nixon-Ford years downplayed specific human rights violations behind the Iron Curtain. Yet while

President Ford, concerned about the fate of ongoing arms control negotiations with the Soviet Union, declined to receive Aleksandr Solzhenitsyn at the White House, the Ford administration was simultaneously negotiating the Basket Three human rights provisions of the 1975 Helsinki Final Act, which would turn out to be a powerful weapon in the hands of human rights activists throughout the Warsaw Pact countries in the endgame of the Cold War.

In response to the realism of the Nixon-Ford years, a new, morally urgent human rights activism was born in the mid-1970s within those elements of the Democratic Party aligned with Senator Henry M. Jackson, including pro-democracy social democrats and the trade union movement. After Jimmy Carter defeated Jackson for the 1976 Democratic presidential nomination and bested President Ford in the subsequent general election, the Carter administration adopted the language of an assertive human rights policy but filled it with New Left content, aiming its criticism primarily at authoritarian American allies rather than at America's totalitarian enemies. President Carter's announcement at Notre Dame in 1977 that Americans had gotten over their "inordinate fear of communism,"[2] and Secretary of State Cyrus Vance's statement that Carter and Soviet leader Leonid Brezhnev shared "similar dreams and aspirations about the most fundamental issues,"[3] demonstrated that moralism—the degradation of moral judgment into moral posturing—could coexist with breathtaking strategic myopia (and indeed moral blindness) in minds for whom the evocation of the specter of "Vietnam" marked an end to moral reasoning, or indeed any other form of reasoning.

Ronald Reagan challenged the realism of the Nixon and Ford administrations in 1976, but without articulating an alternative strategic vision that drew on the human rights themes being developed by the Jackson wing (or "Jackson feather," as Ben Wattenberg sometimes called us) of the Democratic Party. That had changed by 1980, thanks in part to the work of Jeane J. Kirkpatrick, Norman Podhoretz, Carl Gershman, Elliott Abrams, and others; their intellectual and policy advocacy filled out the contours of Reagan's longstanding anticommunism (first forged in battles over control of the Screen Actors Guild) by adding to it the concept of an America once again acting as the international champion of liberty, on the model of Kennedy's inaugural. The election of Pope John Paul II and his triumphant Nine Days in Poland in June 1979 accelerated Reagan's sense that the Soviet emperor had fewer clothes than realists often imagined, and that the Cold War might be, not simply managed, but actually won by the West.

The Revolution of 1989 in east central Europe—a world-historical series of events ignited by moral passion, informed by moral conviction, sustained by deft and morally sophisticated politics, and supported by a resolute demonstration that the Soviet Union could not compete with the United States and its British and West German allies in a serious arms race—raised further questions about classic foreign policy realism and its narrow focus on "hard power" as the sole analytic prism for understanding both the dynamics of world politics and the exigencies of U.S. foreign policy. Nonetheless, the administration of George H. W. Bush restored something of a realist perspective to the White House, through the work of Secretary of State James A. Baker III and national security adviser Brent Scowcroft. This more conventional approach to the world was successful in managing the endgame of the Cold War and effecting the reunification of Germany; it proved far less capable of managing the genocidal dissolution of Yugoslavia, or seeing off the Saddam Hussein regime in Iraq.

Then there came the Clinton years, the years when America took something of a holiday from history—and from serious thought about the relationship among ideals and realities, moral norms and prudential judgments, in formulating and executing U.S. foreign policy. Staffed primarily by veterans of the Carter administration—meaning men and women whose views had first been shaped by the shattering of liberal nerve that forged the McGovernite consensus about "Vietnam"—the Clinton administration seemed content to test Francis Fukuyama's notion that history had in fact ended with the triumph of democracy and the free economy in 1989–1991. In truth, of course, this blindness was shared across a wide swath of the American foreign policy community, of both parties; where it could lead was made unmistakably clear on September 11, 2001, previous signals about history's implacable turbulence having been insufficiently understood when they erupted in Kenya, Tanzania, and Aden.

President George W. Bush came to office promising a modest approach to America's engagement with the world, but the 9/11 watershed compelled his administration to a profound reexamination of the premises of U.S. foreign policy, particularly with reference to the despotic regimes in the Arab Middle East from which so much of the world's turmoil seemed to emerge. Thus having gone into both Afghanistan and Iraq with the full force of American might, Bush dedicated his second inaugural address, in January 2005, to articulating a "Freedom Agenda" that was no less breathtaking in its moral passion and political scope than the Kennedy inaugural:

> We are led, by events and common sense, to one conclusion: The survival of liberty in our land increasingly depends on the success of liberty in other lands. The best hope for peace in our world is the expansion of freedom in all the world.
>
> America's vital interests and deepest beliefs are now one. From the day of our Founding, we have proclaimed that every man and woman on this earth has rights, and dignity, and matchless value, because they bear the image of the Maker of heaven and earth. Across the generations we have proclaimed the imperative of self-government, because no one is fit to be a master and no one deserves to be a slave. Advancing these ideals is the mission that created our nation. It is the honorable achievement of our fathers. Now it is the urgent requirement of our nation's security, and the calling of our time.
>
> So it is the policy of the United States to seek and support the growth of democratic movements and institutions in every nation and culture, with the ultimate goal of ending tyranny in our world.[4]

And thus we are brought to the most recent turn-of-the-wheel. For in reaction to the difficulties of Bush's second term, and informed by an uncritical absorption of the New Left themes that corrupted the strategic perceptions of the Carter and Clinton administrations, the administration of President Barack Obama spent much of its first year in office proclaiming what it called a new "realism" in foreign policy: a strange hybrid that saw the administration declining to defend human rights activists in Russia, China, and Iran, apologizing for what it took to be the suffering caused by American exceptionalism, and retooling the human rights component of U.S. foreign policy to stress "reproductive choice" and what Secretary of State Hillary Rodham Clinton called the imperative of people being "free ... to love in the way they choose."[5]

A Defective Concept of Morality

Now, by my count, that makes at least ten significant shifts of perspective in the definition and execution of U.S. foreign policy between 1914 and 2009: an average of one major shift every nine and a half years. Those shifts were surely influenced by events in the world and by domestic political exigencies. And, if the truth be told, these oscillations eventually resolved themselves, in most cases, by the American people and their leaders doing what they ought to have done: thereby validating Winston Churchill's observation that the Americans will always do the right thing—after they've tried everything else.

Nonetheless, these oscillations between the idealist and realist poles of the ongoing debate over the national interest and the national purpose are jarring, both within our own political culture and for the world; and so it is important to understand their sources, with an eye to setting a steadier course. My proposal here is that, while circumstances surely played their role, these oscillations have also been shaped by a defective understanding within our culture of how moral truths bear on world politics. If I may risk offending ecumenical proprieties, it seems to me that one significant part of our problem can be defined in these terms: This nation of high moral expectation and deep moral commitments has never had an adequate public philosophy for translating moral truths into a framework for strategic analysis and prudent foreign policymaking—and it has lacked such a public philosophy because the American debate over morality and foreign policy, the national interest and the national purpose, has been dominated by one form or another of an inadequate account of morality that derives from the left wing of the Reformation and its adoption of an Ockhamite, or voluntarist, notion of the moral life.

As John Courtney Murray pointed out in the late 1950s, this Protestant way of conceiving the moral life found good and evil, not in the moral "structure" God built into the world and into us—a "structure" we could discern by reason—but in the will of God alone. Good was good because God commanded it; evil was evil because God forbade it. The notion of "moral reason" found little purchase here; reason was untrustworthy because reason might be the tool of passions or interests, both of which were thought to be bad things. This Protestant concept of morality was also biblicist, often imagining that conclusions about complex issues of public policy, including foreign policy, could be derived without much exegetical ado from, say, the Sermon on the Mount. It set a high value on motive or intention and was not much concerned with an analysis of possible consequences (the purity of the actor's will being what most counted); and for that reason it was wary of the very idea of a "national interest." As for society, including world society, the individualism endemic to this understanding of morality often led to a curiously apolitical view of public policy: This form of morality tended to think in highly individualistic terms—there would be no policy conundra at home or abroad, it seemed to suggest, if all men would simply observe the Great Commandment (or its secular equivalents).

This was the moral*ism*—for it cannot be regarded as a form of true moral *reasoning*—that dominated American Protestantism in the first half of the twentieth century, giving rise, by way of reaction, to the neo-orthodoxy of the Niebuhr brothers, on the one hand, and to the foreign policy realism of Hans Morgenthau and his school on the other. But neo-orthodoxy, despite its powerful critique of moralism and its more trenchant reading of the moral obligations of public authority in the face of the totalitarianism threat, had no solution to the more basic problem of moral reasoning. For it, too, declined to adopt the classic morality of right reason (or natural law), substituting for what it found objectionable in the old liberal Protestant moralism such categories as "paradox" or "ambiguity," all the while trying to maintain its equilibrium in what Reinhold Neibuhr would regard as the unresolvable tension between "moral man and immoral society."[6]

As for the realism of Morgenthau and his school, that, too, would provide no means of escape from America's cyclical oscillation between the idealist and realist poles of the national character. Realism proved incapable of crafting an adequate analytic lens for reading the signs of the times in the last two decades of the Cold War: Both liberal realists (such as those in the "arms control community") and conservative realists missed the dynamics of the revolution of conscience that made possible the Revolution of 1989. And realism missed those dynamics because its notion of the relationship between moral truth and world politics was just as deficient as the moralism it rightly criticized. Hans Morgenthau's claim, for example, that "to know with despair that the political act is inevitably evil, and to act nonetheless, is moral courage,"[7] is so silly as to almost beggar belief. This is histrionics, not reason—neither political reason nor moral reason.

If we are to escape the past century's pattern of an American foreign policy that lurches back and forth between an idealism and a realism that are imagined to be two horns of a dilemma when they are in fact two dimensions of a problem, America needs a new template for thinking about the national interest and the national purpose. Such a template would give due weight to the defense of the national interest as an inescapable responsibility of government. Yet it would also recognize that the securing of the national interest must be located within the more ample horizon of a national aspiration to advance what Pope John XXIII called the "universal common good"[8]—which I take to mean the pursuit, on the international plane, of the five rationally knowable ends of any morally serious politics: justice, freedom, security, the general welfare, and the peace of order.

Let me try to translate this general description of the template we need by outlining the connection between the national interest and a broader sense of national purpose in a series of propositions or theses. Taken together, these ten propositions might form a new intellectual grid for disciplining the American public moral debate in the twenty-first century about the goods to be sought in world politics and the means appropriate to the pursuit of those goods.

A New Template

1. There is no escape from moral reasoning in politics, including international politics. Politics, even world politics, inevitably engages questions of what is good and what is evil, what is noble and what is base, what is congruent with the truths we can know to be true and what is incongruent with those truths. Why? Because politics is a human activity, and human beings are characterized by their capacity to reflect and to choose—by their reason and their free will. Politics, as Aristotle and the classic Western philosophical tradition have long affirmed, is an extension of ethics. Attempts to subtract or bracket the moral dimension of politics from our calculus of ends and means in the formulation and execution of foreign policy debases public life, warps strategy, and leads to imprudent tactics.

2. History can be bent to our reason and our will—to the human capacity to know the good, to choose it, and to act upon it. Those who deny the possibility of purposefulness in this kind of world—by appeals either to "complexity" or to the "impersonal dynamics of history"—have not reflected very carefully on modern history. The twentieth century was replete with examples of men whose "purposeful" policies bent events, and the course of history, to their wills: Lenin, Hitler, Mao, and Ho Chi Minh are among the odious examples; Churchill, the founders of the State of Israel, Reagan, Thatcher, and John Paul II are among the admirable examples. In the admirable cases, as in the odious ones, concepts of "purpose" were informed and tempered by issues of "interest." "Interest" and "purpose" thus seem to be linked, empirically. And this linkage has something of the appearance of a dialectic, in which interest and purpose interact and are thereby mutually refined.

3. The two twentieth-century forms of American moralism are both antithetical to clear thought about the national interest and the national purpose and are thus deleterious to serious statecraft. The traditional, culturally transmitted Protestant understanding of morality in America—voluntarist, subjectivist, biblicist, and individualist in its conception of the moral life and moral decision-making—is inadequate to the tasks of moral reasoning and practical action required of statesmen. Its suspicions about the very idea of a "national interest," like its discomfort with the exercise of power, render it a less than useful counselor to those with responsibility for the common good, who must try to drive principles into the hard soil of reality while taking care to safeguard the security of those whom they serve.

The secularist moralism that characterized the Vietnam-era New Left and that shaped U.S. foreign policy in the Carter and Clinton administrations—which looks rather like the old liberal Protestant moralism with God and the Bible tossed over the side—is also inadequate to the tasks of statecraft in the twenty-first-century world. Its ideological blinders preclude its seeing things as they are, which is the essential prerequisite to wise policy. For we cannot advance toward how things ought to be if we do not grasp the nature of things as they are.

4. Protestant neo-orthodoxy's critique of the older American moralism remains important in devising wise policy in the

twenty-first century. Understanding the inevitable irony, pathos, and tragedy embedded in history; being alert to the dangers of unintended consequences; maintaining a robust skepticism about all schemes of human perfection (especially those in which politics is the chosen instrument of salvation); cherishing democracy without worshipping it—these elements of the moral sensibility articulated in the pre–World War II Protestant neo-orthodox critique of twentieth-century American Protestant moralism remain essential intellectual furnishing for anyone who would think wisely about interest and purpose in U.S. foreign policy.

In the twenty-first century, however, the Christian realist critique of the older American moralism will be less a comprehensive framework for thinking about foreign policy than an important set of cautions essential to the exercise of practical reasoning about America's action in the world, especially in light of the cyclical return of New Left moralism.

5. **Realist conceptions of world politics and foreign policy must be completed by a concept of human creativity in history.** Paying close attention to the cautions raised by the realist critique of the older American Protestant moralism and its New Left–influenced successor cannot lead to a form of intellectual paralysis in which the strategist and policymaker simply accepts things as they are. Rather, any genuine realism, and certainly any genuine Christian realism, must guard against premature closure in its thinking about the possibilities of human action in this world. Things can change—things can be *made* to change—for the better: sometimes.

6. **Social ethics, including that subset of social ethics known as "ethics and international affairs," is a distinctive moral discipline.** The moral reasoning appropriate to foreign policy will reflect the distinctive nature of political action. As John Courtney Murray put it, the obligations of society and the state are "not coextensive with the wider and higher range of obligations that rest upon the human person (not to speak of the Christian).... [Thus] the morality proper to the life and action of society and the state is not univocally the morality of personal life, or even of familial life.... The effort to bring the organized action of politics and the practical art of statecraft under the control of the Christian values that govern personal and familial life is inherently fallacious. It makes wreckage not only of public policy but of morality itself."[9] This is the crucial point missed by the old Protestant moralism,

New Left moralism, and the approach to political theology developed in recent decades by Stanley Hauerwas and by representatives of the Radical Orthodoxy school.

Thus, the moral reasoning appropriate to foreign policy will not confuse politics with interpersonal relationships, nor will it apply moral norms appropriate to interpersonal relationships to world politics in a simple-minded, one-to-one correspondence. Rather, the moral reasoning we need will demonstrate to the statesman and policymaker that our choices are not between an immoral or amoral Realpolitik, on the one hand, and naiveté on the other; international outlaws are not to be dealt with as one would deal with refractory children, nor are international negotiations exercises in therapy. By the same token, the moral reasoning we need will keep statesmen and policymakers alert to the possibilities of nudging history in a more humane direction through a variety of means, by keeping public authority's attention focused on the imperative of pursuing the rationally knowable "international common good" in our engagement with the world.

7. **It is in the American national interest to defend and enlarge the sphere of order in international public life, through prudent efforts at changing what can be changed in the trajectory and conduct of world politics.** The irreducible core of the American national interest is composed of those basic security concerns to which responsible public authorities must attend. Those security concerns are not unrelated to a larger sense of national purpose, however: We defend America because America is worth defending, in itself and because of what it means for the world. Therefore, those security concerns that make up the core of the national interest rightly understood should not be understood in classic Realpolitik terms; rather, they should be understood as the necessary inner dynamic of the pursuit of the national purpose.

And the larger American purpose in world affairs is to contribute as best we can to the long, hard, never-to-be-fully-realized "domestication" of international public life: to the quest for ordered freedom in an evolving structure of international public life capable of advancing the classic goals of politics (justice, freedom, security, the general welfare, peace). As a matter of hard fact and as a matter of moral truth, the United States cannot adequately defend its national interest without seeking concurrently to advance these goals in the world. As a matter of hard fact and as a matter of moral truth, those goals will not be advanced when they are pursued in ways that gravely threaten the security of the United States.

8. "National purpose" is not national messianism. The "national purpose," as defined just above, should be understood as a horizon of aspiration toward which our policy (and our polity) should strive. That horizon of purpose helps us measure the gap between things as they are and things as they ought to be, even as it provides an orientation for the long haul. But the "national purpose" as defined above is not something that can be achieved in any final sense, because international public life will never be fully "domesticated," save under a particularly stringent global tyranny. Understanding the "national purpose" as an orienting horizon of aspiration is a barrier against both the cynicism that is the shadow side of realism and the dangers of a moralistic, even messianic, notion of national "mission," which implies a far shorter timeline and the possibility of final accomplishment.

9. Casuistry is the moral art appropriate to international statecraft. For both the moral analyst and the policymaker, the relationship between national interest and national purpose in the practical order is defined through casuistry—that is, through the moral art of applying principles to world politics by means of the mediating virtue of prudence. Prudence does not necessarily guarantee wise policy. Prudence does, however, reduce the danger of stupid policy based on moralistic or Realpolitik confusions.

The classic casuistry most in need of renovation in early twenty-first-century thinking about morality and foreign policy is the just war tradition, which must be revitalized as a tradition of collaborative reflection on the nature of sovereignty, and on the legitimate sovereign's use of proportionate and discriminate armed force in the pursuit of peace. Conceptions of the just war tradition, often found today among philosophers, theologians, and churchmen, that begin with a prima facie "presumption against war" and that conceive the tradition as a set of hurdles for statesmen to jump through are less than helpful in shaping the kind of reflection required by both the tradition of reason and wise statecraft.

10. The debate over the national interest and the national purpose is perennial, but not necessarily circular. The dialectic of interest

and purpose, described above, will remain unresolved. Pursuing a narrow concept of "interest" without reference to "purpose" risks crackpot realism. Pursuing grand and noble purposes without regard for the responsibilities of safeguarding the national interest risks crackpot idealism, or utopianism—and great danger. The world being what it is, these two temptations—crackpot realism and utopianism—may be unavoidable. Succumbing to them is not unavoidable, given a clear understanding of both the inherently moral character of political choice and the distinctive canons of social ethics.

Thus, the debate over the right relationship between the American national interest and the American national purpose will be a perennial one, given the nature of politics itself as well as the historical character of the American people and their democracy. If it is informed, however, by a proper understanding of the moral reasoning appropriate to thinking about world politics, the argument will not be circular and may yield a measure of wisdom from time to time.

Indeed, had such a template to discipline and guide the U.S. foreign policy debate been in place in the century just past, America might have helped prevent the rise of National Socialist totalitarianism by helping craft a more just and sensible peace settlement after World War I; America might have found ways to prevent the Soviet absorption of half of Europe after World War II; America might not have abandoned its commitments and its allies in Southeast Asia, but might have found a way through to a Korea-like settlement, thus preventing the bloodbath that followed our withdrawal from the region; America might not have mistaken the threat posed by the Ayatollah Ruhollah Khomeini, described by President Carter's U.N. ambassador as "some kind of saint";[10] America might have helped prevent genocide in the Balkans; and America might not have made such a hash of the post-major combat phases of the Gulf War and the Iraq War.

Concluding Unscientific Postscript

In politics, of course, as in all things in history, we see through a glass darkly. The opaqueness of the world and its political dynamics is a given; but the opaqueness can sometimes be broken by the clarity of moral vision that comes from a correct understanding of the nature of morality and of moral reasoning. That understanding is what has often been missing in the American debate over the national interest and the national purpose.

Realist appeals to the "national interest" often seem to assume that we know intuitively what that "national interest" is. But we do not. As Charles Frankel, a liberal with some sense, once put it, "The heart of the decision-making process ... is not the finding of the best means to serve a national interest already perfectly known and understood. It is the determining of that interest: the reassessment of the nation's resources, needs, commitments, traditions, and political and cultural horizons—in short, its calendar of values."[11] Bracket the use of that ubiquitous and slippery term "values," and there is genuine insight here.

Determining the content of the "national interest" and the means appropriate to its pursuit is an exercise in moral reasoning, not merely political, economic, or political-economic calculation. That means that the public debate over the national interest in a mature democracy like our own ought to reflect a correct idea of what moral reasoning is, and how the moral reasoning peculiar to international politics functions. The failure to define and culturally instantiate such an idea of moral reasoning is at the heart of the problem of our national oscillation between foreign policy idealism and foreign policy realism.

It is past time for both foreign policy realists and foreign policy idealists to recognize that they share a common tendency to reduce the notion of "morality" to something akin to the injunctions of the Sermon on the Mount. The idealists then seek to apply the dominical counsels to poverty of spirit, meekness, mercy, purity of heart, and so forth to the business of dealing with everyone from the Dalai Lama to Fidel Castro and Mahmoud Ahmadinejad. The realists, agreeing that these dominical counsels sum up the meaning of "morality," insist that they cannot be applied to states or non-state actors in world politics, and conclude that foreign policy is the realm of (at best) amorality. Both camps assume that everyone agrees on what "morality" is, and that the real arguments are about the possible or impossible application of that "morality" to the realm of world affairs.

That assumption is precisely wrong. We do not know, as a political culture, what moral reasoning in foreign policy really means. That is the gap that must be filled. The "morality" we need in foreign policy is one whose principles are derived from reflection on the ends of politics as these can be known by reason, and whose practices are mediated through the virtue of prudence—the moral craft of applying principle to circumstance so as to maximize the chances of doing good and minimize the dangers of making things worse than they already are. This kind of moral analysis, rooted in the tradition of reason, does not easily yield simple answers. It is, however, the kind of moral reasoning appropriate to the distinctive vocation of the statesman, and to the creation of a serious public conversation about the national interest and the national purpose.

Were all of this to be well understood in this great republic, the oscillation between the idealist and realist poles of American foreign policy would abate, and the future of American foreign policy could be placed on a steadier course—which would be a good thing, for us and for the world.

THE JUST WAR TRADITION AND THE WORLD AFTER SEPTEMBER 11

Columbus School of Law, Catholic University of America, Washington, D.C., March 20, 2002

Americans have been telling each other for a long time that our culture is awash to the gunwales in moral relativism. Some have applauded this, for reasons personal, political, or philosophical. Alan Wolfe, for example, has argued recently that the plurality of ethical systems and the wide disparity of moral judgments found in the contemporary United States is a natural and welcome development of democracy: a kind of evolutionary extension of our commitment to equal opportunity and to religious, racial, and ethnic diversity.[1] Others have worried out loud about the very plurality Professor Wolfe applauds, asking how a democracy can function over the long haul if there is no common moral grammar to discipline and direct the public debate over public policy. Still others have deplored the moral relativism of our culture, seeing polymorphous perversity where Alan Wolfe sees healthy plurality, and questioning whether a people incapable of governing their own appetites from within can govern themselves in the public realm.[2]

But whether we applauded it, worried about it, or deplored it, many, many Americans over the past two decades have taken what might be called the Walter Cronkite view of moral relativism: "That's the way it is ..."

This bipartisan, ecumenical, and interreligious agreement about the pervasiveness of moral relativism in twenty-first-century America collapsed on September 11, 2001.

In less than two hours, between the first attack on the World Trade Center and the crash of the fourth hijacked airliner in rural Pennsylvania, Americans discovered, or rediscovered, moral absolutes. Confronted by ruthless, well-planned, and deliberately executed mass murder for evil political ends, the teaching of Pope John Paul II on exceptionless moral norms (or "intrinsically evil acts"), which had caused intense controversy after the 1993 encyclical *Veritatis Splendor*, seemed self-evidently clear: Some things are definitely off-the-board.[3] Some things *must* be off-the-board if there is to be any civilized society. Some acts are evil in themselves, and no putatively mitigating combination of intentions and consequences can possibly justify them. Or, as a shocked Yale undergraduate, a self-confessed product of an education designed to inculcate "tolerance" of "other values" as the *summum bonum*, put it in a *Newsweek* guest column, "We should recognize that some actions are objectively bad, despite differences in cultural standards and values."[4]

Appeals to toleration, cultural diversity, epistemological modesty, the fact/value distinction, and other modern and postmodern arguments for moral relativism cut very little ice when the American people faced the smoldering wreckage in lower Manhattan, the gaping hole in the Pentagon, and the deaths of nearly three thousand innocents. If we were all relativists now, how could one condemn absolutely the attacks of September 11? On the other side of the coin of good and evil, if we were all relativists now, how could we comprehend the self-sacrificial sense of duty that led firefighters to their deaths in the Twin Towers, or the heroism that led doomed passengers on United Airlines flight 93 to deny the hijackers their goal of destroying the White House or the Capitol? There was good, and there was evil. We could tell the difference again, and we could use those words again.

This new moral realism is entirely welcome. It is welcome in itself as a matter of cultural hygiene. It is also essential for the future of the Republic. A society without "oughts" tethered to truths is going to find it difficult to defend itself against aggressors motivated by distorted "oughts." The response to lethally distorted concepts of the good must be a nobler, truer concept of the good; it cannot be a principled skepticism about our capacity to know the good, or a thoroughgoing relativism about possible human goods.[5] Where shall we find the materials with which to build, on this recently unearthed foundation of realist moral intuitions, an understanding of America's responsibilities amidst the new world disorder?

The just war tradition is a venerable form of theologically developed moral realism. It could help fill with real content our often-inchoate national intuitions about the imperatives of moral realism. The just war tradition has also been the normative Catholic tradition for addressing questions of statecraft, war, and peace for a millennium and a half—which should mean that the Catholic Church is in a distinctive position to help our country (and especially its political and military leadership) think through the tangle of issues involved in the war on terrorism that we have been fighting since September 11.

That will not happen, however, unless and until we confront squarely the distortions of just war thinking in the Catholic discussion during the past twenty-five years.

The quarter-century just past has witnessed what can only be described, with regret, as a great forgetting of the classic Catholic just war tradition. This forgetting, which has been particularly acute among Catholic intellectuals and religious leaders, usually presents itself as a development of the just war tradition. In fact, what imagines itself as development is more accurately described as the abandonment of a rich and subtle Catholic understanding of international politics, war, and peace. In the course of this abandonment, the intellectual structure of the just war tradition has been inverted and the notion of the just war tradition as a tradition of statecraft has gotten lost. The net result has been that a species of functional or de facto pacifism has become the new Catholic "default position" on questions of conflict and order in world politics. The terminology of the just war tradition remains; the classic content of the tradition has been largely forgotten.

This Catholic default position has been amply displayed since September 11. It was evident when Church leaders immediately reached for words like "tragedy" or "crime" to describe what the new moral realism instinctively understood to be acts of war.[6] It was evident when the overwhelming majority of Catholic religious leaders and intellectuals laid primary, and sometimes exclusive, stress on the imperative of avoiding noncombatant casualties in our national response to terrorism.[7] It was evident when some Catholic leaders, including senior representatives of the Holy See, deplored the "root causes" of terrorism—an analysis that seemed unacquainted with the history of modern terrorist politics, that ignored the empirical facts of September 11 (when the perpetrators were well-educated, amply funded middle-class people), and that implied a demeaning and deterministic reading of others' moral capabilities (as if the perpetrators of September 11 were people who just did not know any better).[8] The default position was also evident in the ubiquitous warnings one heard from religious leaders and Catholic intellectuals about "violence begetting violence"—as if a proportionate and discriminate use of military force in a just cause were the moral equivalent of turning a 767 into a weapon of mass destruction.[9] Finally, the default position was omnipresent at the local parish level: How many prayers for the vindication of justice, much less for victory in the war against terrorism, have you heard since September 11?[10] Some perhaps, but not many. Somehow, to "pray for peace" has come unglued from praying for justice.[11]

Retrieving, renewing, and extending the just war tradition is essential if the Catholic Church in the United States is to make its proper contribution to the national debate that will shape the war against terrorism—the struggle for world order—in the years, perhaps decades, ahead. It is important at the outset to grasp the nature of that contribution. The primary Catholic contribution to shaping the debate about the war against terrorism does *not* have to do with establishing a series of hurdles that civilian and military officials must overcome before the Church judges a particular military action or set of actions within the broader war justified. That is what the Catholic default position suggests, and that, too, is a misunderstanding of just war thinking. Rather, the first task of the Catholic Church is to teach the principles of the just war tradition, as they have been refined by fifteen hundred years of reflection and experience, so that those principles become ever more explicitly what they are implicitly: the framework for a comprehensive, morally serious, and realistic approach to world politics—an approach that we might call "idealism without illusions." The first task of the Church, according to the classic just war tradition, is to help determine the morally defensible political ends to be sought in the present situation, for those are the ends that give meaning to the debate over means.

In doing this, Catholic religious leaders and scholars today will find intellectual allies—among those few mainline Protestant thinkers who have not succumbed to an even more debilitating form of functional pacifism than is found in many Catholic peace and justice circles; among evangelical Protestants who have begun to discover the just war tradition as an important element of Christian social ethics; and among some secular scholars who have been helping develop just war thinking for some decades now.[12] That ecumenical, interreligious, and interdisciplinary dialogue is entirely welcome. Let me focus here, though, on the crucial themes that would, in my judgment, revitalize just war thinking within the Catholic Church—in the United States and indeed around the world.

Recovering the Just War Tradition as a Theory of Statecraft

In his recent and acclaimed book, *Warrior Politics*, veteran foreign correspondent and analyst Robert Kaplan suggests that only a "pagan ethos" can provide us with the kind of leadership capable of safely traversing the world disorder of the twenty-first century.[13] It is a proposal worth examining as we hone Catholic thinking about the use of military force and its relationship to world politics. Kaplan's "pagan ethos" has several interlocking parts. It is shaped by a tragic sense of life which recognizes the ubiquity, indeed inevitability, of conflict. It teaches a heroic concept of history: Fate is not all, and wise statecraft can lead to better futures. It promotes a realistic appreciation of the boundaries of the possible. It celebrates patriotism as a virtue. And it is possessed by a grim determination to avoid "moralism," which Kaplan (following Machiavelli, the Chinese sage Sun-Tzu, and Max Weber) identifies with a morality of intentions, oblivious to the peril of unintended consequences.[14] For Robert Kaplan, exemplars of this "pagan ethos" in the past century include Theodore Roosevelt, Winston Churchill, and Franklin Roosevelt.

Reading *Warrior Politics* and reflecting on the concept of morality that informs it put me in mind of a story that I had not thought of for years. During the Korean War, the proudly Protestant Henry Luce, son of China missionaries, found himself puzzled by the debate over "morality and foreign policy" that Harry Truman's "police action" had stirred up. What, he asked his friend, Father John Courtney Murray, S.J., did foreign policy have to do with the Sermon on the Mount? "What," Father Murray replied, "makes you think that morality is identical with the Sermon on the Mount?"[15]

Robert Kaplan, a contemporary exponent of foreign policy realism, seems to share Henry Luce's Protestant misimpression that the moral life is reducible to the ethics of personal probity and interpersonal relationships. The implication, which Kaplan and Luce also share, is that issues of statecraft exist somewhere "outside" the moral universe.

The classic Catholic just war tradition takes a very different view, which Kaplan unhappily ignores in *Warrior Politics*. The classic Catholic tradition insists that no aspect of the human condition falls outside the purview of moral reasoning and judgment—including politics. Politics is a human enterprise. Because human beings are creatures of intelligence and free will—because human beings are inescapably *moral* actors—every human activity, including politics, is subject to moral scrutiny.[16] There is no Archimedean point outside the moral universe from which even the wisest "pagan" statesman can leverage world politics.

Indeed, what Robert Kaplan proposes as a "pagan ethos" is a form of moral realism that would be enriched by a serious encounter with the classic Catholic just war tradition. One need not be a "pagan," as Kaplan proposes, to understand the enduring impact of original sin on the world and its affairs; Genesis 1–3 and a good dose of Augustine's *City of God* will do the job just as well, and arguably better. One does not need to be a pagan to act on the conviction that moral conviction, human ingenuity, and wise statecraft can bend history's course in a more humane direction; one need only reflect on the public achievement of Pope John Paul II and the Catholic human rights resistance in central and eastern Europe in helping rid the world of the plague of communism.[17] A realistic sense of the boundaries of the humanly possible in given situations is not foreign to Catholic moral reasoning; prudence, after all, is one of the cardinal virtues. Nor is patriotism necessarily "pagan"; indeed, in a country culturally configured like the United States, patriotism is far more likely to be sustained by biblical rather than "pagan" moral warrants. As for "moralism" and its emphasis on good intentions, classic Catholic moral theology in the Thomistic stream is dubious in the extreme about voluntaristic theories of the moral life and their reduction of morality to a contest of wills between the divine will and my will.[18]

Robert Kaplan notwithstanding, we can get to an ethic appropriate for leadership in world politics without declaring ourselves pagans. And as Brian C. Anderson has argued in a thoughtful review of Kaplan's book, we can get there while retaining "a crucial place for a transcendent *ought* that limits the evil governments can do."[19] An ethic for world politics can be built against an ampler moral horizon than Robert Kaplan suggests.

A recent statement on the post-September 11 situation by sixty American scholars, representing a broad spectrum of American religious conviction and political opinion, challenges Kaplan's pagan ethos on similar grounds. The statement, called "What We're Fighting For: A Letter from America," is worth a lengthy quote:

> We recognize that war is terrible, representative finally of human political failure. We also know that the line separating good and evil does not run between one society and another, much less between one religion and another; ultimately that line runs through the middle of every human heart. Finally, those of us—Jews, Christians, Muslims, and others—who are people of faith recognize our responsibilities, stated in our holy scriptures, to love mercy and to do all in our power to prevent war and live in peace.
>
> Yet reason and careful moral reflection also teach us that there are times when the first and most important reply to evil is to stop it. There are times when waging war is not only morally permitted, but morally necessary, as a response to calamitous acts of violence, hatred, and injustice. This is one of those times.
>
> The idea of a "just" war is broadly based, with roots in many of the world's diverse religious and secular moral traditions. Jewish, Christian, and Muslim teachings, for example, all contain serious reflections on the definition of a just war. To be sure, some people, often in the name of realism, insist that war is essentially a realm of self-interest and necessity, making most attempts at moral analysis irrelevant. We disagree. Moral inarticulacy in the face of war is itself a moral stance—one that rejects the possibility of reason, accepts normlessness in international affairs, and capitulates to cynicism. To seek to apply objective moral reasoning to war is to defend the possibility of civil society and a world community based on justice.[20]

This last claim is crucial—and it is typically missing from the new Catholic default position. For the past quarter century or more, Catholic just war thought and Catholic commentary informed by it have focused so intently on *in bello* questions of proportionality and discrimination (noncombatant immunity) as to forget that, in the classic

Catholic tradition, *war is a moral enterprise*: not only in the assessment of its conduct, but just as importantly in the definition of its legitimate political ends. This forgetting may help explain why so many Catholic leaders and commentators avoided the word "war" (preferring "tragedy" or "crime") in the immediate aftermath of September 11. When we forget that the basic distinction in the just war tradition is the Augustinian distinction between *bellum* and *duellum*, between the use of armed force for legitimate public ends and the illegitimate use of violence for private ends, we can forget that, for the Catholic Church, war is emphatically not a term that implies the abandonment of moral reason; "war" *is* a term of moral reason.[21]

Indeed, the just war tradition is best understood as a sustained intellectual effort to relate the morally legitimate use of proportionate and discriminate military force to morally worthy political ends. In this sense (although Robert Kaplan fails to recognize it), the just war tradition shares Clausewitz's view of the relationship between war and politics: Unless war is an extension of politics, it is simply wickedness. For Kaplan, Clausewitz may be an archetypal "pagan." But on this crucial point, at least, Clausewitz was articulating a thoroughly Catholic view of the matter. Good ends do not justify any means. But as Father Murray was wont to say, "If the end doesn't justify the means, what does?" In the classic Catholic tradition of statecraft, what "justifies" the resort to proportionate and discriminate armed force—what makes the just war tradition make moral sense—is precisely the morally worthy political ends being defended and/or advanced. That is why the just war tradition is a theory of statecraft, not simply a method of casuistry.

The Structure of Just War Analysis

In 1983, the Catholic bishops of the United States issued a pastoral letter entitled "The Challenge of Peace: God's Promise and Our Response" (TCOP). The letter was newsworthy at the time for its discussion of the morality of nuclear deterrence. Its long-term impact on Catholic life and thought in the United States has taken a different form, however. For among its many other assertions, TCOP taught that the just war tradition creates "a set of rigorous conditions which must be met if the decision to go to war is to be morally permissible. Such a decision ... requires extraordinarily strong reasons for overriding the presumption *in favor of peace and against war.*"[22]

This notion of a "presumption against violence" as the starting point of just war analysis was the product of a rereading of intellectual history wedded to several contemporary concerns: the threat to human survival posed by massive numbers of nuclear and other weapons of mass destruction; the determination in some quarters to integrate elements of the pacifist conscience into mainstream Catholic thought and life; and the politics of the moment, in which fears of the alleged bellicosity of the Reagan administration were widespread in U.S. Catholic peace-activist circles. However we parse its origins, however, the "presumption against violence" is perhaps the most enduring effect of TCOP, in the Church in the United States and elsewhere.[23] Indeed, the "presumption against violence" is the core claim in the new Catholic "default position." In the aftermath of September 11, the "presumption against violence" was cited on numerous occasions.[24]

The difficulty is that the classic Catholic just war tradition does not begin with a "presumption against violence." To suggest that it does inverts the structure of the moral analysis in ways that inevitably lead to dubious judgments and distorted perceptions of reality.

The classic Catholic tradition, whose roots are found in Augustine, begins with the presumption—better, the moral judgment—that rightly constituted publicly authority is under a strict moral *obligation* to defend the security of those for whom it has assumed responsibility, even if this puts the magistrate's own life in jeopardy. That is why Saint Thomas locates his discussion of *bellum iustum* within the treatise on charity in the *Summa Theologiae.*[25] That is why the late Paul Ramsey, who revivified Protestant just war thinking in America after World War II, described the just war tradition as an explication of the public implications of the Great Commandment of love of neighbor (even as he argued that the commandment sets limits to the use of armed force).[26]

The leading Anglophone scholar of the just war tradition, James Turner Johnson, has flatly denied that the tradition begins with a "presumption against violence." To argue this, he suggests, is to falsify history and to distort the intellectual structure of the just war tradition.[27]

If the just war tradition is a theory of statecraft, to reduce it to means-tests that begin with a presumption against violence is to begin at the wrong place. The just war tradition *begins somewhere else*: It begins by defining the moral responsibilities of governments, continues with the definition of morally appropriate political ends, and then takes up the question of means. By reversing the analysis of means and ends, the "presumption against violence" starting point tends to collapse *bellum* into *duellum* and ends up conflating the ideas of "violence" and "war" (another typical move in the new Catholic default position). The net result is that warfare is stripped of its distinctive moral texture. Indeed, in certain extreme cases within the new Catholic default position, the very notion of warfare as having a "moral texture" seems to have been forgotten.

The "presumption against violence" starting point is not only fraught with historical and methodological difficulties; it is also theologically dubious. For its effect in moral analysis is to invert the tradition, such that *in bello* questions of proportionality and discrimination take theological precedence over what were traditionally assumed to be the prior *ad bellum* questions: just cause, right intention, competent authority, reasonable chance of success, proportionality of ends, and last resort. This inversion explains why, in much of the Catholic commentary after September 11, considerable attention was paid to the necessity of avoiding indiscriminate noncombatant casualties in the war against terrorism, while little attention was paid to the *prior* question of the moral *obligation* of government to pursue national security and world order, both of which were directly threatened by the terrorist networks.

This inversion is also theologically problematic because it places the heaviest burden of moral analysis on what are inevitably contingent judgments. There is nothing wrong, per se, with contingent judgments; but they are *contingent*. In the nature of the case, we can have less surety about *in bello* proportion and discrimination than we can about what have previously been assumed to be the prior *ad bellum* questions.[28] As I hope I have shown above, the tradition logically starts with *ad bellum* questions because the just war tradition is a tradition of statecraft: a tradition that attempts to define morally acceptable political ends. But there is also a theo-logic that gives priority to the *ad bellum* questions, for these are the questions on which we can have some measure of moral clarity.

The claim that a presumption against violence is at the root of the just war tradition cannot be sustained historically or theologically. As it has worked itself out empirically (and, one might almost say, psychologically), it has contributed immeasurably to the new Catholic default position, which in turn shed little light on the grave issues posed by September 11.[29] Thus the retrieval, renewal, and extension of Catholic just war thinking must include a recovery of the classic structure of the just war argument. How that structure might be developed is a topic I shall address in a moment.

The Peace We Are to Seek

Fifteen years ago, before I had learned something about literary marketing, I published a book entitled Tranquillitas Ordinis*: The Present Failure and Future Promise of American Catholic Thought on War and Peace.*[30] In that book, I argued that the just war tradition, as a theory of statecraft, contained within itself a *ius ad pacem* in addition to the classic *ius ad bellum* and *ius in bello*. By *ius ad pacem*, I meant a concept of the peace that could and should be sought through the instruments of politics, including, if necessary, the use of armed force. Like the just war tradition itself, the classic Catholic concept of peace finds its roots in Augustine: Peace is *tranquillitas ordinis*, the "tranquillity of order," or as I preferred to render it, the peace of "dynamic and rightly ordered political community."

In classic Catholic thinking about statecraft, "peace" is not a matter of the individual's right relationship with God, nor is it a matter of seeking a world without conflict. The former is a question of interior conversion (which by definition has nothing to do with politics), and the latter is impossible in a world forever marked, even after its redemption, by the *mysterium iniquitatis*. In the appropriate political sense of the term, peace is, rather, *tranquillitas ordinis*: the order created by just political community and mediated through law.

This is, admittedly, a humbler sort of peace. It coexists with broken hearts and wounded souls. It is to be built in a world in which swords have not been beaten into plowshares, but remain sheathed, we pray, but ready to be unsheathed in the defense of innocents. Its advantage, as Augustine understood, is that it is the form of peace that can be built through the instruments of politics.

In contemporary Catholic thought, which has been deeply influenced by John XXIII and his 1963 encyclical *Pacem in Terris*, this peace of *tranquillitas ordinis* is composed of justice and freedom. The peace of order, as the Catholic Church understands it, is not the eerily quiet and sullen "peace" of a well-run authoritarian regime; it is a peace built on foundations of legal, commutative, and distributive justice. It is the peace of an order that reflects the core Catholic social ethical principles of personalism, the common good, subsidiarity, and solidarity. It is a peace in which freedom, especially religious freedom, flourishes. The defense of basic human rights is thus an integral component of "work for peace."[31]

This is the peace that has been achieved in and among the developed democracies. It is the peace that has been built in recent decades between such ancient antagonists as France and Germany. It is the peace that we defend within the richly diverse political community of the United States, and between ourselves and our neighbors and allies. It is the peace that we are now defending in the war against global terrorism and against aggressor states seeking weapons of mass destruction.

International terrorism of the sort we have seen since the late 1960s, and of which we had a direct national experience on September 11, is a deliberate assault, through the murder of innocents, on the very possibility of order in world affairs. That is why the terror networks must be dismantled or destroyed. The peace of order is also under grave threat when vicious, aggressive regimes acquire weapons of mass destruction which we must assume, on the basis of their treatment of their own citizens, they will not hesitate to use against others. That is why there is a moral *obligation* to ensure that this lethal combination of irrational and aggressive regimes, weapons of mass destruction, and credible delivery systems does not go unchallenged. That is why there is a moral *obligation* to rid the world of this threat to the peace and security of all. Peace, rightly understood, demands it.

In eradicating global terrorism and denying aggressive regimes' weapons of mass destruction, we are addressing the most threatening problems of global *dis*-order that must be resolved if the peace of order, the peace of *tranquillitas ordinis*, is to be secured in as wide a part of the world as possible in the twenty-first century.

The Development of the Tradition

In addition to *retrieving* the idea of the just war tradition as a tradition of statecraft, *recovering* the classic structure of just war analysis, and *renewing* the concept of peace as *tranquillitas ordinis*, the Catholic Church today must *develop and extend* the just war tradition to meet the political exigencies of a new century, and to address the international security issues posed by new weapons technologies. Permit me to sketch briefly three areas in which the *ad bellum* (or "war-decision") criteria of the just war tradition require development, even as I suggest what the policy implications of these developments might be in the situation we face after September 11.

Just Cause

In the classic just war tradition, "just cause" was understood as defense against aggression, the recovery of something wrongfully taken, or the punishment of evil. As the tradition has developed since World War II, the latter two notions have been largely displaced, and "defense against aggression" has become the primary, even sole, meaning of "just cause."[32] This theological evolution has parallels in international law: The "defense against aggression" concept of "just cause" shapes Articles 2 and 51 of the Charter of the United Nations. In light of twenty-first-century international security realities, it is imperative to reopen this discussion and to develop the concept of "just cause."

As recently as the Korean War (and, some would argue, the Vietnam War), "defense against aggression" could reasonably be taken to mean a defensive military response to a military aggression already underway. New weapons capabilities and outlaw or "rogue" states require a development of the concept of "defense against aggression." To take an obvious, current example, it makes little moral sense to suggest that the United States must wait until North Korea or Iraq or Iran actually launches a ballistic missile tipped with a nuclear, biological, or chemical weapon of mass destruction before we can legitimately do something about it. Can we not say that, in the hands of certain kinds of states, the mere possession of weapons of mass destruction constitutes an aggression—or, at the very least, an aggression waiting to happen? The "regime factor" is crucial in the moral analysis, for weapons of mass destruction are clearly not aggressions waiting to happen when they are possessed by stable, law-abiding states. No Frenchman goes to bed nervous about Great Britain's nuclear weapons, and no sane Mexican or Canadian worries about a preemptive nuclear attack from the United States. Every sane Israeli, on the other hand, is deeply concerned about the possibility of an Iraq or Iran with nuclear weapons and medium-range ballistic missiles. If the "regime factor" is crucial in the moral analysis, can we not say that preemptive military action to deny the rogue state that kind of destructive capacity would not contravene the "defense against aggression" concept of "just cause"?

I think we can; indeed, I think we must. The post-Westphalian notion that all states are equal and enjoy equal sovereign immunity assumes at least a minimum of acquiescence to minimal international norms of order. Today's rogue states cannot, on the basis of their behavior, be granted that assumption. Therefore, they have forfeited that immunity. The "regime factor" is determinative, in these extreme instances.[33]

The debate over "humanitarian intervention" launched in the 1990s by the Somali famine and the genocidal violence of an imploding Yugoslavia also remains to be completed and bears on the development of the just cause criterion. Addressing the U.N. Food and Agricultural Organization on December 5, 1992, Pope John Paul II spoke of humanitarian intervention as a "duty of justice" in cases of impending or actual genocide, or mass starvation caused by political upheaval or ethnic conflict. But the Pope did not specify precisely why this is a moral duty, on whom that duty falls, or how it is to be fulfilled. Development is, again, required.

Can we argue that the mass murder of innocents (or the starvation of entire peoples) constitutes an unacceptable affront to world order and a challenge to international security that must be met? That might have arguably been true in Yugoslavia, but it seems a stretch in regions more marginal to mainstream world politics—no matter how much we deplore (as we should) situations like the Somali famine or the genocide in Rwanda. If, as the Pope proposes, there is a "duty" of humanitarian intervention in these cases, then perhaps it is time to revisit the old notion of "punishment for evil" as satisfying the criterion of "just cause" for the resort to armed force in the vindication of justice and the peace of order. That would not resolve other questions posed by the assertion of a "duty" of humanitarian intervention, but it would get the just cause debate tethered to what are likely to be an increasing number of "real world" situations in the twenty-first century.[34]

Finally, on this matter of "just cause," the tradition needs development in terms of its concept of the relevant actors in world politics. Since September 11, exponents of the new Catholic "default position" have sometimes objected to describing our response to the international terrorist networks as "war" because, they argue, al-Qaeda and similar networks are not states, and only states can, or should, wage "war," properly understood. There is an important point at stake here, but the "default position" misapplies it.

Limiting the legitimate use of armed force to those international actors who are recognized in international law and custom as exercising "sovereignty" has been one of the principle accomplishments of just war thinking as it has shaped world political culture and law; over a period of centuries, the classic distinction between *bellum* and *duellum* has been concretized in international law. At the same time, however, I would argue that it does not fudge or blur this crucial distinction to recognize that al-Qaeda and similar networks function like states, even if they lack certain of the attributes and trappings of sovereignty traditionally understood. Indeed, terrorist organizations provide a less ambiguous example of a legitimate military target, because, unlike conventional states (which are always admixtures of good and evil, against whom military action sometimes threatens the good as well as the evil), the "parasite states" that are international terrorist organizations are unmitigated evils whose only purpose is wickedness—the slaughter of innocents for ignoble political ends.[35] Thus the exigencies of the current situation require us to think outside the Westphalian box, so to speak, but to do so in such a way as to avoid dismantling de facto the distinction between *bellum* and *duellum*.

Competent Authority

Two questions involving the *ad bellum* criterion of "competent authority" have been raised since September 11: the question of the relationship between a government's domestic and foreign policy and its legitimacy as a belligerent, and the question of whether "competent authority" now resides in the United Nations only. Let me address these briefly in turn.

One of the more distasteful expressions of the new Catholic "default position" post-September 11 could be found in suggestions that there were "root causes" to terrorism that not only explained the resort to mass violence against innocents but made the use of such violence humanly plausible, if not morally justifiable. The corollary to this was the suggestion that the United States had somehow brought September 11 on itself, by reasons of its economic and cultural dominance of the world, its Middle East policy, or some combination thereof. The moral-political implication was that such a misguided government lacked the moral authority to respond to terrorism through the use of armed force.

Here, Lutheran scholar David Yeago has been a wise guide. Writing in the ecumenical journal *Pro Ecclesia*, Yeago clarified an essential point:

> The authority of the government to protect the law-abiding and impose penalties on evil-doers is not a reward for the government's virtue or good conduct.... The protection of citizens and the execution of penalty on peace-breakers is the commission which constitutes government, not a contingent right which it must somehow earn. In the mystery of God's providence, many or indeed most of the institutional bearers of governmental authority are unworthy of it, often flagrantly so, themselves stained with crime. But this does not make it any less the vocation of government to protect the innocent and punish evil-doers. A government which refused to safeguard citizens and exercise judgment on wrong out of a sense of the guilt of past crime would only add the further crime of dereliction of duty to its catalog of offenses.[36]

The pursuit of national interest is often understood by exponents of the new Catholic "default position" to be an exercise in amorality—a notion they have, oddly, picked up from certain streams of foreign policy realism. A developed Catholic just war tradition, understanding itself as a theory of statecraft, would insist that the very definition of national interest is an exercise in moral judgment. For among the primary elements of the American "national interest" are, in the first instance, the defense of the core values of American democracy and the institutions that give political content to those values, and, in the second instance, the defense of a measure of order in international public life, sufficient so that those committed to the rule of law can live in the peace of "order." One of the tasks that Catholic just war thinking should take up is to refine our moral understanding of "national interest" and demonstrate the implausibility of the Realpolitik notion of the "amorality" of "national interest."

Finally, on this question of competent authority, there is the question of alliances and international organizations. Must any legitimate military action be sanctioned by the U.N. Security Council? Or, if not that, then is the United States obliged, not simply as a matter of political prudence but as a matter of moral principle, to gain the agreement of allies (or, more broadly, "coalition partners") to any use of armed force in response to terrorism, or any military action against aggressive regimes with weapons of mass destruction?

The manifest inability of the United Nations to handle large-scale international security questions suggests that assigning a moral veto over U.S. military action on these fronts to the Security Council would be a mistake. Building coalitions of support for dismantling the international terror networks and denying rogue states lethal weapons capacities is politically desirable (and in some instances militarily essential). But it may not be morally imperative from a just war point of view. The United States has a unique responsibility for leadership in the war against terrorism and the struggle for world order; that is not a statement of hubris but of empirical fact. That responsibility may have to be exercised unilaterally on occasion. Defining the boundaries of unilateral action while defending its legitimacy under certain circumstances is one task for a developing Catholic just war tradition.

Last Resort

In the new Catholic default position, the classic *ad bellum* criterion of "last resort" is usually understood in mathematical terms: The use of proportionate and discriminate armed force is the last point in a series of options, and prior, nonmilitary options (legal, diplomatic, economic, etc.) must be serially exhausted before the criterion of last resort is satisfied. This is both an excessively mechanistic understanding of last resort and a prescription for danger.

The case of international terrorism again compels a development of this *ad bellum* criterion. For what does it mean to say that all nonmilitary options have been tried and found wanting when we are confronted with a new and lethal type of international actor, which recognizes no other form of power except the use of violence and which is largely immune (unlike a conventional state) to international legal, diplomatic, and/or economic pressures? The charge that U.S. military action after September 11 was morally dubious because all other possible means of redress had not been tried and found wanting misreads the nature of terrorist organizations and networks. The "last" in "last resort" can mean "only," in circumstances where there is plausible reason to believe that nonmilitary actions are unavailable or unavailing.

As for rogue states developing or deploying weapons of mass destruction, a developed just war tradition would recognize that here, too, "last resort" cannot be understood in mathematical terms, as the terminal point of a lengthy series of nonmilitary alternatives. In the case of Iraq, for example, it would always be possible to imagine trying to send in one more international team of weapons inspectors; meanwhile, as the Ba'athist regime stalls on accepting the conditions laid down by the United Nations, the regime's weapons programs grind ahead, increasing the danger to America, its allies, and world order every day. Can we not say that "last resort" has been satisfied in those cases when a rogue state has made plain, by its conduct, that it holds international law in contempt and that no diplomatic solution to the threat it poses is likely, and when it can be demonstrated that the threat the rogue state poses is intensifying?

Some states, because of the regime's aggressive intent and the lack of effective internal political controls on giving lethal effect to that intent, cannot be permitted to acquire weapons of mass destruction. Denying them those weapons through proportionate and discriminate armed force—even displacing those regimes—can, I suggest, be an exercise in the defense of the peace of order, within the boundaries of a developed just war tradition. Until such point as the international political community has evolved to the degree that international organizations can effectively disarm such regimes, the responsibility for the defense of order in these extreme circumstances will lie elsewhere.

An Argument That Cannot Be Avoided

In his *Small Catechism*, Martin Luther suggested that one positive meaning of the commandment against lying is that the Christian ought to put the best construction on everything. Following that counsel, we should assume that one motivation underlying the new Catholic default position is the religious and moral intuition that, in the third millennium of Christian history, humanity ought to be able to develop a more satisfactory way to handle conflict than through organized mass violence. That admirable and understandable intuition, forged in the fires of the bloody twentieth century, has also been influenced by the success of the nonviolent Revolution of 1989 in central and eastern Europe and other late twentieth-century examples of profound and desirable political change effected through nonviolent means.

This should not be dismissed entirely as romanticism or frivolous utopianism, although elements of both maladies all too frequently shape the new Catholic default position. The hope for a better future—the hope that, as the Holy Father put it at the United Nations in 1995, "the tears of this century have prepared the ground for a new springtime of the human spirit"—should not be extinguished in the name of a realism that, on closer examination, is actually a tired cynicism.[37]

The quest for peace, however, must be informed by the moral wisdom of the just war tradition, rightly understood in its history and its logic. There is no way around this argument. If international politics is ever "domesticated"—if a genuine, law-governed international political community were to emerge over time (which the Catholic tradition of statecraft and the modern papal magisterium both suggest is our goal)—it would have to wrestle with the questions I have posed above, just as much as we do in this age of stable, unstable, and crumbling nation states. For the moral "logic" within the criteria of the just war tradition is also the moral "logic" that must guide any meaningful political action. To put it another way, the just war criteria are the "moral economy" that tempers and orders the use of armed force, which, this side of the coming Kingdom, is an inescapable part of all political life.

To suggest that the just war tradition is obsolete is to suggest that politics—the organization of human life into purposeful political communities—is obsolete. To reduce the just war tradition to an algebra is to deny the tradition its capacity to shed light on the irreducible moral component of all political action. What we must do, in this generation, is to retrieve, renew, and extend the just war tradition to take account of the new political and technological realities of the twenty-first century. September 11 and what has followed have demonstrated just how urgent that task is.

Let us get on with it.

ACKNOWLEDGMENTS

I am grateful to the late Cardinal William Keeler, then the Archbishop of Baltimore, and to Father Robert Leavitt, S.S., then the president-rector of St. Mary's Seminary and University, for the invitation to deliver "The Vocation of Theology in the Image of John Paul II" at my undergraduate alma mater. A similar analysis of theology's debt to the inspiration of John Paul II was given in commencement addresses delivered at Sacred Heart Major Seminary in Detroit, at the invitation of then-Bishop Allen Vigneron, and at Saint Vincent Seminary in Latrobe, Pennsylvania, at the invitation of the late Archabbot Douglas R. Nowicki, O.S.B.

Monsignor Milam Joseph, then the president of the University of Dallas, invited me to give the address entitled "Christian Humanism vs. Inhuman Humanism."

Father Terence Henry, T.O.R., then the president of the Franciscan University of Steubenville, invited me to deliver the commencement address entitled "No Ordinary People," which in a somewhat different form I also delivered at Anna Maria College in Paxton, Massachusetts, at the invitation of President William D. McGarry, and at Felician College in Lodi, New Jersey, at the invitation of Sister Theresa Mary Martin, C.S.S.F.

Dr. Thomas Powell, then the president of Mount St. Mary's University, invited me to deliver the commencement address entitled "Making Your Soul." The address subsequently appeared in *National Review Online*, May 12, 2009, under the title "Un-Obama Commencement Address."

Stephen Minnis, president of Benedictine College, invited me to deliver the commencement address entitled "Defending Religious Freedom in Full." I struck similar themes in a commencement address given at Thomas More College of Liberal Arts in Merrimack, New Hampshire, at the invitation of college president William Edmund Fahey.

Then-Father Borys Gudziak, president of the Ukrainian Catholic University, invited me to deliver the commencement address entitled "The Truths about Truth."

Then-Bishop Kevin Farrell and Dr. Thomas Keefe, then the president of the University of Dallas, invited me to deliver the commencement address entitled "Agents of the New Evangelization."

Dr. Tina Holland, president of Franciscan Missionaries of Our Lady University (then known as Our Lady of the Lake College), invited me to deliver the commencement address entitled "More Than Stardust."

Kevin Cieply, then the dean of the Ave Maria School of Law, invited me to deliver the commencement address entitled "Lawyering as a Vocation." The address was published in *National Review Online* on May 13, 2018, under the title "The Vocation of Law."

Deacon Brad Watkins, headmaster of St. Thomas More Academy (STMA) in Raleigh, North Carolina, invited me to address the graduation ceremonies of the academy's Class of 2024, which included my grandson, William Spaeder, and a remarkable group of young people. Thanks, too, to Robert Luddy, chairman of the academy's board of directors, whose philanthropy has made STMA and other educational institutions on the front lines of American educational reform possible.

Archeparch Borys Gudziak of the Ukrainian Greek Catholic Archeparchy of Philadelphia invited me to give the address entitled "Twentieth-Century Witness and Twenty-First-Century Mission."

The late, great Peter L. Berger invited me to participate in a Boston University conference on religion, modernity, and pluralism for which I wrote "Ironies of Modern Catholic History"—which later grew into my book *The Irony of Modern Catholic History* (Basic Books, 2019). The lecture was subsequently published in *Society* 53 (Spring 2016) under the title, "Modernity, Pluralism, and Catholicism."

My lecture entitled "The Catholic University of the Twenty-First Century" was arranged by friends in FASTA, the *Fraternidad de Agrupaciones Santo Tomás de Aquino*, and by Mr. Mario Paredes.

"On Beauty," "Voltaire Confounded: The Church in Defense of Reason," "*Veritatis Splendor*: A Gift to the Church and the World," and "John Paul II, Doctor of the Church?" were commissioned by the organizing committee for the annual John Paul II Days hosted by various institutions of higher learning in Kraków, in which Dr. Teresa Malecka played a key role.

"John Paul II, the Priority of Culture, and the Contemporary Culture Wars" was the result of the invitation extended to me to teach at Rome's Angelicum by Dr. Dariusz Karłowicz of the institute *Teologia Politczyna* in Warsaw and Father Thomas Joseph White, O.P., the Angelicum's rector.

The origins of "Benedict XVI: Voice in the Secular Wilderness" are described in the note appended to the text.

Jean Duchesne, longtime aide to Cardinal Jean-Marie Lustiger, arranged for me to deliver the lecture on that noble churchman and the future of the West.

The aforementioned Father Thomas Joseph White, O.P., invited me to offer the opening lecture at an Angelicum conference on John Henry Newman held the day before Newman's canonization, which appears here as "Lead, Kindly Light: John Henry Newman and Us."

The faculty and administration of Ave Maria University were kind enough to ask me to conclude a conference on an old friend with the lecture "Michael Novak: An American Catholic Achievement."

"The National Interest and the National Purpose: Moral Reasoning and U.S. Foreign Policy" was given as Baylor University's Laura B. Jackson Endowed Lecture in World Affairs, at the invitation of professors David Smith and Thomas Hibbs.

Douglas Kmiec, then-dean of the Columbus School of Law at the Catholic University of America, invited me to give the school's annual Pope John XXIII Lecture, which appears here as "The Just War Tradition and the World after September 11." The lecture was subsequently published in the *Catholic University of America Law Review* 51:3 (Spring 2002).

I am grateful to these men and women for the invitations to address their faculty and students and for the hospitality extended to me on those occasions, and to the editors of the aforementioned publications for their cooperation in reprinting these materials.

Helen Schlueter helped prepare the manuscript for publication. I am also grateful to my colleagues at the Ethics and Public Policy Center, my professional home for thirty-five years, for their friendship and an abundance of simulating conversations.

It is with pleasure and gratitude that I dedicate this book to two exemplary educators, Fran and Mary Kane, friends for over a half-century.

George Weigel
October 22, 2024
Memorial of Pope Saint John Paul II

ENDNOTES

Preface

1. This demand was delivered by one Johannah King-Slutzky (a name beyond the parodic talents of Charles Dickens, Anthony Trollope, or P. G. Wodehouse), whose biography page on the website of Columbia University included this description of her doctoral research, which deserves preservation in a time capsule:

> My dissertation is on fantasies of limitless energy in the transatlantic Romantic imagination from 1760–1860. My goal is to write a prehistory of metabolic rift, Marx's term for the disruption of energy circuits caused by industrialization under capitalism. I am particularly interested in theories of the imagination and poetry as interpreted through a Marxian lens in order to update and propose an alternative to historicist ideological critiques of the Romantic imagination.

The Vocation of Theology

1. On these points, see Hans Urs von Balthasar, *In the Fullness of Faith: On the Centrality of the Distinctively Catholic* (San Francisco: Ignatius Press, 1988), pp. 55–57.
2. See Hans Urs von Balthasar, *Theo-Drama IV: The Action* (San Francisco: Ignatius Press, 1994), pp. 92–93.
3. John Paul II, Address to the Pontifical Gregorian University (December 15, 1979), no. 4, https://www.vatican.va/content/john-paul-ii/it/speeches/1979/december/documents/hf_jp-ii_spe_19791215_universita-gregoriana.html.
4. Ibid.
5. Ibid.
6. Ibid., no. 9.
7. Ibid.
8. Ibid.
9. Ibid., quoting Saint Thomas Aquinas, *Summa Theologiae* II-II, q. 162, a. 3, ad 1.
10. From the first line of Hopkins' poem "God's Grandeur."

Christian Humanism vs. Inhuman Humanism

1. John Paul II, Address to the Fiftieth General Assembly of the United Nations Organization (United Nations Headquarters, New York, October 5, 1995), no. 2, https://www.vatican.va/content/john-paul-ii/en/speeches/1995/october/documents/hf_jp-ii_spe_05101995_address-to-uno.html.
2. Henri de Lubac, S.J., *The Drama of Atheist Humanism*, 1st English ed. (London: Sheed & Ward, 1949; repr., San Francisco: Ignatius Press, 1995).
3. On these points, see ibid.
4. Aldous Huxley, *Brave New World* (London: Chatto & Windus, 1932).
5. See C. S. Lewis, "The Weight of Glory," preached originally as a sermon in the Church of St. Mary the Virgin, Oxford, June 8, 1942; published in *Theology*, November 1941, and by the S.P.C.K., 1942, https://www.doxaweb.com/assets/weight_of_glory.pdf.

No Ordinary People

1. Roger Kahn, *The Boys of Summer* (New York: Signet, 1973), p. 358.

2. C. S. Lewis, "The Weight of Glory," preached originally as a sermon in the Church of St. Mary the Virgin, Oxford, June 8, 1942; published in *Theology*, November 1941, and by the S.P.C.K., 1942, https://www.doxaweb.com/assets/weight_of_glory.pdf.

3. Ibid.

Defending Religious Freedom in Full: A Generation's Challenge

1. John Courtney Murray, S.J., *We Hold These Truths: Catholic Reflections on the American Proposition* (Garden City, N.Y.: Doubleday Image Books, 1964), p. 52.

2. Dr. King was arguing in the terms of Saint Thomas Aquinas, in Martin Luther King, Jr., "Letter from Birmingham Jail," April 16, 1963, published in *The Christian Century*, June 12, 1963, p. 769, https://www.christiancentury.org/sites/default/files/downloads/resources/mlk-letter.pdf.

3. John Paul II, Address to the Fiftieth General Assembly of the United Nations Organization (United Nations Headquarters, New York, October 5, 1995), no. 3, https://www.vatican.va/content/john-paul-ii/en/speeches/1995/october/documents/hf_jp-ii_spe_05101995_address-to-uno.html.

4. Hillary Rodham Clinton, "Remarks on the Human Rights Agenda for the 21st Century" (Georgetown University's Gaston Hall, Washington, D.C., December 14, 2009), available on the website of the U.S. Department of State, https://2009-2017.state.gov/secretary/20092013clinton/rm/2009a/12/133544.htm.

The Truths about Truth

1. See John Paul II, encyclical *Fides et Ratio* (September 14, 1998), https://www.vatican.va/content/john-paul-ii/en/encyclicals/documents/hf_jp-ii_enc_14091998_fides-et-ratio.html.

2. Cardinal Joseph Ratzinger, Homily at the Mass *Pro Eligendo Romano Pontifice* (For the Election of the Roman Pontiff) (St. Peter's Basilica, April 18, 2005), https://www.vatican.va/gpII/documents/homily-pro-eligendo-pontifice_20050418_en.html#:~:text=We%20are%20building%20a%20dictatorship%20of%20relativism%20that,man.%20He%20is%20the%20measure%20of%20true%20humanism.

3. Francis, Address to the Diplomatic Corps Accredited to the Holy See (March 22, 2013), https://www.vatican.va/content/francesco/en/speeches/2013/march/documents/papa-francesco_20130322_corpo-diplomatico.html.

Agents of the New Evangelization

1. John Paul II, *Novo Millennio Ineunte* (January 6, 2001), nos. 1, 15, https://www.vatican.va/content/john-paul-ii/en/apost_letters/2001/documents/hf_jp-ii_apl_20010106_novo-millennio-ineunte.html.

2. Ibid., no. 17.

3. See Pope Francis, *Evangelii Gaudium* (November 23, 2013), 27.

4. G. K. Chesterton, *Orthodoxy*, chap. 4, "The Ethics of Elfland."

5. Henri de Lubac, S.J., *The Drama of Atheist Humanism* (San Francisco: Ignatius Press, 1995).

More Than Stardust

1. Cited in William D. Miller, *A Harsh and Dreadful Love; Dorothy Day and the Catholic Worker Movement* (New York: Liveright, 1973), p. 221.

Lawyering as a Vocation

1. Martin Luther King, Jr., "Letter from Birmingham Jail," April 16, 1963, https://minio.la.utexas.edu/webeditor-files/coretexts/pdf/1963_mlk_letter.pdf (source is from Teaching AmericanHistory.org).

2. On these points, see Russell Hittinger, "Pope Leo XIII," in *The Teachings of Modern Roman Catholicism on Law, Politics and Human Nature*, eds. John Witte, Jr., and Frank S. Alexander (New York: Columbia University Press, 2007), pp. 48–55.

3. Cardinal Joseph Ratzinger, Homily at the Mass *Pro Eligendo Romano Pontifice* (For the Election of the Roman Pontiff) (St. Peter's Basilica, April 18, 2005), https://www.vatican.va/gpII/documents/homily-pro-eligendo-pontifice_20050418_en.html#:~:text=We%20are%20building%20a%20dictatorship%20of%20relativism%20that,man.%20He%20is%20the%20measure%20of%20true%20humanism.

Your Own Westerplatte

1. John Henry Newman, *Meditations on Christian Doctrine*, Part III, March 7, 1848, https://www.newmanreader.org/works/meditations/meditations9.html.

2. John Paul II, Homily during his Apostolic Journey to Poland (June 12, 1987), https://www.vatican.va/content/john-paul-ii/it/homilies/1987/documents/hf_jp-ii_hom_19870612_giovani-danzica.html, my translation.

Twentieth-Century Witness and Twenty-First-Century Mission: Eastern Catholics and the Universal Church

1. Robert Louis Wilken, *The Spirit of Early Christian Thought: Seeking the Face of God* (New Haven: Yale University Press, 2003), p. 35.

2. Ibid.

3. Ibid.

4. Cap. 9, 223: *Patrologia graeca*, 32:110, cited in Office of Readings for Tuesday of the Seventh Week of Lent in *The Liturgy of the Hours II* (New York: Catholic Book Publishing, 1976), p. 976.

5. Vatican II, Pastoral Constitution on the Church in the Modern World *Gaudium et Spes* (December 7, 1965), no. 22, https://www.vatican.va/archive/hist_councils/ii_vatican_council/documents/vat-ii_const_19651207_Gaudium-et-spes_en.html.

6. Cited in *Catechism of the Catholic Church*, no. 690.

7. *Catechism of the Catholic Church*, no. 703.

8. John Paul II, *Novo Millennio Ineunte* (January 6, 2001), nos. 1, 15, https://www.vatican.va/content/john-paul-ii/en/apost_letters/2001/documents/hf_jp-ii_apl_20010106_novo-millennio-ineunte.html.

Ironies of Modern Catholic History: The Church and Pluralism

1. See Peter L. Berger, "The Pluralist Phenomenon", *The Many Altars of Modernity: Toward a Paradigm for Religion in a Pluralist Age* (New York: De Gruyter Mouton, 2014).

2. The classic work here is Robert A. Graham, S.J., *Vatican Diplomacy: A Study of Church and State on the International Plane* (Princeton: Princeton University Press, 1959).

3. See Gertrude Himmelfarb, *The Roads to Modernity: The British, French, and American Enlightenments* (New York: Alfred A. Knopf, 2004).

4. See Eamon Duffy, *The Stripping of the Altars: Traditional Religion in England 1400–1580* (New Haven: Yale University Press, 1992).

5. See Michael Gross, *The War against Catholicism: Liberalism and the Anti-Catholic Imagination in Nineteenth-Century Germany* (Ann Arbor: University of Michigan Press, 2005), and

Owen Chadwick, *A History of the Popes 1830–1914* (Oxford: Oxford University Press, 2003), pp. 254–65, 285–303.

6. J. N. D. Kelly, *The Oxford Dictionary of Popes* (New York: Oxford University Press, 1986), p. 308.

7. At one point in his brief exile, Pius IX became the first pope to set foot on sovereign American territory, when he visited U.S.S. *Constitution*, popularly known as "Old Ironsides," which was then keeping a watch on European affairs at the Italian harbor of Gaeta. When the armed forces of the *Risorgimento* closed in on the remaining papal forces at Rome's Porta Pia, Pius IX ordered his troops to fire one volley over the heads of their Italian foes "for honor's sake" and then lay down their arms.

8. See Russell Hittinger, "Two Modernisms, Two Thomisms: Reflections on the Centenary of Pius X's Letter against the Modernists," *Nova et Vetera* 5, no. 4 (2007): 843–80, and Russell Hittinger, "Pope Leo XIII," in *The Teachings of Modern Roman Catholicism on Law, Politics, and Human Nature*, eds. John Witte, Jr., and Frank S. Alexander (New York: Columbia University Press, 2007), pp. 39–75.

9. I describe the broad outlines of the evolution of this tradition in *Against the Grain: Christianity and Democracy, War and Peace* (New York: Crossroad, 2008), pp. 11–36.

10. See George Weigel, *Soul of the World: Notes on the Future of Public Catholicism* (Grand Rapids, Mich.: Eerdmans, 1996), pp. 99–124.

11. See, for example, John XXIII's noteworthy opening address to the Council, *Gaudet Mater Ecclesia* (October 11, 1962), https://jakomonchak.files.wordpress.com/2012/10/john-xxiii-opening-speech.pdf.

12. For more on what the Pastoral Constitution "missed," see George Weigel, "Rescuing *Gaudium et Spes*: The New Humanism of John Paul II," *Nova et Vetera* 8, no. 2 (2010): 251–67.

13. David Bentley Hart, "Religion in America: Ancient and Modern," *The New Criterion*, March 2004, p. 16.

14. *Gaudium et Spes*, no. 36.

15. Ibid.

16. See John Courtney Murray, *We Hold These Truths: Catholic Reflections on the American Proposition* (Garden City, N.Y.: Doubleday Image Books, 1964), pp. 17–35, 126–39.

17. On *Centesimus Annus, Veritatis Splendor, and Evangelium Vitae*, see George Weigel, *Witness to Hope: The Biography of Pope John Paul II* (New York: HarperCollins, 1999), pp. 612–19, 688–98, 757–60; on *Ecclesia in Europa*, see George Weigel, *The End and the Beginning: Pope John Paul II—The Victory of Freedom, the Last Years, the Legacy* (New York: Doubleday, 2010), pp. 337–41. Benedict XVI's September addresses are discussed below in this lecture.

18. As I wrote at the time, this would seem to mean that nothing of positive consequence for twenty-first-century European public life had happened between Marcus Aurelius and Descartes, which was an awfully long time for nothing to have happened.

19. See J. H. H. Weiler, *Un'Europa cristiana? Un saggio esplorativo* (Milano: Biblioteca Universale Rizoli, 2003).

20. Richard John Neuhaus, *The Naked Public Square: Religion and Democracy in America* (Grand Rapids, Mich.: Wm. B. Eerdmans Publishing, 1984).

21. Benedict XVI, Regensburg Lecture: "Faith, Reason and the University: Memories and Reflections" (September 12, 2006), https://www.vatican.va/content/benedict-xvi/en/speeches/2006/september/documents/hf_ben-xvi_spe_20060912_university-regensburg.html.

22. Benedict XVI, Address to Representatives from the World of Culture (Collège des Bernardins, Paris, September 12, 2008), https://www.vatican.va/content/benedict-xvi/en/speeches/2008/september/documents/hf_ben-xvi_spe_20080912_parigi-cultura.html

http://w2.vatican.va/content/benedict-xvi/en/speeches/2008/september/documents/hf_ben-xvi_spe_20080912_parigi-cultura.html.

23. Benedict XVI, Address to the Representatives of British Society (Westminster Hall, London, September 17, 2010), http://w2.vatican.va/content/benedict-xvi/en/speeches/2010/september/documents/hf_ben-xvi_spe_20100917_societa-civile.html.

24. Benedict XVI, Address to the Members of the German Bundestag (Berlin, September 22, 2011), https://www.vatican.va/content/benedict-xvi/en/speeches/2011/september/documents/hf_ben-xvi_spe_20110922_reichstag-berlin.html.

25. Ibid.

26. Cardinal Joseph Ratzinger, Homily at the Mass *Pro Eligendo Romano Pontifice* (For the Election of the Roman Pontiff) (St. Peter's Basilica, April 18, 2005), https://www.vatican.va/gpII/documents/homily-pro-eligendo-pontifice_20050418_en.html#:~:text=We%20are%20building%20a%20dictatorship%20of%20relativism%20that,man.%20He%20is%20the%20measure%20of%20true%20humanism.

27. Owen Chadwick, *The Secularization of the European Mind in the Nineteenth Century* (Cambridge: Cambridge University Press, 1975).

28. On the German situation, see Dietrich von Hildebrand, *My Battle against Hitler: Faith, Truth, and Defiance in the Shadow of the Third Reich* (New York: Image, 2015). On the antiliberal, antipluralist vision of the French École Nationale des Cadres, see John Hellman, *The Knight-Monks of Vichy France: Uriage, 1940–45* (Montreal and Kingston: McGill-Queen's University Press, 1997).

29. For a more detailed discussion of this shift in Catholic self-understanding, the roots of which also go back to the Leonine Revolution described above, see George Weigel, *Evangelical Catholicism: Deep Reform in the Twenty-First Century Church* (New York: Basic Books, 2013).

The Catholic University of the Twenty-First Century

1. Interview with the author, April 7, 1997.

2. John Paul II, apostolic constitution *Ex Corde Ecclesiae* (August 15, 1990), no. 4, https://www.vatican.va/content/john-paul-ii/en/apost_constitutions/documents/hf_jp-ii_apc_15081990_ex-corde-ecclesiae.html.

3. Ibid.

4. Cited in Henri de Lubac, S.J., *At the Service of the Church: Henri de Lubac Reflects on the Circumstances That Occasioned His Writings* (San Francisco: Ignatius Press, 1993), pp. 171–72.

5. Karol Wojtyła, *The Lublin Lectures and Works on Max Scheler* (Washington, D.C.: Catholic University of America Press, 2023), pp. 195–231.

6. Aldous Huxley, *Brave New World* (New York: Bantam Books, 1968), p. 119.

7. John Paul II, *Novo Millennio Ineunte* (January 6, 2001), nos. 1, 5, https://www.vatican.va/content/john-paul-ii/en/apost_letters/2001/documents/hf_jp-ii_apl_20010106_novo-millennio-ineunte.html.

8. Benedict XVI, Address to Catholic Educators (Catholic University of America, Washington, D.C., April 17, 2008), https://www.vatican.va/content/benedict-xvi/en/speeches/2008/april/documents/hf_ben-xvi_spe_20080417_cath-univ-washington.html.

9. Ibid.

10. John Paul II, encyclical *Fides et Ratio* (September 14, 1998), opening remarks, https://www.vatican.va/content/john-paul-ii/en/encyclicals/documents/hf_jp-ii_enc_14091998_fides-et-ratio.html.

11. Servais Pinckaers, O.P., *The Sources of Christian Ethics* (Washington, D.C.: Catholic University of America Press, 1995), pp. 354–78.

12. Leo XIII, encyclical *Rerum Novarum* (May 15, 1891), https://www.vatican.va/content/leo-xiii/en/encyclicals/documents/hf_l-xiii_enc_15051891_rerum-novarum.html.

13. Pius XI encyclical *Quadragesimo Anno* (May 15, 1931), https://www.vatican.va/content/pius-xi/en/encyclicals/documents/hf_p-xi_enc_19310515_quadragesimo-anno.html.

14. John Paul II, encyclical *Centesimus Annus* (May 1, 1991), https://www.vatican.va/content/john-paul-ii/en/encyclicals/documents/hf_jp-ii_enc_01051991_centesimus-annus.html.

On Beauty: The Forgotten Transcendental in a Post-Cultural World

1. A "post-cultural world" may be contrasted to the "exegetical world" in which Christian art first flourished: "By the age of Justinian, the period when the evidence for Christian veneration of images is most copious, the Roman empire especially in the East was what [Jas] Elsner terms an 'exegetic culture,' that is, as he explains, one in which 'Every event, text and image could be used as an exegesis of one fundamental and real event—namely, the Incarnation as represented by the narrative of Christ's life and Passion.'" (Aidan Nichols, O.P., *Redeeming Beauty: Soundings in Sacral Aesthetics* [Aldershot, England: Ashgate, 2007], p. 30.)

2. The sad truth of the matter is that the "continuum" may be collapsing into a single, pornographic reality. Here is a description of a recent production at the *Komische Oper*, directed by Calixto Bieito:

> Mozart's lighthearted opera *The Abduction from the Seraglio* does not call for a prostitute's nipples to be sliced off and presented to the lead soprano. Nor does it include masturbation, urination as foreplay, or forced oral sex. Europe's new breed of opera directors, however, know better than Mozart what an opera should contain. So not only does the *Abduction* at Berlin's *Komische Oper* feature the aforementioned activities; it also replaces Mozart's graceful ending with a Quentin Tarantino-esque bloodbath and the promise of future perversion....
>
> Other Regietheater directors may not yet have achieved the sheer volume of gratuitous perversion and bloodletting that Bieito managed to cram into his *Abduction*—but their aesthetic obeys the same impulse. Gérard Mortier ... staged a *Fledermaus* at the Salzburg Festival that dragooned Johann Strauss's delightful confection into service as a cocaine-, violence-, and sex-drenched left-wing "critique" of contemporary Austrian politics.... Don Giovanni is almost invariably an offensive slob who masturbates and stuffs himself with junk food and drugs, surrounded by equally repellant psychotics, perverts, and sluts.... Handel's Romans and nobles come accessorized with machine guns, sunglasses, and video cameras, while jerking like rappers to delicate Baroque melodies. (Heather MacDonald, "The Abduction of Opera," *City Journal*, Summer 2007.)

3. Aleksandr Solzehenitsyn, "Nobel Lecture in Literature 1970", The Nobel Prize, https://www.nobelprize.org/prizes/literature/1970/solzhenitsyn/lecture/.

4. One of the key texts here is John Paul II's 1987 Christmas address to the Roman Curia: "Annual Address to the Roman Curia," *L'Osservatore Romano* (English Weekly Edition), January 11, 1988, pp. 6–8.

5. Cited in George Weigel, *Witness to Hope: The Biography of Pope John Paul II* (New York: HarperCollins, 1999), pp. 713–15.

6. John Paul II, *Letter to Artists* (April 4, 1999), no. 7, https://www.vatican.va/content/john-paul-ii/en/letters/1999/documents/hf_jp-ii_let_23041999_artists.html.

7. Paul VI, Address to Artists (December 8, 1965), https://www.vatican.va/content/paul-vi/en/speeches/1965/documents/hf_p-vi_spe_19651208_epilogo-concilio-artisti.html#:~:text=To%20all%20of%20you%2C%20the%20Church%20of%20the,her%20temples%2C%20celebrated%20her%20dogmas%2C%20enriched%20her%20liturgy.

8. Paul VI, Address to the Rulers (December 8, 1965), https://www.vatican.va/content/paul-vi/en/speeches/1965/documents/hf_p-vi_spe_19651208_epilogo-concilio-governanti.html.

9. John Paul II, *Letter to Artists*, no. 2.

10. See ibid., no. 3.

11. Ibid., no. 15.

12. Saint Augustine, *Confessions*, 10.

13. Václav Havel, "The Power of the Powerless," in Václav Havel et al., *The Power of the Powerless: Citizens against the State in Central-Eastern Europe* (Armonk, N.Y.: M.E. Sharpe, 1990), p. 30.

14. On this point, Aidan Nichols notes: "God in himself, of himself, is not only beauty. He is, in a Latin word-form ... *superpulcher*, 'beautiful to excess'. It is because his divine excess of beauty is the cause of all things, the loveliness of each of those things a participated likeness of his own, that there can be innumerable relative beauties without surrender of beauty's objectivity. All of which helps to explain why the beautiful can seem to carry the soul beyond the created realm.... Without the transcendentals we would be immured in our private needs. The transcendentals allow us to communicate in a common intellectual and spiritual meaning." (Nichols, *Redeeming Beauty*, pp. 136–37.)

15. George Weigel, "Tales from the Vienna Woods," *Denver Catholic*, May 31, 2006, https://denvercatholic.org/tales-vienna-woods/.

16. Ibid.

Voltaire Confounded: The Church in Defense of Reason

1. John Paul II, Homily for the Celebration of the Word at Mount Sinai (St. Catherine's Monastery, February 26, 2000), no. 3, http://www.vatican.va/holy_father/john_paul_ii/travels/documents/hf_jp-ii_hom_20000226_sinai_en.html.

2. *Catechism of the Catholic Church*, Glossary.

3. Drew Gilpin Faust, "Installation Address: Unleashing Our Most Ambitious Imaginings" (Harvard University, Cambridge, Mass., October 12, 2007), https://www.harvard.edu/president/speeches-faust/2007/installation-address-unleashing-our-most-ambitious-imaginings/.

4. John Paul II, encyclical *Centesimus Annus* (May 1, 1991), no. 46, https://www.vatican.va/content/john-paul-ii/en/encyclicals/documents/hf_jp-ii_enc_01051991_centesimus-annus.html.

5. Cardinal Joseph Ratzinger first used the phrase "dictatorship of relativism" in his Homily at the Mass *Pro Eligendo Romani Pontificis* (For the Election of the Roman Pontiff), April 18, 2005 (St. Peter's Basilica, April 18, 2005), https://www.vatican.va/gpII/documents/homily-pro-eligendo-pontifice_20050418_en.html#:~:text=We%20are%20building%20a%20dictatorship%20of%20relativism%20that,man.%20He%20is%20the%20measure%20of%20true%20humanism. This theme was developed in Benedict XVI, Address to the Representatives of British Society (Westminster Hall, London, September 17, 2010), http://w2.vatican.va/content/benedict-xvi/en/speeches/2010/september/documents/hf_ben-xvi_spe_20100917_societa-civile.html, and Benedict XVI, Address to the Members of the German Bundestag (Berlin, September 22, 2011), https://www.vatican.va/content/benedict-xvi/en/speeches/2011/september/documents/hf_ben-xvi_spe_20110922_reichstag-berlin.html.

6. Henri de Lubac, S.J., *The Drama of Atheist Humanism* (San Francisco: Ignatius Press, 1995), p. 14.

7. Pierre Manent, "Autumn of Nations," *Azure*, Winter 2004, p. 37.

8. John Paul II, encyclical *Fides et Ratio* (September 14, 1998), https://www.vatican.va/content/john-paul-ii/en/encyclicals/documents/hf_jp-ii_enc_14091998_fides-et-ratio.html.

9. Ibid., no. 5.

10. Ibid., opening remarks.

11. See ibid., nos. 7–15.

12. Ibid., no. 79, citing St. Augustine, *De Praedestinatione Sanctorum*, 2, 5 (PL 44, 963).

13. This "anthropological crisis" was the principal concern of John Paul II's inaugural encyclical, *Redemptor Hominis* (March 4, 1979), https://www.vatican.va/content/john-paul-ii/en/encyclicals/documents/hf_jp-ii_enc_04031979_redemptor-hominis.html. In *Fides et Ratio* 81ff. it is linked to late modernity's "crisis of meaning."

14. Beatitude as the telos of the moral life was one key theme in John Paul II's encyclical *Veritatis Splendor*. See also Servais Pinckaers, O.P., *The Sources of Christian Ethics* (Washington, D.C.: Catholic University of America Press, 1995). The development of twenty-first-century moral theology in a renewed dialogue with theology is discussed in John Paul II, *Fides et Ratio*, nos. 67 and 98.

15. See John Paul II, *Fides et Ratio*, no. 36.

16. John Paul II, Address to the Fiftieth General Assembly of the United Nations Organization (United Nations Headquarters, New York, October 5, 1995), https://www.vatican.va/content/john-paul-ii/en/speeches/1995/october/documents/hf_jp-ii_spe_05101995_address-to-uno.html.

17. As John Paul II notes,

> Faced with contemporary challenges in the social, economic, political, and scientific fields, the ethical conscience of people is disoriented. In the Encyclical Letter *Veritatis Splendor*, I wrote that many of the problems of the contemporary world stem from a crisis of truth. I noted that 'once the idea of a universal moral truth about the good, knowable by human reason, is lost, inevitably the notion of conscience also changes. Conscience is no longer considered in its prime reality as an act of a person's intelligence, the function of which is to apply the universal knowledge of the good in a specific situation and thus to express a judgment about the right conduct to be chosen here and now. Instead, there is a tendency to grant to the individual conscience the prerogative of independently determining the criteria of good and evil and then acting accordingly. (John Paul II, *Fides et Ratio*, no. 98.)

18. John Paul II, encyclical *Redemptoris Missio* (December 7, 1990), no. 39, https://www.vatican.va/content/john-paul-ii/en/encyclicals/documents/hf_jp-ii_enc_07121990_redemptoris-missio.html. On the "*diakonia* of the truth," see *Fides et Ratio*, no. 2.

19. John Paul II, *Fides et Ratio*, no. 1.

20. See ibid., no. 4.

21. Ibid., no. 5.

22. Ibid.

23. As John Paul II put it,

> The world and all that happens within it, including history and the fate of peoples, are realities to be observed, analyzed, and assessed with all the resources of reason, but without faith ever being foreign to the process. Faith intervenes not to abolish reason's autonomy nor to reduce its scope for action, but solely to bring the human being to understand that in these events it is the God of Israel who acts. Thus the world and the events of history cannot be understood in depth without professing faith in the God who is at work in them. Faith sharpens the inner eye, opening the mind to discover in the flux of events the workings of Providence.... This is to say that with the light of reason human beings can know which path to take, but they can follow that path to its end, quickly and unhindered, only if with a rightly tuned spirit they search for it

> within the horizon of faith. Therefore, faith and reason cannot be separated without diminishing the capacity of men and women to know themselves, the world, and God in an appropriate way. (John Paul II, *Fides et Ratio*, no. 16.)

24. Ibid., no. 32.

25. John Paul II, *Redemptor Hominis*, no. 8, citing Vatican II, Pastoral Constitution on the Church in the Modern World *Gaudium et Spes* (December 7, 1965), no. 22, in *AAS* 58 (1966): 1042–43.

26. According to John Paul II,

> This sapiential dimension is all the more necessary today, because the immense expansion of humanity's technical capability demands a renewed and sharpened sense of ultimate values. If this technology is not ordered to something greater than a merely utilitarian end, then it could soon prove inhuman and even become a potential destroyer of the human race....
>
> [Humanity needs] a philosophy of genuine metaphysical range, capable, that is, of transcending empirical data in order to attain something absolute, ultimate, and foundational in its search for truth.... Here I do not speak of metaphysics in the sense of a specific school or a particular historical current of thought. I only want to state that reality and truth do transcend the factual and the empirical, and to vindicate the human being's capacity to know this transcendent and metaphysical dimension in a way that is true and certain, albeit imperfect and analogical. In this sense, metaphysics should not be seen as an alternative to anthropology, since it is metaphysics that makes it possible to ground the concept of personal dignity in virtue of [men's] spiritual nature. In a special way, the person constitutes a privileged locus for the encounter with being, and hence with metaphysical enquiry. (John Paul II, *Fides et Ratio*, nos. 81, 83.)

27. Ibid., no. 105, citing St. Bonaventure, *Prologus*, 4.

Veritatis Splendor: A Gift to the Church and the World

1. Servais Pinckaers, O.P., *The Sources of Christian Ethics* (Washington, D.C.: Catholic University of America Press, 1995), pp. 327–79.

John Paul II, the Priority of Culture, and the Contemporary Culture Wars

1. Rod Dreher, *The Benedict Option: A Strategy for Christians in a Post-Christian Nation* (New York: Sentinel, 2017).

2. Jennifer Rubin, "It's the Cruelty That Will Undo the Forced-Birth Crusade," *The Washington Post*, July 5, 2022, https://www.washingtonpost.com/opinions/2022/07/05/forced-birth-abortion/.

3. Antony J. Blinken, "Transgender Day of Remembrance," U.S. Department of State, press statement, November 20, 2023, https://www.state.gov/transgender-day-of-remembrance-2/.

4. Cited in Henri de Lubac, *At the Service of the Church: Henri de Lubac Reflects on the Circumstances That Occasioned His Writings* (San Francisco: Ignatius Press, 1993), pp. 171–72.

5. Richard Rex, "A Church in Doubt," *First Things*, April 2018, https://www.firstthings.com/article/2018/04/a-church-in-doubt.

6. Richard Rex, "The Church's Revolutions," *First Things*, October 2023, https://www.firstthings.com/article/2023/10/the-churchs-revolutions.

7. Leon R. Kass, "Where Are We?", Herzl Prize Address at the Jewish Leadership Conference, The Tikvah Fund, New York, October 29, 2023, https://www.aei.org/research-products/speech/where-are-we/.

8. Interview was published in "End of Priest Celibacy Nigh, Says Brisbane Catholic Archbishop Mark Coleridge," *The Australian*, August 11, 2023.

9. The phrase "culture of death" appears a dozen times in the encyclical.

John Paul II, Doctor of the Church?

1. Cited in Henri de Lubac, S.J., *At the Service of the Church: Henri de Lubac Reflects on the Circumstances That Occasioned His Writings* (San Francisco: Ignatius Press, 1993), pp. 171–72.

2. John Paul II, *Novo Millennio Ineunte* (January 6, 2001), nos. 1, 5, https://www.vatican.va/content/john-paul-ii/en/apost_letters/2001/documents/hf_jp-ii_apl_20010106_novo-millennio-ineunte.html.

Benedict XVI: Voice in the Secular Wilderness

1. This pungent observation closed John Maynard Keynes' seminal work, *The General Theory of Employment, Interest, and Money* (Stansted, UK: Wordsworth Editions Classics, 2017).

2. These and subsequent quotes from Ratzinger's Senate lecture are taken from Joseph Ratzinger and Marcello Pera, *Without Roots: The West, Relativism, Christianity, Islam* (New York: Basic Books, 2006).

3. The two lectures are available in a small volume published in 2007 by Ignatius Press: *The Dialectics of Secularization: On Reason and Religion.* All subsequent quotes are from this source.

4. See Richard John Neuhaus, *The Naked Public Square: Religion and Democracy in America* (Grand Rapids, Mich.: Wm. B. Eerdmans Publishing, 1984).

Cardinal Jean-Marie Lustiger and the Future of the West: Retrieving the Truths within Christian Ideas Gone Mad

1. John Paul II, post-synodal apostolic exhortation *Ecclesia in Europa* (June 28, 2003), no. 8, https://www.vatican.va/content/john-paul-ii/en/apost_exhortations/documents/hf_jp-ii_exh_20030628_ecclesia-in-europa.html.

2. Ibid., no. 3.

3. Ibid., no. 4.

4. Jean-Marie Lustiger, "Europe, the Pope, and Universality," in *Dare to Live* (New York: Crossroad, 1988), p. 75.

5. Jean-Marie Lustiger, "The Christian Origins of European Culture," in *Dare to Live*, pp. 66–67.

6. John Paul II, *Ecclesia in Europa*, no. 47.

7. Lustiger, "Christian Origins of European Culture," p. 67.

8. Cardinal Joseph Ratzinger, Homily at the Mass *Pro Eligendo Romano Pontifice* (For the Election of the Roman Pontiff) (St. Peter's Basilica, April 18, 2005), https://www.vatican.va/gpII/documents/homily-pro-eligendo-pontifice_20050418_en.html#:~:text=We%20are%20building%20a%20dictatorship%20of%20relativism%20that,man.%20He%20is%20the%20measure%20of%20true%20humanism.

9. Jean-Marie Lustiger, "Europe's Spiritual Future," in *Dare to Live*, pp. 59, 61. See also Jean-Marie Lustiger, "Pour L'Europe, un Nouvel Art de Vivre," in *L'Europe a Venir* (Paris: Communio/Editions Parole et Silence, 2010), pp. 48ff.

10. John Paul II, *Ecclesia in Europa*, no. 76.

11. Henri de Lubac, S.J., *The Drama of Atheist Humanism* (San Francisco: Ignatius Press, 1995).

12. Benedict XVI, Address to Representatives from the World of Culture (Collège des Bernardins, Paris, September 12, 2008), https://www.vatican.va/content/benedict-xvi/en/speeches/2008/september/documents/hf_ben-xvi_spe_20080912_parigi-cultura.html.

13. See Jürgen Habermas and Joseph Ratzinger, *Dialectics of Secularization: On Reason and Religion* (San Francisco: Ignatius Press, 2007).

14. Romano Guardini, Brague's predecessor in the Chair of Christian Worldview at Munich, foresaw all this shortly after the Second World War, when he wrote of the "interior disloyalty of modern times," a betrayal of "the structure of reality itself." (Cited in John Courtney Murray, S.J., *We Hold These Truths: Catholic Reflections on the American Proposition* [Garden City, N.Y.: Doubleday Image Books, 1964], p. 208.)

15. See J.H.H. Weiler, *Un'Europa cristiana: Un saggio esplorativo* (Milano: Rizzoli, 2003). See also the discussion of Weiler's analysis in George Weigel, *The Cube and the Cathedral: Europe, America, and Politics Without God* (New York: Basic Books, 2005), pp. 72–77.

16. John Paul II, encyclical *Centesimus Annus* (May 1, 1991), no. 46, https://www.vatican.va/content/john-paul-ii/en/encyclicals/documents/hf_jp-ii_enc_01051991_centesimus-annus.html.

17. See John Paul II, *Man and Woman He Created Them: A Theology of the Body*, translated and with an introduction by Michael Waldstein (Boston: Pauline Books and Media, 2006). This is the most reliable translation in English, and Waldstein's introduction is a masterpiece of philosophical and theological analysis.

18. On the Crusades, see Thomas F. Madden, *The New Concise History of the Crusades* (Lanham, Md.: Rowman & Littlefield, 2006). On the Thirty Years' War, see Peter Wilson, *The Thirty Years War: Europe's Tragedy* (Cambridge, Mass.: Belknap/Harvard, 2009).

19. On the Inquisition, see Henry Kamen, *The Spanish Inquisition: Historical Revision* (New Haven: Yale University Press, 1999), and B. Netanyahu, *The Origins of the Inquisition in Fifteenth-Century Spain* (New York: New York Review Books, 2001). On communist depredations, see Stéphane Courtois et al., *The Black Book of Communism* (Cambridge, Mass.: Harvard University Press, 1999), and Anne Applebaum, *Gulag: A History* (New York: Doubleday, 2003).

20. See Ronald L. Numbers, ed., *Galileo Goes to Jail and Other Myths about Science and Religion* (Cambridge, Mass.: Harvard University Press, 2009), and the numerous works of Stanley L. Jaki on the influence of Christian doctrine on the culture from which modern science emerged.

21. For examples of such a joining of forces, see Joseph Ratzinger and Marcello Pera, *Without Roots: The West, Relativism, Christianity, Islam* (New York: Basic Books, 2006), and Pera's introduction ("*Una Proposta da Accetare*") to Joseph Ratzinger, *L'Europa di Benedetto: Nella Crisi delle Culture* (Rome: Cantagalli, 2005).

Lead, Kindly Light: John Henry Newman and Us

1. John Colville, *Footprints in Time: Memories* (London: Michael Russell, 1984), p. 22.

2. "Who Was Cardinal Newman?," History Extra, October 7, 2019, https://www.historyextra.com/period/victorian/john-newman-cardinal-saint-history-facts-profile-biography-life-death-who/.

3. Cardinal John Henry Newman, "Biglietto Speech," EWTN.com, taken from *L'Osservatore Romano* (English Weekly Edition), April 14, 2010, p. 9, https://www.ewtn.com/catholicism/library/biglietto-speech-5245.

4. Paul Shrimpton, "Newman and the White Rose Resistance", St. John Henry Newman Canonisation Resource, October 20, 2019, https://www.newmancanonisation.com/blog/how-newman-inspired-the-white-rose-resistance-in-nazi-germany.

5. Vincent of Lerins, "First Instruction" (Cap. 23: PL 50, 667–68), Office of Readings, Friday of the Twenty-Seventh Week of Ordinary Time, in *The Liturgy of the Hours*, copyright © 1973, 1974, 1975 by International Commission on English in the Liturgy Corporation.

6. John Henry Newman, *Apologia pro Vita Sua* 65, May 26, 1864, chap. 5, https://www.newmanreader.org/works/apologia65/chapter5.html.

Michael Novak: An American Catholic Achievement

1. John Paul II, encyclical *Centesimus Annus* (May 1, 1991), no. 13, https://www.vatican.va/content/john-paul-ii/en/encyclicals/documents/hf_jp-ii_enc_01051991_centesimus-annus.html.

2. Richard John Neuhaus, *The Naked Public Square: Religion and Democracy in America* (Grand Rapids, Mich.: Wm. B. Eerdmans Publishing, 1984).

3. John Paul II, encyclical *Redemptoris Missio* (December 7, 1990), no. 39, https://www.vatican.va/content/john-paul-ii/en/encyclicals/documents/hf_jp-ii_enc_07121990_redemptoris-missio.html.

4. Jimmy Carter, "Address at Commencement Exercises at the University of Notre Dame," May 22, 1977, available online by Gerhard Peters and John T. Woolley, American Presidency Project, https://www.presidency.ucsb.edu/documents/address-commencement-exercises-the-university-notre-dame.

The National Interest and the National Purpose: Moral Reasoning and U.S. Foreign Policy

1. Transcript is available on the website of the National Archives, at https://www.archives.gov/milestone-documents/president-john-f-kennedys-inaugural-address.

2. Jimmy Carter, "Address at Commencement Exercises at the University of Notre Dame," May 22, 1977, available online by Gerhard Peters and John T. Woolley, American Presidency Project, https://www.presidency.ucsb.edu/documents/address-commencement-exercises-the-university-notre-dame.

3. "Nation: People Want to See Coonskins", *Time Magazine*, April 24, 1978, https://time.com/archive/6849859/nation-people-want-to-see-coonskins/.

4. George W. Bush, "Second Inaugural Address", January 20, 2005, Voices of Democracy, https://voicesofdemocracy.umd.edu/bush-second-inaugural-speech-text/.

5. Hillary Rodham Clinton, "Remarks on the Human Rights Agenda for the 21st Century" (Georgetown University's Gaston Hall, Washington, D.C., December 14, 2009), available on the website of the U.S. Department of State, https://2009-2017.state.gov/secretary/2009 2013clinton/rm/2009a/12/133544.htm.

6. Reinhold Neibuhr, *Moral Man and Immoral Society: A Study in Ethics and Politics* (New York: Charles Scribner's Sons, 1932).

7. Cited in Anatol Lieven, "The Lesser Evil: Using American Force Wisely", *Boston Review*, November 2006, https://www.bostonreview.net/articles/lieven-lesser-evil/.

8. John XXIII, encyclical *Pacem in Terris* (April 11, 1963), nos. 100, 132–34, 137–38, 140, 155, https://www.vatican.va/content/john-xxiii/en/encyclicals/documents/hf_j-xxiii_enc_11041963_pacem.html.

9. Cited in George Weigel, Tranquillitas Ordinis: *The Present Failure and Future Promise of American Catholic Thought on War and Peace* (New York: Oxford University Press, 1987) p. 124.

10. "Young Praises Islam as 'Vibrant' and Calls the Ayatollah a Living Saint," *New York Times*, February 8, 1979, https://www.nytimes.com/1979/02/08/archives/young-praises-islam-as-vibrant-and-calls-the-ayatollah-a-saint.html#:~:text=Andrew%20Young%2C%20the%20chief%20United%20States%20delegate%20to,leader%2C%20would%20eventually%20be%20hailed%20as%20%E2%80%9Ca%2.

11. Charles Frankel, *Morality and U.S. Foreign Policy* (New York: Foreign Policy Association, 1975).

The Just War Tradition and the World after September 11

1. See Alan Wolfe, *Moral Freedom: The Search for Virtue in a World of Choice* (New York: W. W. Norton, 2001).

2. For an important analysis of the sociological dimensions of moral plurality in the United States, see James Davison Hunter, *Culture Wars: The Struggle to Define America* (New York: Basic Books, 1991). For analysis of the specifically religious dimensions of this phenomenon, see Richard John Neuhaus, *The Naked Public Square: Religion and Democracy in America* (Grand Rapids, Mich.: Wm. B. Eerdmans Publishing, 1984), and Richard John Neuhaus, *America against Itself: Moral Vision and the Public Order* (Notre Dame, Ind.: University of Notre Dame Press, 1992). My own parsing of the problem of plurality may be found in George Weigel, *Catholicism and the Renewal of American Democracy* (Mahwah, N.J.: Paulist Press, 1989).

3. See John Paul II, encyclical *Veritatis Splendor* (August 6, 1993), nos. 79–83, https://www.vatican.va/content/john-paul-ii/en/encyclicals/documents/hf_jp-ii_enc_06081993_veritatis-splendor.html.

4. Alison Hornstein, "The Questions That We Should Be Asking," *Newsweek*, December 17, 2001, p. 14.

5. On this point, see George Weigel, "A Better Idea of Freedom," *First Things* 121 (March 2002): 14–20.

6. The Administrative Committee of the United States Conference of Catholic Bishops (USCCB) was meeting in Washington, D.C., on September 11, 2001. Its episcopal members immediately issued a statement that began by describing September 11 as a "day of national tragedy." (*Origins* 31, no. 15 [September 20, 2001]: 253.) At a hastily organized Mass at noon that day in the Basilica of the National Shrine of the Immaculate Conception, Cardinal Theodore McCarrick spoke of a "moment of national tragedy" and a "horrible crime." (Ibid., p. 255.) Cardinal Edward Egan of New York also spoke of a "tragedy" on the night of September 11, as did Archbishop-elect John Myers of Newark in a joint statement with Newark's apostolic administrator, Bishop Paul Bootkoski. (Ibid.) The same language of "tragedy" was used on September 11 by Bishops Kenneth Untener of Saginaw, Walter Sullivan of Richmond, and Robert Lynch of St. Petersburg. (Ibid., pp. 256–58.) On the night of September 11, Bishop Paul Loverde of Arlington, whose diocese includes the Pentagon, spoke of "diabolical acts of terrorism" that had led to an "unspeakable tragedy." (*Origins* 31, no. 16 [September 27, 2001]: 279.) Archbishop Thomas Kelly of Louisville spoke of a "tragedy with unthinkable implications for our nation and our world." (Ibid., p. 282.)

In a letter to President Bush on September 19, 2001, Bishop Joseph Fiorenza, president of the USCCB, only spoke of "warlike acts." (*Origins* 31, no. 17 [October 4, 2001]: 294.) In a service on September 22 at his cathedral in Lake Charles, Louisiana, Bishop Edward Braxton spoke of a " 'war' against terrorism," as if the very notion were dubious. (Ibid., p. 296.)

This same reluctance to use the word "war" was evident in the initial commentary on September 11 by the chief intellectual architect of the new Catholic default position, Father J. Bryan Hehir. Writing in *America* shortly after September 11, Father Hehir had this to say:

> How is it possible to broaden the horizon of policy debate and contextualize the military issues? Begin with the definition of what we are planning to do. Both the government and the press have decided the best term is "war." Given the enormity of what the nation has suffered, there is a clear rhetorical reason for reaching for the term "war" to define what we face and what we should do. But beyond rhetoric there lie serious reasons to distinguish war from what is ahead of us. Even if one is convinced that there must be a military dimension to an effective response to terrorism, it is better not to locate the whole effort under war. Many who use the term "war" quickly say this will not be like our normal conception of war. It is better to forfeit the rhetorical bounce that comes from invoking war and define more precisely what we can and should do. Enough to say we need an internationally coordinated, long-term effort to erode the basis for terrorism in the life of states and nations. This is deadening rhetoric, but the purpose is to take

> some of [the] passion out of the immediate sense of what must be done. (J. Bryan Hehir, "What Can Be Done? What Should Be Done?", *America*, October 8, 2001, http://www.america@ americapress.org/articles/hehir-terror.htm.)

In the classic just war tradition, as I shall argue below, "war" is not a matter of rhetoric, but of moral reasoning and moral action. To reduce the invocation of war to a question of which rhetoric least inflames passions nicely illustrates just where the Catholic default position leads.

A month or so after September 11, in an interview with the popular Italian Catholic magazine *Famiglia Cristiana*, Cardinal Roger Etchegaray, a Frenchman who served for many years as president of the Pontifical Council for Justice and Peace and had undertaken numerous private diplomatic missions for Pope John Paul II, questioned the very concept of a just war, condemning the characterization of warfare as "divine, holy, or just." (Interview by *Famiglia Cristiana* with Cardinal Roger Etchegary, cited in *Catholic World Report*, December 2001, p. 7.)

In terms of the immediate responses to September 11 from Catholic religious leaders, some might object to my questioning the use of the language of "tragedy" and "crime," on the grounds that these were responses made under great time pressure. That, however, is precisely when a default position, by definition, manifests itself most clearly. The default position can be overcome, as some Catholic leaders demonstrated, in later, more refined statements. But it remains the default position—the first, instinctive response.

7. See note 6 above. (The issues of *Origins* cited include numerous examples of this tendency.)

8. In a column in his diocesan newspaper shortly after September 11, Bishop Frank Rodimer of Paterson, New Jersey, wrote that "nothing, absolutely nothing, justifies the evil that has been done to our American family, but once we have dealt with the terrorists who have caused such devastation, we must do everything we can to eliminate the root causes of the hatred that spawns terrorism." (*Origins* 31, no. 16 [September 27, 2001]: 281.) The Commission of Episcopal Conferences of the European Community, in a statement issued shortly after September 11, wrote:

> Injustices exist in the world; they are the source of many social and political conflicts. The world is divided into rich and poor, not by religions and cultures.... Our classical categories of justice seem inadequate to address the terrorist attacks on New York and Washington. The massive use of force is not an appropriate response for restoring law and justice. ("European Bishops Oppose Massive Use of Force: Classical Categories of Justice Seem Inadequate," ZENIT, September 19, 2001.)

Archbishop Renato Martin, the Holy See's permanent observer at the United Nations, said in November that, while

> terrorism is unjustifiable ... you can't free the world from terrorism by police action, because it will only return if you don't address what caused it in the first place. Any serious campaign against terrorism needs to address the social, economic, and political conditions that nurture the emergence of terrorism. (Interview with Archbishop Renato Martino, "General in the Fight for Peace," *National Catholic Register*, November 25–December 1, 2002, p. 1.)

World religious leaders, meeting in Assisi on January 24, 2002, at the invitation of Pope John Paul II, pledged themselves to "doing everything possible to eliminate the root causes of terrorism." (*L'Osservatore Romano* [English Weekly Edition], January 30, 2002, p. 2.)

The Jesuit Conference Board, which includes the Jesuit provincials of the United States, wrote President Bush on October 1, 2001, and, mixing a "root causes" analysis with a psychiatric approach to foreign policy, urged "that our government radically examine the roots of suffering and anger in the Middle East." The psychologization often evident in the new

Catholic default position was also evident in more immediate responses to September 11. In his National Shrine homily of September 11, Cardinal McCarrick speculated that what had happened "may be the acts of a few irrational terrorists"; yet modern terrorism, from the mid-nineteenth century on, has been quite deliberate and "rational." Bishop Loverde of Arlington, in a statement issued on September 11 itself, urged prayers for "an end to the madness of terrorism." (See *Origins* 31, no. 15 [September 20, 2001]: 253, 255.)

A further variant within the "root causes" element of the "default position" is the notion that contemporary wars are driven by economic tensions. Thus the archbishop of Madrid, Cardinal Antonio Maria Rouco Varela, while addressing the question of the "peace of order" in an impressive speech to Spain's Royal Academy of Moral and Political Sciences, also said that war has too often been caused by "the injustices that stem from excessive economic inequalities and delay in the necessary remedies." ("Response to Terrorism Must Be a Just World Order," ZENIT, December 21, 2001.) It is noteworthy that, whenever an exponent of the default position cites economic inequalities as the source of contemporary wars, examples are rarely, if ever, adduced.

9. Speaking for the Holy See at the United Nations on October 22, 2001, Archbishop Renato Martino said the following:

> Acts of revenge will not cure such hatred. Reprisals, which strike indiscriminately at the innocent, continue the spiral of violence and are illusory solutions that prevent the moral isolation of the terrorists. We must rather remove the most obvious elements that spawn conditions for hatred and violence and which are contrary to any move toward peace. (Interview with Martino, "General in Fight for Peace.")

In an interview a month later, the archbishop completely conflated war and violence, saying that "violence on top of violence will only lead to more violence." (Ibid.) In late October 2001, the Federation of Asian Bishops' Conferences issued the following statement:

> In the Spirit of the Sermon on the Mount, we say "no" to a response of revenge in the sense of "a tooth for a tooth and an eye for an eye." As disciples of Jesus, we reject in equal terms both violence and terrorism that destroy life and dehumanize humanity. We also note that the seeds of violence and terrorism lie in the many injustices and the unjust system in the world. Violence cannot be overcome by revenge that traps us in the spiral of violence. ("Statement of the Federation of Asian Bishops," ZENIT, October 28, 2001.)

A similar pattern was observable domestically. Thus, on September 14, Bishop Tod Brown of Orange, California, chairman of the U.S. Bishops' Committee on Ecumenical and Interreligious Affairs, signed a joint statement with five American Muslim leaders, condemning "terrorist acts and hate crimes" in the same sentence—thus implying a kind of moral equivalence between September 11 and the rare (but always deplorable) acts of random vandalism that had been committed against U.S. mosques and Islamic centers. (See *Origins* 31, no. 16 [September 27, 2001]: 275–76.) One of the signatories of this statement was the executive director of the American Muslim Council, an organization not previously known for the rigor of its opposition to Islamic-based terrorism.

Lutheran scholar David Yeago had this to say a few weeks after September 11, on the question of "violence begetting violence":

> The argument from principle—"violence never solves anything"—seems to be harnessing a valid point to a conclusion which does not follow from it. The valid point is this: government action cannot redemptively alter the human condition in any decisive way.... At most, government action can clear a little temporary space amidst the

> chaos of the present age, throw up a bit of transitory shelter, in which people may for a moment enjoy a modicum of safety and fair dealing ... [but] no action of government can end the larger "cycle of violence" in human history.... Only the self-surrendered Lamb of God, who takes away the sin of the world, can grant the world peace in this sense. (David S. Yeago, "Just War: Reflections from the Lutheran Tradition in a Time of Crisis," *Pro Ecclesia* X, no. 4 [2001]: 415–16.)

On the roots and history of modern terrorism, see Walter Laqueur, *Terrorism* (Boston: Little, Brown, 1977).

10. For the default position evident in an episcopal prayer, see the "September 11 Homily of Seattle Archbishop Alex J. Brunett," *Origins* 31, no. 16 (September 27, 2001): 276–77.

11. Some alternative voices, reflecting more accurately the main themes of the classic Catholic just war tradition, could be heard in the aftermath of September 11. See Archbishop John Myers, "Faith and Terrorism: Reflections on the Questions People Ask," *Origins* 31, no. 24 (November 22, 2001): 408–11. See also Bishop William E. Lori, "A Nation's Response to Terrorism: Six Moral Considerations," *Origins* 31, no. 20 (September 25, 2001): 333, 335–36. Bishop Lori was one of the few Catholic leaders to describe September 11 unambiguously as "an aggression" and to state that military action (as well as other measures) against international terrorism was "imperative." The Catholic bishops of Missouri avoided the "presumption against violence" reading of the just war tradition in their October 1, 2001, statement and acknowledged the government's "obligation to defend against unjust attacks." (Ibid., 336–38.)

12. See Darrell Cole, "Good Wars," *First Things* 116 (October 2001): 7–31; Yeago, "Just War"; and Michael Walzer, *Just and Unjust Wars*, 2nd ed. (New York: Basic Books, 1992), presenting a thoroughly secular perspective. In particular, Catholic religious leaders and scholars must attend far more seriously to the work of the English-speaking world's premier just war historian and theorist, James Turner Johnson, whose major works include *Can Modern War Be Just?* (New Haven: Yale University Press, 1984), *The Quest for Peace: Three Moral Traditions in Western Cultural History* (Princeton: Princeton University Press, 1987), and *Morality and Contemporary Warfare* (New Haven: Yale University Press, 1999).

13. Robert D. Kaplan, *Warrior Politics: Why Leadership Demands a Pagan Ethos* (New York: Random House, 2001).

14. Brian C. Anderson, "Men o' War," *National Review*, February 25, 2002, p. 46.

15. This story is recounted in a slightly more generic form in John Courtney Murray, *We Hold These Truths: Catholic Reflections on the American Proposition* (Garden City, N.Y.: Doubleday Image Books, 1964), p. 262.

16. The most prominent contemporary exponent of this form of Catholic personalism is, of course, Pope John Paul II. Prior to his pontificate, he analyzed the capacity for moral action as the distinguishing characteristic of the human being in *Osoba y czyn, oraz inne studia antropologiczne. Osoba y czyn, oraz inne studia antropologiczne*, eds. Tadeusz Styczen et al. (Lublin: Catholic University of Lublin, 1994). This is the revised Polish edition of Karol Wojtyła's principal philosophical work. *Osoba y czyn* is intelligently discussed in Kenneth L. Schmitz, *At the Center of the Human Drama: The Philosophical Anthropology of Karol Wojtyła/Pope John Paul II* (Washington, D.C.: Catholic University of America Press, 1993), and Jarosław Kupczak, O.P., *Destined for Liberty: The Human Person in the Philosophy of Karol Wojtyła/John Paul II* (Washington, D.C.: Catholic University of America Press, 2000).

17. See George Weigel, *The Final Revolution: The Resistance Church and the Collapse of Communism* (New York: Oxford University Press, 1992).

18. For a Catholic critique of voluntaristic (i.e., will-centered) conceptions of the moral life, see Servais Pinckaers, O.P., *The Sources of Christian Ethics* (Washington, D.C.: Catholic

University of America Press, 1995), and Servais Pinckaers, O.P., *Morality: The Catholic View* (South Bend, Ind.: St. Augustine's Press, 2001).

19. Anderson, "Men o' War," p. 48.

20. "What We're Fighting For: A Letter from America," February 13, 2002, https://avalon.law.yale.edu/sept11/letter_002.asp.

21. On *bellum* and *duellum*, see James Turner Johnson's comments in "Just War Tradition and the New War on Terrorism," available at https://www.pewresearch.org/religion/2001/10/05/just-war-tradition-and-the-new-war-on-terrorism/.

22. "The Challenge of Peace: God's Promise and Our Response; A Pastoral Letter on War and Peace by the National Conference of Catholic Bishops, May 3, 1983," USCCB.org, https://www.usccb.org/upload/challenge-peace-gods-promise-our-response-1983.pdf; emphasis in original.

23. It shaped, for example, the U.S. bishops' letter to Secretary of State James A. Baker III in November 1990, when military action against Iraq was being debated. In a November 7, 1990, letter to Baker, which was later adopted by the entire body of bishops as their own, then-Archbishop Roger Mahony of Los Angeles, chairman of the bishops' international policy committee, stated flatly, "In our tradition, while the use of force is not ruled out absolutely, there is a clear presumption against war." (Cited in James Turner Johnson and George Weigel, eds., *Just War and the Gulf War* [Washington, D.C.: Ethics and Public Policy Center, 1991], p. 101.) A similar tack was taken in "The Harvest of Justice Is Sown in Peace," the U.S. bishops' statement on the tenth anniversary of "The Challenge of Peace"; here, TCOP's "presumption *in favor of peace and against war*," which had already elided into Mahony's "clear presumption against war," now became "a strong presumption against the use of force." (*Origins* 23, no. 26 [December 29, 1993]: 254.)

24. See, for example, the developed statement by the U.S. bishops, "Living with Faith and Hope After September 11":

> Some Christians profess a position of principled nonviolence, which holds that nonmilitary means are the only legitimate response in this case. This is a valid Christian response. While respecting this position and maintaining a strong presumption against the force by legitimate authority in self-defense and as a last resort, the Church has sanctioned the use of the moral criteria for a just war to allow the use of force by legitimate authority in self-defense and as a last resort. (*Origins* 31, no. 25 [November 29, 2001]: 417.)

There are multiple confusions here. First, the statement confuses principled pacifism and a commitment to nonviolence, which are not identical. A Christian committed to the just war tradition could, in some circumstances, judge nonviolent means of resisting evil more effective—or, in the case of resistance against particularly repressive regimes, the only means of resistance available. These judgments have nothing to do with pacifism, which is based on the premise that, for a disciple of Jesus Christ, any resort to violence is *malum in se*. As for pacifism's place in the Catholic Church, another confusion is evident in the new default position. It is true that the Catholic Church now teaches that the pacifist conscience is a legitimate option for individuals (although the moral-theological grounds of that legitimacy have not been clarified in a definitive way). But the Catholic Church has never taught, and does not teach, that pacifism is a morally possible option for governments, which have an obligation to defend the common good, by the use of armed force if necessary. "Living with Faith and Hope" manifests these default position confusions, for before the section just quoted (and after the now-obligatory nod to a form of the "presumption against violence"), the bishops "acknowledge ... the right and duty of a nation and the international community to use military force if necessary to defend the common good by protecting the innocent against mass terrorism." (Ibid., p. 416.)

"Living with Faith and Hope" is also notable for its lack of reflection on the "order" (*tranquillitas ordinis*) component of the just war tradition, which would be stressed by Pope John Paul II six weeks later in his 2002 World Day of Peace message. But then the concept of peace as *tranquillitas ordinis* has never gotten much traction among the staff of the bishops' international policy committee, who had a considerable hand in shaping "Living Faith and Hope."

25. Saint Thomas Aquinas, *Summa Theologiae* II-II, q. 40, a. 1.

26. Ramsey's principal works in this field are *War and the Christian Conscience: How Shall Modern War Be Conducted Justly* (Durham: Duke University Press, 1961) and *The Just War: Force and Political Responsibility* (New York: Scribner's, 1968). James Turner Johnson describes Ramsey's specifically Christian understanding of the just war tradition in these terms:

> Ramsey argued that Christian just war theory is based on the moral duty of love of neighbor. The obligation to protect the neighbor who is being unjustly attacked provided justification for Christians to resort to force; at the same time, love also imposes limits on such force, requiring that no more be done to the unjust assailant than is necessary to prevent the evil he would do, and that no justified use of force can ever itself directly and intentionally target the innocent. (James Turner Johnson, "The Just War Tradition and the American Military," in Johnson and Weigel, *Just War and the Gulf War*, pp. 8–9.)

27. Johnson, *Morality and Contemporary Warfare*, pp. 35–36.

28. On this point, see James Turner Johnson, "Just Cause Revisited," in *Close Calls: Intervention, Terrorism, Missile Defense and "Just War" Today*, ed. Elliott Abrams (Washington, D.C.: Ethics and Public Policy Center, 1998).

29. The presumption against violence and its distortion of the just war way of thinking led to a serious misreading of the world politics of the 1980s in the U.S. bishops' pastoral letter, "The Challenge of Peace." TCOP was deeply influenced by the emphasis laid on questions of proportionality and discrimination because of the threat of nuclear war. No doubt these were important issues. But when that emphasis drove the moral analysis, as it did in TCOP, the result was a distorted picture of reality and a set of moral judgments that contributed little to wise statecraft. Rather than recognizing that nuclear weapons were one (extremely dangerous) manifestation of a prior conflict with profound moral roots, the bishops' letter seemed to suggest that nuclear weapons could be factored out of the conflict between the West and the Soviet Union by arms control. And in order to achieve arms control agreements with a nervous, even paranoid, foe like the Soviet Union, it might be necessary to downplay the moral and ideological (i.e., human rights) dimensions of the Cold War. That, at least, was the policy implication of the claim that the greatest threat to peace (identified as such because *in bello* considerations trumped everything else) was the mere possession of nuclear weapons.

The opposite, of course, turned out to be true. Nuclear weapons were not the primary threat to peace; communism was. When communism went, so did the threat posed by the weapons. As the human rights resistance in central and eastern Europe brought massive regime change inside the Warsaw Pact, creating dynamics that eventually led to the demise of the USSR itself, the risks of nuclear war were greatly diminished, and real disarmament (not "arms control") began. The Catholic default position, as manifest in TCOP, produced a serious misreading of the political realities and possibilities. "The Harvest of Justice Is Sown in Peace," the bishops' 1993 statement on the tenth anniversary of TCOP, unhappily fails to acknowledge this misreading or analyze its intellectual roots. For a representative sampler of Catholic intellectuals' reading of the immediate post–Cold War situation, see *Peacemaking: Moral and Policy Challenges for a New World*, eds. Gerard F. Powers et al. (Washington, D.C.: Georgetown University Press, 1994), which includes the full text of "The Harvest of Justice Is Sown in Peace."

30. George Weigel, Tranquillitas Ordinis: *The Present Failure and Future Promise of American Catholic Thought on War and Peace* (New York: Oxford University Press, 1987).

31. Pope John Paul II has made important contributions to this idea, especially in his World Day of Peace message in 1981. See *Ways of Peace: Papal Messages for the World Day of Peace 1968–1986* (Vatican City: Libreria Editrice Vaticana, 1987), pp. 147–61. The Pope's most recent World Day of Peace statement refines the discussion of the components of *tranquillitas ordinis* further by teaching that there is no peace without justice and no justice without forgiveness. Forgiveness helps create the conditions of civil society in which the peace of order, composed of justice and freedom, can flourish. In a comment on the message, Richard John Neuhaus notes:

> The title of the message has it right: there is no peace without justice, and temporal justice is secured by the acknowledgment of a transcendent judgment that reveals our need to be forgiven and to forgive. This is said [by the Pope] without any blurring of the line between good and evil, or any obscuring of the duty to defend the innocent. Rather, it anticipates the day when, beyond the present battles, there may be a new order based on a shared recognition of God's justice and mercy. Some call that idealistic. The right word is prophetic. (See John Paul II, "No Peace without Justice, No Justice without Forgiveness," *Origins* 31, no. 28 [December 20, 2001]: 461–66; Richard John Neuhaus, "The Public Square," *First Things* 88 [February 2002]: 120.)

32. See Johnson, "Just Cause Revisited," for a historical survey and contemporary arguments.

33. Denying rogue states weapons of mass destruction and the means to deliver them, and effecting regime change if necessary to accomplish this, could also have a salutary effect on changing the state-of-the-question in Islamic societies. Political modernization in the Arab Islamic world has not, typically, meant liberation. Rather, the importation of Western revolutionary ideologies has generally led to repression. In a recent study, Bernard Lewis argues that Arab Islamic states "looked for the secret of Western success in those features of the West that were most distinctive, most different from anything in their own experience—and not tainted with Christianity." (Bernard Lewis, *What Went Wrong? Western Impact and Middle Eastern Response* [New York: Oxford University Press, 2001].) This, as Christopher Caldwell notes in a review of Lewis' work, led Arab Islamic states to modern Western political ideologies. Caldwell writes:

> The French Revolution was a major influence, but also, eventually, nationalism, socialism, and National Socialism, whose baleful influence Lewis still sees at work in the Ba'athist regimes of Iraq and Syria. The move to political modernization in Islam did not enhance freedom and autonomy, but strengthened states through modern approaches to enforcement, surveillance, propaganda, and the consequent depredations against civil society. (Christopher Caldwell, "The Closing of the Muslim Mind," *Weekly Standard*, January 21, 2002, p. 39.)

This, in turn, has led to a blame-the-West phenomenon throughout the Arab Islamic world, with the United States currently replacing European colonialism, which replaced the Turks, who replaced the Mongols, as the source of Islamic decline. It is crucial, Bernard Lewis argues, to change the question, so that the Islamic world stops asking, "Who did this to us?" and starts asking the question, "What did we do wrong?" Regime change in places like Iraq could well contribute to changing the question, as well as to clearing the ground on which the seeds of a new Islamic civil society could be planted. (See Lewis, *What Went Wrong?*; Caldwell, "Closing of the Muslim Mind"; and Joshua Muravchik, "Freedom and the Arab World," *Weekly Standard*, December 31, 2001, pp. 15–16.)

34. For a stark reading of the likely evolution of twenty-first-century world politics which, however exaggerated in parts, nevertheless poses important questions for the just war tradition, see Robert D. Kaplan, *The Coming Anarchy: Shattering the Dream of the Post-Cold War World* (New York: Alfred A. Knopf, 2000).

35. On this point see the editorial "In a Time of War," *First Things* 118 (December 2001): 11–17.

36. Yeago, "Just War," pp. 414–15.

37. John Paul II, Address to the Fiftieth General Assembly of the United Nations Organization (United Nations Headquarters, New York, October 5, 1995), nos. 16, 18, https://www.vatican.va/content/john-paul-ii/en/speeches/1995/october/documents/hf_jp-ii_spe_05101995_address-to-uno.html.